Crystal Beach Park ~ A Century of Screams

Published by:

Buffalo, New York
www.crystalbeachhistory.com

First Printing: October 2011
Second Printing: January 2012
Third Printing: May 2013
Fourth Printing: January 2015
Fifth Printing: October 2017

ISBN: 978-0-9796632-3-9
Library of Congress Control Number: 2011915282
Kae, William E., 1959 -
Crystal Beach, Ontario; Buffalo, New York.

Crystal Beach Park - A Century of Screams
The History of Crystal Beach, Volume 3
-1st ed.
262 pp. : photos
Includes bibliographic references and index.

Summary: History of the Crystal Beach Park midway in Ontario, Canada, near Buffalo, New York. Text, images, blueprints and site plans explore the development and history of the midway, and the rides that occupied it for a century.

Also from the author:

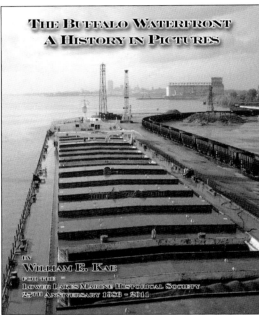

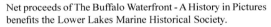

Net proceeds of The Buffalo Waterfront - A History in Pictures
benefits the Lower Lakes Marine Historical Society.

www.crystalbeachhistory.com

Cover Photo: A front seat view on the Giant Coaster as the train nears the top of the lift hill in 1984. Courtesy John B. deHass.
Back Cover: View from the top of the Giant Coaster. Courtesy Cathy Herbert.

Table of Contents

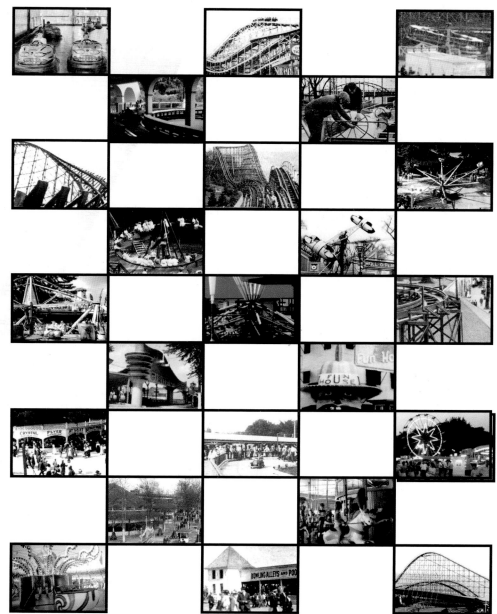

Acknowledgements

"A picture is worth a thousand words" is a banal, clichéd adage but an accurate one. Throughout the years I amassed an impressive collection of photographs, postcards and other Crystal Beach ephemera that appear in this and the previous two volumes of the History of Crystal Beach series. However, without the contributions of photos and other documents from the collections of others, the series would be visually inadequate. Their contributions provided the WOW factor and transformed each volume from a history book into a time machine.

John Bosco of Oakland, California collects and preserves plate glass and celluloid negatives. Among John's collection are glass negatives of the Backety Back Scenic Railway. John provided prints from these negatives for use in this volume - images that probably have not been seen in over a century.

Pianist, composer and music director, John B. deHaas of Ocoee, Florida is also a roller coaster and amusement park enthusiast. He attended the American Coaster Enthusiasts convention at Crystal Beach in 1984. Some of his photos from his visit appear within, including the front cover.

A resident of Ridgeway, Rick Doan could hear the screams from Comet riders and the whistle of the miniature railway locomotive from his house when the wind was right. Through the years he amassed an impressive collection of Crystal Beach photos, postcards, artifacts, and ephemera that includes correspondence between Crystal Beach management and Laff in the Dark manufacturer R. E. Chambers. He co-produced 2 DVD's on Crystal Beach and contributed to and appeared in WNED TV's Crystal Beach DVD. Material from his collection has appeared in many other Crystal Beach works. Rick has composed web pages for the Internet sites Laff in the Dark.com (http://www.laffinthedark.com/articles/magicpalace/magic_1.htm) and Tunnel of Laffs.com (http://www.elvision.com/tunneloflaffs/crystalbeach/crystal-1.html).

Cathy Herbert also resides in Ridgeway and spent thousands of hours at the park. Cathy is *The Source* for primary Crystal Beach documents. She produced the first historic calendars and photo books of Crystal Beach. Photos and other material from her collection continue to enhance works in local newspapers, videos, and books on the history of Fort Erie and Southern Ontario.

Bob Hall, along with his cousin Van, operated Crystal Beach during the 1970s and early 1980s. During this project's infancy, I tracked Bob down to Davie, Florida where he continued to make Crystal Beach salt-water taffy. Operating under the name Carousel Confections, one of his biggest clients was Busch Gardens. Bob was a pleasant and unassuming man who passed away shortly after my second meeting with him in 1999. During our two visits, he shared the few images of the park he had that appear in this volume and Volume 2. I know he loved fishing, and docked his boat at his mother's home in Fort Lauderdale. He liked the car I drove at the time, a 1972 Chevelle Malibu 350 and he gave me a peek at the classic car he restored and drove only occasionally. If memory serves, it was a '68 Barracuda. I wish I had had the opportunity to get to know him better.

Harvey Holzworth passed away on February 8, 2010 at the age of 85. He was an icon; well known on both sides of the border. A resident of Buffalo, he maintained a summer residence at Point Abino with his life partner Jean McCabe. In spite of battling cancer for over 20 years, he worked ceaselessly collecting and preserving remnants of the *S.S. Canadiana* – the fabled "Crystal Beach Boat." Harvey opened up his archives of photos and postcards for inclusion in Volumes 1 and 2 asking only to be credited. Sadly, Harvey passed before this volume reached first draft stage. Jean perpetuated Harvey's generosity and continued to make available Harvey's collection, wanting nothing more than Harvey to be remembered.

Michael J. Losi generously consented to the use of his nighttime color images. Crystal Beach Park had a dreamlike quality that is beyond my ability to describe but Michael's images do what words cannot.

While I lived Tampa, I purchased an image of Crystal Beach from Richard Schwegler through Ebay. After some correspondence, he sent me a disk of his midway photos. I caught up with Richard in 2011 and he was able to supply high resolution scans of his images that appear within.

Nick DeWolf was an engineer and entrepreneur who founded a company called Teradyne. Nick catalogued his life and travels in photographs. He died in 2006 at the age of 77. In Nick's library are some fantastic images of the one-of-a-kind *Holiday Bounce*. On my behalf, Nick's archivist and son-in-law, Steve Lundeen, arranged with Nick's wife Maggie DeWolf, permission to include the *Holiday Bounce* photos.

Roller Coaster enthusiasts Michael and Celia Horwood formerly of Brampton, Ontario, plowed through a mound of shaving cream piled on the Comet's tracks. I have known Mike and Celia since the early 1990s and had no idea they had ever participated in such an escapade until coming across it in a newspaper about a year ago. They provided some excellent shots.

I became acquainted with Lower Lakes Marine Historical Society in Buffalo, New York while working on Steamers of the Crystal Beach Line (Volume 1) in 2005. Their photographic contributions and support throughout this project are immeasurable. Their extensive maritime news clippings, to my surprise, contained many articles about Crystal Beach, especially during the 1940s and 1950s.

I started this project when I was 36 years old and it is rooted in the news clippings files and other primary source documents in archives at the Fort Erie Historical Museum in Ridgeway, Ontario. There I began the research, but not with the intent to write books, but merely to satisfy my curiosity about the formative years of the park. Joan Lyons Felstead, formerly of the Museum, was very accommodating. During the years that followed, Jane Davies, Jude Scott, and Erin Wilson from the Fort Erie Historical Museum were a constant source

of support and encouragement. Many rare photos from the museum's archives appear in all three volumes.

Thank you's also go out to Thomas Rebbie of Philadelphia Toboggan Coasters (formerly Philadelphia Toboggan Company), the Public Library of Niagara Falls, Ontario, Robert Cartmell and the American Coaster Enthusiasts, Chance Rides, Greg Gibbs, Michael and Celia Horwood, Tom Love, Karl R. Josker, Jim Conklin, Thomas Martin Smith, Steve Urbanowicz, Lewellen Amusements, Richard Munch, and the National Foundation for Carnival Heritage, Kinsley, Kansas, in partnership with the Kinsley Library.

Finally, to those doing the dirty work: Keith Hansult, Robert Radominski, and Arlene Swank for reading and critiquing the drafts - a truly tedious chore. - *WEK*

Michael Losi is accepting inquiries for prints of his night images at: mclosi@verizon.net.com

Many images from the collection of Cathy Herbert are available through her website: http://www.crystalbeachmemories.com/

Rick Doan's DVDs of the park are available through http://www. crystalbeachpark.net/

Evening aerial of Crystal Beach Park, circa 1978.
Fort Erie Historical Museum collection.

For

Paul S. Walczak

and the shared summer days
at Crystal Beach
during the 1960s and 1970s.

 # Introduction

Crystal Beach Park - A Century of Screams (Screams) is the third and final volume of the History of Crystal Beach series. It focuses on the growth and development of the midway, its rides, and the people behind the park. Like the previous two volumes, *Screams* was developed from primary source material - blueprints, correspondence, photographs, census data back to 1850; and secondary sources - period newspapers dating back to 1887, period amusement industry trade magazines and journals, city directories, and similar sources.

While primary source material is limited, secondary source material is abundant for those with the wherewithal to search through hundreds of reels of microfilm. Although primary source material is preferred, for subjects as innocuous as Crystal Beach Park, most newspaper print is sufficiently reliable but with caveats. They require filtering to distinguish between press releases from the park (that had are prone to exaggeration) and hard news. News from the late 19th and early 20th centuries requires scrutiny to filter through the sensationalism that was the reporting trend of the era. For example, basic laws of physics prevent the Comet roller coaster from achieving 100 miles per hour even under ideal operating conditions - contrary to local press in 1948.

Interviews are limited because of the inherent weaknesses of oral history when used for historical research. During 1931, John E. Rebstock was interviewed and reportedly claimed that Crystal Beach started as a religious retreat in 1888. Details from the period press from 1887 through 1896 contradicts the 1931 account and are discussed in the "Origins" chapter. These contradictions underscore the weaknesses of interviews as part of historical research that render the 1931 article unreliable. This an example of inherent interview weakness - the failings of human memory. In 1931 John Rebstock was 79 years old and not in the best of health. With age comes memory loss and other cognitive impairments. Who can say how well Rebstock's memory was? Many scientific studies on memory-recall demonstrate the unreliability of the human memory at any age.

The second weakness inherent in interviews are self-serving motives of the interviewee (Rebstock did open a religious retreat in 1895 and closed it in 1896 – he may have been trying to but a positive spin on a failed enterprise by claiming that he changed the venue to an amusement park. No one likes to admit failure.)

An unconscious tendency of the interviewed is the creation of inaccurate narratives of past events, which is the third weakness inherent in interviews (the previous example also applies here).

Anyone interviewing Rebstock in his senior years would not have pressed him about his accuracy and would not have felt it necessary. This illustrates the fourth weakness of interviewing accuracy: The impact of the relationship between the interviewer and his subject – which could be exacerbated if a personal relationship pre-existed.

What has become the accepted history of the park, a history I call the "traditional" or "romantic" history is borne from misinformation. Baked into the traditional history are urban myths such as those surrounding the Cyclone: The nurse at the station; The 75,000 people that mobbed the coaster on opening day 1927 and tore down the fence.

The reader can make up his/her own mind after reading this volume, but the author contends that these and other elements of the traditional history of the park were all precipitated by interview shortcomings, and ulterior motives of park owners to promote the park by exaggerating history to the point of fiction.

Another reason for the limited use of interviews in the Crystal Beach series is the obvious one: most of the people who had anything to do with the park are deceased. The few that are still around declined to be interviewed.

Layouts that illustrate the growth and development of the park are unique to this volume. Not only do they illustrate the physical changes over a century; some include markers for the location of a camera and its point of view for select images. This is most helpful, especially to orient the reader when viewing early photos.

The layouts were developed from a series of high altitude reconnaissance aerial photos from 1968, 1973, 1980 and 1988 photographed by the Department of Energy, Mines and Resources, Canada. A fireplug map from the 1920s (courtesy of Cathy Herbert) and a real estate site plan of Crystal Beach from 1893 where invaluable to develop the site plans for the park's early years. The layouts are not to scale and are for illustrative purposes only; the very early layouts are based on available descriptions from secondary sources.

Presenting 100 years of Crystal Beach history for this volume became problematic. Early drafts were strictly chronological – presenting the midway history year over year. Inasmuch as it seems a logical approach, it made for very choppy reading. A hybrid chronology, compartmentalizing the history into eras marked by watershed events in the park's history, eliminated the chop. Details of each ride and their entire histories at the park are contained in the era when the ride debuted.

Jungle Land is one of a few exceptions. This "old mill" went through a number of themes of which details are scant and obscure. Jungle Land was a radical departure from its previous iterations that garnered significant press and photographs that presented better when separated from its ancestors.

History of the portable rides on the midway that appeared, disappeared, and reappeared are also presented, but it most cases, these rides do not have a narrative history as their existence at Crystal Beach was uneventful. Therefore general background information of the ride is provided.

Tracking the life span of rides was both easy and difficult depending upon the ride and the era. The life span of permanent midway rides such as the Laff in the Dark are well documented. Rides during the early eras were considered diversions from the picnics, athletics, the beach, and a ride on the steamers. These rides rarely garnered any press on an individual basis. This is not surprising as Crystal Beach owners during the early decades made a large percentage of their money from the steamboat trade so the focus of their advertising was a lake cruise to Crystal Beach. Concessionaires, not the park, owned what few rides existed during the first fifteen years. If there were references to rides, it was often in general terms such as "improved midway attractions" or "the midway features were well patronized." References to specific rides did happen occasionally and increased in frequency as the years passed.

Occasional advertisements contained the entire ride line-up for a season. These helped to build a ride inventory found in the appendix. No illusions about its completeness are implied. Portable rides that made the inventory were culled from Crystal Beach coverage in newspapers, journals, and trade magazines for a particular year. Rare photos containing rides or glimpses of rides also made the inventory, but their life spans on the midway remain uncertain. There may have been other rides on the midway that missed the inventory because they did not make the press or were missed while researching. Space considerations did not allow for coverage of Kiddie Land rides.

The reader will not find any nostalgia in this book. The author trusts that the reader will provide his or her own memories. For anyone reading this tome who did not have the privilege of summer visits to the park, there are no words or images that can adequately convey the experience of a day at "Crystal." – *WEK*.

Chapter 1:
1890 ~ 1906

Except for improvements that would be found in the picnic grove, initially, Crystal Beach was in its natural state. There was a bath house on the beach and picnic tables in the grove, but little else. Slowly, typical amusement park elements found their way onto the grove, but the transformation of the grove into an amusement park would take 15 years.

Cathy Herbert collection.

Above: The first steamer to sail to Crystal Beach was the Dove, seen at the Crystal Beach pier in 1890. Note there is no sheltered area for passengers waiting to board. Right: Crystal Beach in 1890.

John E. Rebstock officially opened Crystal Beach on July 16, 1890. There were no banner headlines in the local press, only an inconspicuous ad among dozens of others. The announcements of the development of the resort and its imminent opening were more prominent than the opening ad and described a sylvan setting with a pristine beach and acres of shaded picnic groves. Except for a pier for steamers to dock, Crystal Beach was rustic, primitive.

Construction of the first pier marked the beginning of the physical transformation of Crystal Beach. There were three pier designs - the first two designs were constructed primarily of wood and vulnerable to fierce winter storms and ice jams in the bay. Both wood piers were partially washed away or completely destroyed numerous times. It is difficult to count the number of wood piers built because each edition varied only slightly unless the design was changed entirely. The wood piers were perhaps the most maintenance intensive element of the resort until the reinforced concrete pier emerged more than 25 years after the debut season (and that pier was not entirely without maintenance from storm and ice damage and required extensions when lake levels were low).

Photos and postcards of the piers throughout the decades show a canopied area of the pier that sheltered waiting passengers seeking passage to Buffalo. The first edition of the first pier was nothing more than a wood-planked walkway. Arthur Hickman, president of the Crystal Beach Steamboat and Ferry Company (CBSFC) announced in 1893 that a shelter on the dock was constructed *"so that people going down to the boat will not be obliged to stand out in the open air."*

The first substantial improvement to the park was on the bluff overlooking the dock – the Crystal Beach Hotel opened for business for the first time on July 1, 1891. J. A. Jordan, manager of the hotel touted the therapeutic benefits of a stay:

"The attention of sufferers of hay fever and kindred affections is called to the wonderful healing properties of the air of the north shore of Lake Erie. For years, thousands of victims of Hay Fever have flocked to ... northern Michigan resorts for relief. The atmosphere of Crystal Beach is equally effective, and the facilities for quick communication to the city commend the beach to businessmen and others who have hitherto sought relief in the backwoods."

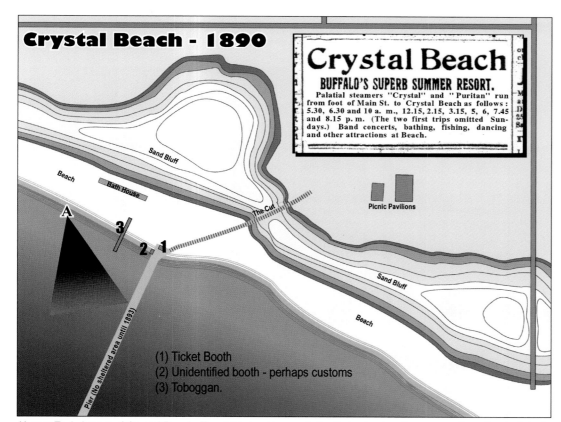

Crystal Beach - 1890

Sand Bluff

Beach

Bath House

The Cut

Picnic Pavilions

A

3
2 1

Sand Bluff

Beach

Pier (No sheltered area until 1893)

(1) Ticket Booth
(2) Unidentified booth - perhaps customs
(3) Toboggan.

Crystal Beach

BUFFALO'S SUPERB SUMMER RESORT.

Palatial steamers "Crystal" and "Puritan" run from foot of Main St. to Crystal Beach as follows : 5.30, 6.30 and 10 a. m., 12.15, 2.15, 3.15, 5, 6, 7.45 and 8.15 p. m. (The two first trips omitted Sundays.) Band concerts, bathing, fishing, dancing and other attractions at Beach.

B pg. 12

Cathy Herbert collection.

C pg. 12

Above: Early layout of Crystal Beach. Top right: Looking east, the first raised walkway goes from the dock to the bluff and the Crystal Beach Hotel. The raised walkway behind it leads to the Cut. Above right: A view down the ramp from the bluff near the Crystal Beach Hotel.

The Crystal Beach Hotel would eventually be called the Bellaire, and finally the Bon Air.

There was a restaurant in the grove during the 1891 season evidenced in the 1892 season opening announcement that indicated a "new" restaurant replaced the "old one."

There was no press indicating Rebstock built a dance hall in the grove, but there was a pavilion of sufficient size to host a dance for the first time late in the 1891 season. The large pavilion, no longer adequate for dances, prompted construction of a new dance hall that debuted in 1896. Advertised as the largest dance hall in Western New York, it contained a 6,000 square foot dance floor free of any posts or obstructions.

The only access to the grove from the pier and the beach was a narrow wooden catwalk with steps and inclines through a natural depression in the sand bluffs that became known as the Cut. This passage became a bottleneck as the popularity of Crystal Beach grew and would undergo a number of widening projects in the coming years.

Early popularity of Crystal Beach belies the financial problems of the CBSFC that became apparent before the 1895 season when the

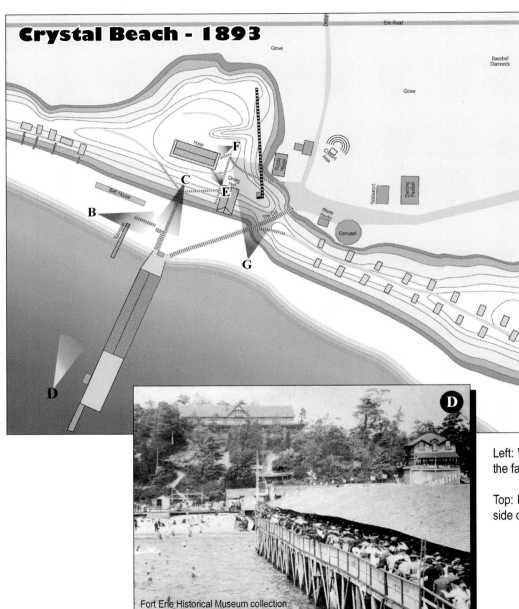

Crystal Beach - 1893

Left: View of the dock, the Crystal Beach Hotel on the Bluff, the hotel's restaurant on the far right photographed from the bow of one of the park's steamers.

Top: Eventually the Crystal Beach Hotel became the Hotel Bon-Air. Above: The east side of the Bon-Air.

Fort Erie Historical Museum collection.

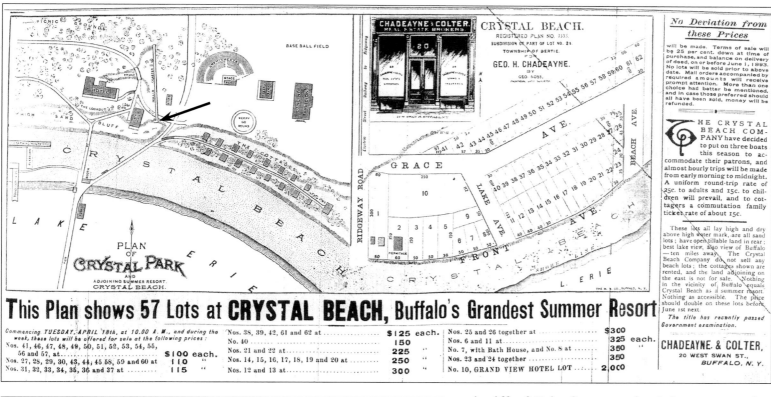

The arrow in the site plan (left) points to the loading platform of a roller coaster. The image below left is that platform but this is not enough to confirm the coaster's existence.

No Deviation from these Prices

will be made. Terms of sale will be 25 per cent. down at time of purchase, and balance on delivery of deed, on or before June 1, 1893. No lots will be sold prior to above date. Mail orders accompanied by required amounts will receive prompt attention. More than one choice had better be mentioned, and in case those preferred should all have been sold, money will be refunded.

THE CRYSTAL BEACH COMPANY have decided to put on three boats this season to accommodate their patrons, and almost hourly trips will be made from early morning to midnight. A uniform round-trip rate of 25c. to adults and 15c. to children will prevail, and to cottagers a commutation family ticket rate of about 15c.

These lots all lay high and dry above high water mark, are all sand lots; have open tillable land in rear; best lake view, also view of Buffalo — ten miles away. The Crystal Beach Company do not sell any beach lots; the cottages shown are rented, and the land adjoining on the east is not for sale. Nothing in the vicinity of Buffalo equals Crystal Beach as a summer resort. Nothing as accessible. The price should double on these lots before June 1st next.

The title has recently passed Government examination.

CHADEAYNE & COLTER,
20 WEST SWAN ST.,
BUFFALO, N.Y.

This Plan shows 57 Lots at CRYSTAL BEACH, Buffalo's Grandest Summer Resort

Commencing TUESDAY, APRIL 18th, at 10.00 A.M., and during the week, these lots will be offered for sale at the following prices:

Nos. 41, 46, 47, 48, 49, 50, 51, 52, 53, 54, 55, 56 and 57, at $100 each.	Nos. 38, 39, 42, 61 and 62 at $125 each.	Nos. 25 and 26 together at $300	
Nos. 27, 28, 29, 30, 43, 44, 45 58, 59 and 60 at 110 "	No. 40 150	Nos. 6 and 11 at 325 each.	
Nos. 31, 32, 33, 34, 35 and 37 at 115 "	Nos. 21 and 22 at 225 "	No. 7, with Bath House, and No. 8 at 350 "	
	Nos. 14, 15, 16, 17, 18, 19 and 20 at 250 "	Nos. 23 and 24 together 350 "	
	Nos. 12 and 13 at 300 "	No. 10, GRAND VIEW HOTEL LOT 2,000	

Buffalo Express, April 16, 1893.

sheriff of Erie County seized the company's two steamers and put them up for auction to pay back creditors for $36,000 worth of unpaid coal deliveries during 1894. Just before the auction was to commence, the CBSFC and its creditor, coal dealer H. K. Wicks, reached an agreement that was not disclosed.

The financial vicissitudes of the CBSFC may have started when a fire reduced the Crystal Beach Hotel to a pile of burnt timbers and smoldering ash in a matter of minutes during early May 1893. By the time anyone was aware of the fire, smoke was belching through the roof. If forensics of the era are accurate, then the destruction of the hotel began when workers built a fire in a wood stove or fireplace. Embers had blown through a crack in the flue or stovepipe into the attic starting the fire. Valued at $12,000, it was a total loss and insured for only

$3,000. After taking into account the value of the furnishings saved, Crystal Beach began the 1893 season with a $7,000 loss. The Crystal Beach Hotel reopened in 1894. That same year, inspectors heavily fined the CBSFC for an inadequate number of life preservers for its passengers, sailing without enough water buckets for extinguishing fires, and missing other safety equipment on the steamer *Tymon* that the company leased that year. The fine levied was not disclosed.

Bowling alleys began their long time presence on the midway in 1896.

Announcements for the 1900 season note that the pier was lengthened and widened to relieve overcrowding. In the middle of September, a severe storm destroyed the dock, the bathhouse, and the raised wood walkways. Two months later, the park's steamer *Pearl* sank in the Erie Basin. Overwhelmed with damages and apparently lacking funds to underwrite all the necessary repairs, the CBSFC leased the Crystal Beach operations to the Lake Erie Excursion Company (LEEC) in 1901. The LEEC rebuilt the dock and complimented the beach front with a wide boardwalk at the base of the sand bluffs, forgoing the raised walkways. Incorporated in the State of New York on May 24, 1899, the immediate function of the LEEC is not clear, however, Joseph Rebstock (John Rebstock's brother), and Oliver Jenkins (John Rebstock's friend and business partner) were the directors when the LEEC incorporated.

The LEEC purchased Crystal Beach in 1902 for $48,000. It is uncertain whether the company purchased the all the assets of the Crystal Beach Steamboat and Ferry Company or just the park, leaving the Steamer operations to the CBSFC.

Transformation of the grove into a formal midway began in 1906. The LEEC widened the Cut and lowered its base and built a structure through it that resembled a covered bridge. On the Cut's east side appeared a roller skating rink. Its unclear whether this rink replaced an older one, or if it was the park's first. The rink required a number of floor replacements, and underwent minor expansions and improvements until its removal after the 1924 season. In 1906, the

park's first penny arcade appeared in the grove, and the dance hall was enlarged and a stage was added. The grove began to look more like a midway with the introduction of a number of rides: *Razzle-Dazzle, Circle Swing,* and *Bump the Bumps.* To power the new attractions, the park built a new electric generating station that would power *"3 times as many lights than in previous years."*

An ulterior motive to the improvements may have been to enhance the grounds so perspective buyers could see the potential of Crystal Beach. Henry S. Fisher was the Buffalo agent for the Cleveland and Buffalo Transit Company (C&B Line) and a stockholder of the LEEC. He believed that Crystal Beach would be a good acquisition for the C&B Line and presented his ideas to the C&B Line officers. The C&B Line passed on the acquisition because it was not in the scope of the company's core business - transportation. But some of its officers did see Crystal Beach as an attractive business venture. Initially these officers invested $15,000 in capital stock, then they upped their investment in July 1907 to $600,000. At this point, the CBSFC ceased operations and went out of existence. After 1907, John Rebstock's official duties with Crystal Beach also ended. A new era of Crystal Beach began.

Rides at Crystal Beach during the Rebstock era were not well documented. In some cases the alleged presence of a particular ride remains speculative for lack of confirmation through a second reference or photograph.

The map on the previous page is the earliest known official map of Crystal Beach. It appeared in a newspaper ad in 1893 when parcels of land at Prospect Point were put on the market. The map shows the existence of a carousel, and a roller coaster. There are confirmations of the carousel, but none for the coaster. If the coaster existed, it is of the earliest type of wood coaster known as a Switch Back.

Switch Backs were simple devices of two parallel tracks with very gentle hills between two platform towers. As the layout on the map illustrates, they are devoid of curves. Pushed off one platform, a car that could seat about 10 people, gently traversed a series of hills to the opposite side. There, a moveable track on the platform was pushed over to the parallel track where the car was pushed off for the return trip. Its unlikely there is any true scale to the 1893 map, but the roller coaster layout suggests it had a single track with riders possibly facing sideways rather than forward in the single car.

There were no other references to this roller coaster in any of the Crystal Beach research material; however, the photo below and the one on page 13 contain possible evidence of its existence. The photo on page 13, in comparison to the map, appears to be the loading platform as seen from the beach. In the photo below the arrow points to structure that resembles a single-track roller coaster structure but the date of the photo is unknown and there is not enough of the structure exposed to eliminate the slightest doubt it could be something else. The existence of the Crystal Beach Switch Back Railway remains speculative.

Existence of the carousel depicted in the 1893 map is confirmed with 1893 research references. Photos show a large tent in the proximity of the carousel in the map. Also, there were at least two carousel manufacturers near by that could have supplied the machine. These early machines were steam powered and the one at Crystal Beach was most likely a steam-powered machine from the Armitage-Herschell Company, which began manufacturing carousels around 1880 in North Tonawanda, New York. The menagerie on these early machines was mounted on oblong wheels to create the up-down motion as they rolled on a circular track under the platform. Another nearby carousel manufacturer, though an obscure one was Gillie, Goddard and Company of Tonawanda, New York.

A Ferris Wheel was another diversion for Crystal Beach visitors during the early years of the park. It debuted circa 1895 and confirmed

H pg. 17

Fort Erie Historical Museum collection.

Above: Invented by LaMarcus Thompson, the Switchback Railway debuted at Coney Island in 1884.

Left: The Supply House had the food basics for long term resort residents and was also the office of the resort superintendent. The arrow points to a graded structure that could possibly be the Crystal Beach Switch Back, but there is not enough structure visible to distinguish it from a raised walkway.

Fort Erie Historical Museum collection.

Harvey Holzworth collection.

Fort Erie Historical Museum collection.

Crystal Beach - 1896

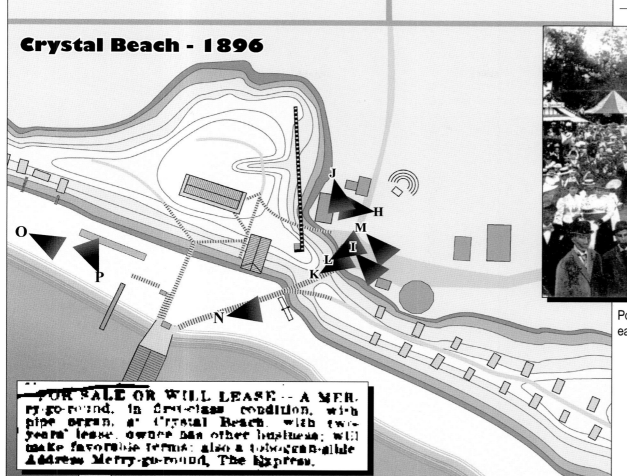

Postcard of crowded grove at Crystal Beach circa 1895 looking east. The large, peaked circus tent likely houses the carousel.

FOR SALE OR WILL LEASE — A MER-ry-go-round, in first-class condition, with pipe organ, at Crystal Beach, with two years' lease, owner has other business; will make favorable terms; also a toboggan-slide. Address Merry-go-round, The Express.

Inset: An ad looking for a buyer or lessee of the carousel at Crystal Beach. Buffalo Express, April 5, 1896, p22c4.

ARMITAGE HERSCHELL CO'S. PATENT STEAM RIDING GALLERY.
NORTH TONAWANDA NY USA.

Gillie Goddard ad (right); Left: Armitage-Hershell Carousel ad resembles the postcard image above.

1892-3
STEAM · RIDING · GALLERY AND **WHIRLING PANORAMA.**

Grand Magnified Panorama.   Music, Chariots, and Galloping Horses.
THE RIDING A DELIGHTFUL EXERCISE!
The Panorama an Unrivalled Attraction.

Cathy Herbert collection.

Left: Ferris Wheel on the beach at the Cut. Bottom: On the left side of this grainy shoreline image there is a spoke-like structure with the bluff in the background indicated by the arrow. Just to the left of this spoke-like structure is a clearing through the trees which is the Cut. Below: A close-up of the spokes that too closely mirrors the wheel at left for it to be anything else.

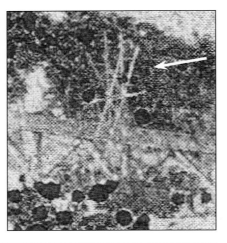

to exist in an 1896 news article. Throughout the history of the park, amusement devices on the beach were rare. The location of the wheel in the image at left is on the beach at the "Cut." Such devices typically require set-up on ground firmer than sand. It wasn't until the images at left surfaced in an advertisement that confirmed that the Ferris Wheel was indeed on the beach. Although the images are far from sharp, the spokes of the wheel are visible just to the right of the gap in the trees.

Due to the instability of the sand, it is unlikely the Ferris Wheel remained on the beach longer than a season. The length of time this particular wheel remained as part of the Crystal Beach ride line-up is unknown. Images of a Ferris Wheel on the Crystal Beach midway circa 1915 show a wheel that is larger than the one on the beach (see page 67).

The image of the Ferris Wheel on the beach is also significant because it clearly shows the Cut before major modifications were done to it to relieve the congestion it created.

The second of the rare beach rides appeared around the time the LEEC leased the park in 1901. The images of the ride (at right) show the wood boardwalk erected by the LEEC along the base of the bluffs and the absence of the raised wood walkways destroyed by a winter storm. It was a simple swing ride that rotated around a vertical axis sweeping its riders out over the water at a gentle speed. Horses provided the power. Images of this ride at the Buffalo and Erie County Historical Society show a ticket booth that calls the ride the Aerolite Swing and a ride cost five cents. The number of years it was a park diversion are unknown. If it lasted more than one season, it most likely was removed after each season as it would not survive the winter ice and storms.

Bicycle riding was a semi-controversial rage during the mid-1890s and local governments imposed many restrictions on the "infernal machines" that dictated where and how fast one could ride. As late as 1904 these rules were still in place, even in small towns such as nearby Ridgeway where the following was reported, *"Boys will be boys! Three Buffalonians were found guilty of scorching on Main Street in Ridgeway. This bicycle speeding is dangerous."* Bicycle riders were afforded considerably more freedom on private bicycle tracks which were being constructed everywhere including Crystal Beach for the 1896 season. Rebstock strategically installed the track near the athletic field in the area that the Giant Coaster occupied later.

Little is known about a merry-go-round that arrived in the park in 1904.

The *Razzle Dazzle* was a very simple device that relied on human muscle and gravity. The ride operator(s) set it in motion by giving it a spin. Then they would pull down on the ring to set it rocking. Its precise years on the midway are uncertain but range from as early as 1895 and lasting to 1906 or 1907. The modern day version is motorized and known by a variety of names: Trabant (German for Satellite), Casino, Satellite, Hully Gully, and Schwabinchen.

R pg. 22

Above: This post card shows the boardwalk built by the Lake Erie Excursion Company in 1901, therefore this image could not have been taken any earlier. On the beach is the ride called the Aerolite Swing with its horizontal spokes orbiting the vertical axis. Below: Horses or mules gently propel the Aerolite Swing sweeping its riders over the water and back.

Q pg. 22

RAZZLE DAZZLE

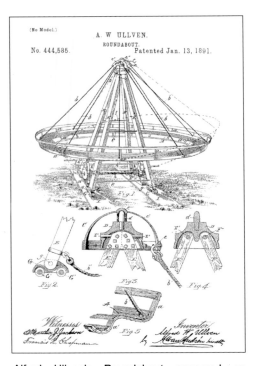

S
pg. 22

Above: From a postcard, visitors at Crystal Beach are enjoying the Razzle-Dazzle, a gently spinning oscillating device put in motion by human muscle. Note the three men standing just within the ring propelling it with their hands. There is an unidentified amusement device to the left of the Razzle-Dazzle. This image, and the inset at left were taken in sequence. Study the people and how they are grouped on the ring. They are in the same position relative to each other, but the ring has changed position. The arrow points to the same boy in both images.

Alfred Ullven's Roundabout appeared on midways across North America as the Razzle-Dazzle. Its local installations included Fort Erie Grove (Erie Beach), Eagle Park on Grand Island, and Bellevue Park in Buffalo.

The patent illustration indicates that the base of the fulcrum widened to lower the ring for easy loading and unloading of passengers, but in actual photos of the ride a series of stairs on wheels that were moved under the ring instead of a widening fulcrum. Other images of Razzle-Dazzles show options such as back rests for the riders, decorative skirting hanging from the inside perimeter of the ring, and varying fulcrum constructions.

A ride named *Circle Swing* debuted in 1906. A popular ride, postcards reveal that Crystal Beach named their unit "Air Ships." Various versions of the Circle Swing would come and go. This one remained for approximately ten years. Invented by Harry Traver, the Circle Swing was the first of a number of his rides that would appear on the midway during the ensuing years.

Another 1906 debut was *Bump-the-Bumps*. Not a ride in the traditional sense, Bump-the-Bumps was an exceptionally wide slide in which riders slid down on a padded mat. The surface of the slide resembled moguls on a ski slope – the bumps. The bumps would propel riders from one side of the slide to the other and frequently into others. At the base people would gather to watch people "Bump the Bumps." It had a relatively long life at Crystal Beach. It was added to the midway for the 1906 season and was removed after the 1924 season.

During the early 1900s, there was mention of another ride called Aerial Swing, which could be a reference to the amusement device to the left of the Razzle Dazzle in the photo on the previous page, or it could have been a reference to the ride on beach seen on page 19.

pg. 22

Above: A postcard circa 1900 looking west showing the midway taking shape. On the left is a partial image of the Razzle-Dazzle. In background is the tented roof of the carousel. The series of buildings on the right housed the midway restaurant, the bowling alleys, and a dance hall.

Above left: The modern version of the Razzle Dazzle, the Trabant resembles an off balance roulette wheel. They are found with various themes and lighting packages, like Schwabinchen (above right) formerly of Cedar Point has an Octoberfest look.

Above: View of the Crystal Beach midway with the Bump the Bumps entrance on the right side.
Below: Postcard image of an open air Bump the Bumps clearly showing the bumps.

Crystal Beach - 1906

CIRCLE SWING

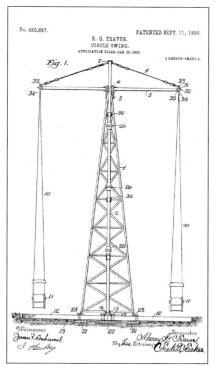

pg. 26

Gulls circling a ship's mast served as Harry Traver's inspiration for the Circle Swing that was a fixture on virtually every midway on the globe during the early 20th Century. Variations of the Circle Swing would come and go in the decades to follow. Above left: Traver's patent diagram. Above right: A portion of a postcard that captures the Venetian style of the rider gondolas. Right: An enlargement of a section of the image on page 57 that captured the ride in motion.

Chapter 2:
1907~1923

A substantial cash infusion by the new management of the Lake Erie Excursion Company (LEEC) put Crystal Beach on the map almost overnight. Although the former owners were successful men in their own right, they were either unwilling or unable to underwrite the necessary improvements to modernize the enterprise. Within a year, the LEEC had a steamer with a capacity greater than all the steamers that previously sailed to the park in a single season. The grounds had undergone a major layout reorganization with landscaping, and the appearance of big-ticket rides transformed Crystal Beach into a major amusement park.

Henry S. Fisher Buffalo Courier, March 20, 1904

Thomas F. Newman Lower Lakes Marine Historical Society

Morris A. Bradley A History of Cleveland and its Environs

H. Bert Rogers Rochester Democrat and Chronicle February 17, 1913

The takeover of the LEEC by Cleveland businessmen began in the fall of 1906 and was completed at some point before July 1907 when the Cleveland investors pumped $600,000 into the company. Thomas F. Newman became the new president and John B. Richards – a prominent Cornell-educated Buffalo attorney became vice president. Henry S. Fisher, instrumental in bringing the LEEC to the attention of the C&B Line was named secretary and general manager, and at Crystal Beach, Herbert Rogers was named general manager. Notable directors included Morris A. Bradley, Edward Smith and A.T. Zillmer.

Zillmer was the secretary and treasurer of the C&B Line. He wrote a synopsis of the LEEC for *Inland Seas* and notes that Henry S. Fisher was a stockholder of the early LEEC and that Fisher also was the Buffalo agent for the C&B Line. According to Zillmer, Fisher promoted the LEEC and its Crystal Beach operations as an acquisition for C&B Line. He and the other original stockholders of the LEEC probably envisioned a grander future for Crystal Beach - a future that would never be realized because the company was undercapitalized.

Fisher was not acting alone. John Rebstock met with Thomas Newman on February 19, 1907 to discuss reorganizing the LEEC in order to put the company in good financial standing.

The C&B Line declined the acquisition offer but its officers took controlling interest of the LEEC, keeping the two companies as separate enterprises.

A Cleveland native born in 1858, Thomas F. Newman began learning about transportation on the Great Lakes when he went to work as a general utility boy for the Detroit & Cleveland Steam Navigation Company in 1875. Three years later he received a promotion to chief clerk, then became the general agent for the line in the Cleveland district in 1884. He resigned this position in 1893 to organize the Cleveland and Buffalo Transit Company with Morris A. Bradley. Bradley became the president of the C&B Line, Newman held the office of secretary and general manager.

Morris A. Bradley was a Cleveland industrial magnate of considerable wealth. All prior investors in Crystal Beach would appear to be living in poverty in comparison to Bradley. He joined his father's shipbuilding firm in Cleveland in 1868. When his father died in 1885, he inherited a fortune that was invested in real estate and iron and steel enterprises. He held a number of offices with a number of companies including the U.S. Coal Company (president), Erie Building Company (sec./treas.), Alva Realty Company (sec./treas.), St. Claire Realty Company (sec./treas.), Bradley Electrical Company (president), Bradley Light Heat and Power (owner operator with his sons), and State National Bank of Cleveland (president). The Bradley Real Estate Company became one of the largest holders of downtown Cleveland real estate. He was on now the board of directors of the LEEC.

Details of Henry S. Fisher are sparse outside his association with the C&B Line. He and Newman worked for the Detroit and Cleveland Line, Newman recruited Fisher as the C&B Line's Cleveland agent. Fisher later relocated to Buffalo to replace the C&B Line agent who resigned. His experience and connections through the C&B Line made his role as agent for the LEEC a natural fit.

Improvements at the park began in 1907, but once again, the first improvements were more disaster recovery as a major storm in January destroyed the pier again. The second pier design debuted that summer. It consisted of two sections: the 24-foot wide pier that stretched from the shoreline out 500 feet into the bay; the second section, built on the beach, served as the waiting area and was 50 feet wide, 200 feet long, with a second deck with decorative railings around its perimeter. Just before this new pier was completed, another storm in May damaged a portion farthest from the shore that was still under construction.

In the grove, from the Cut to the dance hall, all the trees where cleared for an open court that would be lined on both sides with concession stands, a theater, games and other attractions. The first new attraction on the midway for 1907 was the *Figure-8* roller coaster. Season announcements described the *Backety-Back Scenic Railway* for 1907, but it did not materialize until 1908.

The second pier under construction along with a boardwalk along the base of the bluff to a covered bridge-style pass through the Cut. Left of the pier ice accumulates from the steady winds from the west, and an addition to the bathhouse is also under construction.

To unburden themselves of the necessity to lease a fleet of steamboats that had been the practice during most years since 1890 the LEEC contracted with American Shipbuilding Company in 1907 to build an elegant steamer specifically for the Crystal Beach Line. Construction

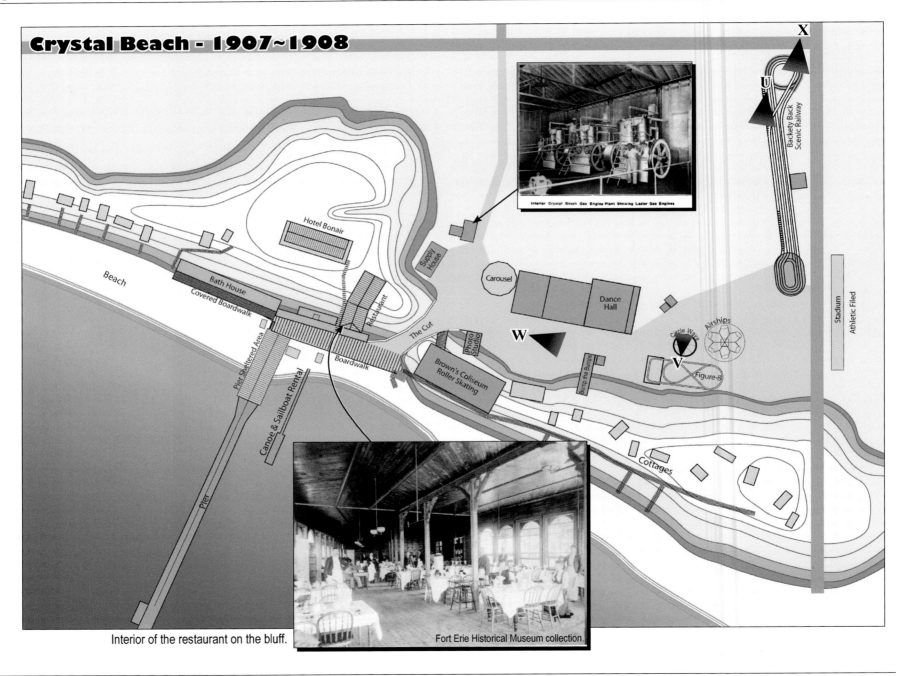

Crystal Beach - 1907~1908

Interior of the restaurant on the bluff.

Fort Erie Historical Museum collection.

of the steamer began that fall at the Buffalo Dry Dock Company in Buffalo. Edward Smith, one of the new directors of the LEEC was also president of the American Shipbuilding Company and the Buffalo Dry Dock Company. The new steamer, *S.S. Americana,* debuted in 1908.

As earlier noted, the *Backety-Back Scenic Railway* debuted in 1908. Another infrastructure improvement was the installation of a "drainage" system. It is assumed that this system was to remove access water from the grove, but with ever increasing crowds on the midway, whatever cisterns were employed for human by-products had to have had reached their limit, so it is also possible that this drainage system was a sewer system. The LEEC also constructed a new electric generating plant on the grounds that supplied power to the rides, over 15,000 lights, water supply pumps, and other equipment. The generators where fueled with natural gas from local wells. The public was invited to view the generators (see inset on the previous page).

It was clear that the new management of the LEEC wanted to disenfranchise themselves from the old management when this comment appeared in one of their press releases, *"It is not the old Crystal Beach of the sand, and the cheap, ramshackle concessions."*

A year later the first incarnation of the "Old Mill" called *Scenic Rivers of the World* made its debut. Announcements for the 1909 season note that a miniature railway was now an attraction at Crystal Beach that would transport its riders to the grove behind the sand bluffs. Romantic history of Crystal Beach contends that this railway was the same one used at the Pan American Exposition in Buffalo during 1901, but there is no evidence to support this, and no references to the Pan American in any 1909 Crystal Beach press. Peter and Thomas McGarigle of Niagara Falls, New York manufactured the Pan Am miniature railway and the Crystal Beach miniature, but whether it came from the Pan Am remains to be proved.

The launching of the *S. S. Canadiana* in 1910 marked expenditures of $565,000: $250,000 for each steamer, $50,000 for the *Backety-Back* and $15,000 for the *Figure-8*. Rebuilding the pier in 1907 along with the drainage system, and the various other improvements probably

exceeded the initial $615,000 pumped into the LEEC. George Hall, who would later have a pivotal role in the park's development, began selling confections on the midway around 1910.

With two palatial steamers that could deliver 3,500 people to the Crystal Beach pier every hour the congestion at the Cut became a critical bottleneck. To relieve the pedestrian gridlock, management focused their efforts on widening the pass for the 1911 season. Herbert B. Rogers, manager of the park, received bids for the excavation, but the lowest quote came in it at $7,000 – a price he felt was too high. Rather than remove the sand and gravel with shovels, wheelbarrows, and horses hitched to scrapers, Rogers fabricated a long 4-foot wide trough with 12-inch sidewalls that sloped downward from the Cut to the shoreline. With four fire hoses and water from the park's fire-fighting system, crews washed the sand and gravel from the steep banks of the Cut into the trough. After six days, the Cut had been widened from forty feet to 250 feet, but traditional earth-moving equipment leveled and graded the rough-hewn pass for terraces and sod on the banks, and a cement walkway. Keeping with this trend, and as a cost avoidance measure, Rogers replaced the boardwalk along the beach with one of cement that was able to withstand severe winter storms (but it was not completely impervious to Lake Erie surf).

NEW DANCE HALL TO BE BUILT AT CRYSTAL BEACH.
From drawing by the architect

Rendering of the dance hall proposed in 1919 by the LEEC that did not materialize.
Buffalo Express, April 27, 1919

Also in 1911, a new restaurant on the midway was rebuilt to accommodate the ever-growing patronage.

On the midway, *Scenic Rivers of the World* had been redone and renamed *Dreamland*. The exact year of this change is uncertain, but on July 11, 1912, the second fire at Crystal Beach destroyed it. Newspaper accounts record that a burning cigarette ignited the fire in what the ride's owner, Henry Oges, claimed was the *"Biggest Waterway Tunnel Building in the World."* The fire erupted at 6:30 PM with smoke billowing from the rear of the tunnels. Pegged at a loss of $14,000, Oges reported that Dreamland was fully insured and would be rebuilt.

Just before the 1914 season was about to begin, Herbert Rogers resigned as general manager of the park to become the general manager of Maple Beach Park (also known as Altro Park) which was on an island in the Hudson River between Albany and Troy, New York. This long forgotten park operated from about 1907 into the 1920s.

Buffalo restaurateur Charles Laube began a long affiliation with Crystal Beach in 1914 when he, along Henry S. W. Simon assumed management of the restaurant and food services at the park.

After the 1916 season, construction of new roller coaster began that would eventually be known as the *Giant Coaster*. Reportedly, to make room for it, the *Figure-8* had to be removed. In reality, there was plenty of room for both, so the real reason for the LEEC to remove it is unknown. The Giant debuted in 1917, and a walk-through attraction called *Steeplechase* occupied a portion of the Figure-8 site.

The drainage system installed on the grounds during 1908 proved inadequate ten years later when a cloudburst flooded the midway.

A new dance hall planned by the LEEC in 1919 never materialized (see page 27). They also announced $500,000 of improvements in 1919 that included lengthening and widening of the pier and removal of the sand hill that separated the midway from the beach – presumably it included a protective seawall. This too did not materialize under the LEEC. A year later, they dedicated a grandstand for the athletic field.

The 1919 announcement of pier improvements materialized in 1921 in the form of a massive reinforced concrete pier with a price tag of $250,000. According to the LEEC, construction on it began

Fort Erie Historical Museum collection.

Whatever the drainage system installed in 1907, a summer cloudburst flooded the midway circa 1920 with more than it could handle.

Fort Erie Historical Museum collection.

This image captures the flooded midway from the Giant Coaster station (left) to the Backety-Back Scenic Railway in the background.

Cathy Herbert collection.

five years earlier when they began construction of the pylons that reached from the bedrock to several feet above the waterline. This may have been a slight exaggeration, but planning for it may have started in 1916. This was also the last major investment by the LEEC in Crystal Beach operations.

The second pier under siege during a winter storm in 1921 before major construction on the third pier began. These images are dated December 1921. The concrete, double deck pier that exists today was dedicated before the 1921 season but is clearly not in this photo. So the date cannot be correct.

Cathy Herbert collection.

Above: High surf batters the shoreline.

Cathy Herbert collection.

After the storm: The surf undermined the foundation of a section of the concrete walkway causing it to collapse.

Top left and right: Comparison of images of the first pier reveal subtle differences precipitated by total and partial reconstruction. The top left image circa 1895 reveals the uneven crib construction. The top right image from 1901 image reveals cribs of more uniform timbers. Note the deck overhangs are better reinforced and the sheds are gone.

The second pier was a sturdier construction but not sturdy enough.

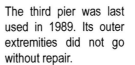

The third pier was last used in 1989. Its outer extremities did not go without repair.

Cathy Herbert collection.

Below: Artist rendering of the third dock. The rendering shows the double deck section extending back to what was the boardwalk at the base of the sand bluffs. When built, this section terminated at the arrow, which corresponds to the arrow in the two images above. It also marks the point of the west terminus of the sea wall constructed during the summer of 1924.

PROPOSED·REINFORCED·CONCRETE-
-DOUBLE·DECK·DOCK-
-FOR THE-
-CRYSTAL·BEACH·Co.-

Cathy Herbert collection.

The third pier takes shape over the ice with the first deck partially complete. The reinforcing rebar for the second deck supporting pillars are ready for cement.

Construction workers raise a hoist that will be used to pour cement into the forms that will become supportive pillars for the second deck.

Looking outward, the first deck floor is nearing completion and one of the pillars is wrapped against the cold to so the cement can harden and not freeze.

Fort Erie Historical Museum collection.

A grainy image, but one that illustrates the third pier nearing completion. The arrow indicates the western terminus of the seawall to come in a few more years.

Fort Erie Historical Museum collection.

A close up looking east from the beach showing the second deck forms and supportive structure. The cribs from the second dock are still in place under the third dock.

Above and below: Circa 1926 images of an extension to the third pier under construction. Low water levels may have forced the extension so the steamers would not bottom when docking.

Construction of the extension was already underway when the Buffalo and Crystal Beach Corp. filed for permits to build it. The district engineer, S.E. O'Brien, secretary of the Department of Public Works Canada, recommended the project for approval and also recommended that the 1921 cement dock be considered part of the project as it was constructed without approvals required by the Navigable Waters Protection Act, Chapter 33 of 1918. The Governor in Council could have forced the removal of all of it. Everything was approved on March 4, 1927 - long after completion.

Fort Erie Historical Museum collection.

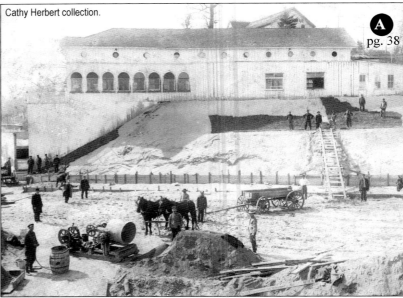

Cathy Herbert collection.

A
pg. 38

Top left: The Cut after the 1906 lowering and the construction of the covered bridge-like passage.

Above: This photo was taken in 1907 as landscaping work on the Cut continued after Burt Rogers' sluice had done its job. Now, workers are building the forms for cement terraces and laying sod. The grove and midway are to the right, the beach to the left. This would eventually be the site of the water slides during the 1970s.

Left: One year later the results of infusion of cash into Crystal Beach and the subsequent improvements are evident. The dotted line approximates the profile of the bluff and illustrates the volume of sand that had been removed.

SCENIC RIVERS OF THE WORLD

This circa 1910 image shows Scenic Rivers of the World - the first incarnation of the Old Mill - at Crystal Beach. An in-the-dark water ride, small boats were propelled by the gentle current of water through a channel with view ports to scenes of famous rivers recreated in miniature dioramas or depicted in murals.

Fort Erie Historical Museum collection.

HILARITY HALL

This pre-1917 image of Hilarity Hall stands to the left of Scenic Rivers of the World. What it contained is a mystery, but a "Cake Walk" (p. 66) also occupied this location.

Harvey Holzworth collection.

Fair
Japan

Cane
Bakery

Red
Hots

Box Ball
Alleys

Bump the
Bumps

Rifle
Range

Amusement
Parlor

Paper
House

There were always changes on the main midway. In this image, the Box Ball Alleys were removed and replaced with the "The Dolls Cane Rack" and the "Play Ball" game.

B

pg. 38

Right side of
Box Ball Alleys

In this image shows the formal midway under construction. The Supply House for the summer colony remains in the background. Immediately above it is the hotel on the ridge. The Paper House, Amusement Parlor and Box Ball Alleys are under construction.

CIRCLE WAVE

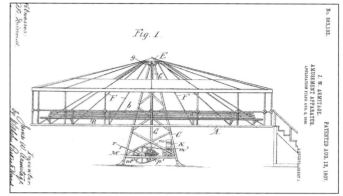

Above: This photo is an enlargement of a portion of the photo on page 57. A partial view appears on page 62. Below: A Circle Wave somewhere in the U.K.

Circle Wave was a larger motorized version of the Razzle Dazzle and assumed to be its replacement in 1907 added to the formalized midway. Since people rode the Circle Wave facing outward, (and it was doubtful there any rider restraints), its rotation speed had to have been relatively slow otherwise the centrifugal force would have flung riders out across the park.

According to the patent, there were mechanisms that controlled the degree of the ride's rocking.

Circle Wave was most likely removed from the midway when another attraction, The House That Jack Built, debuted on its site.

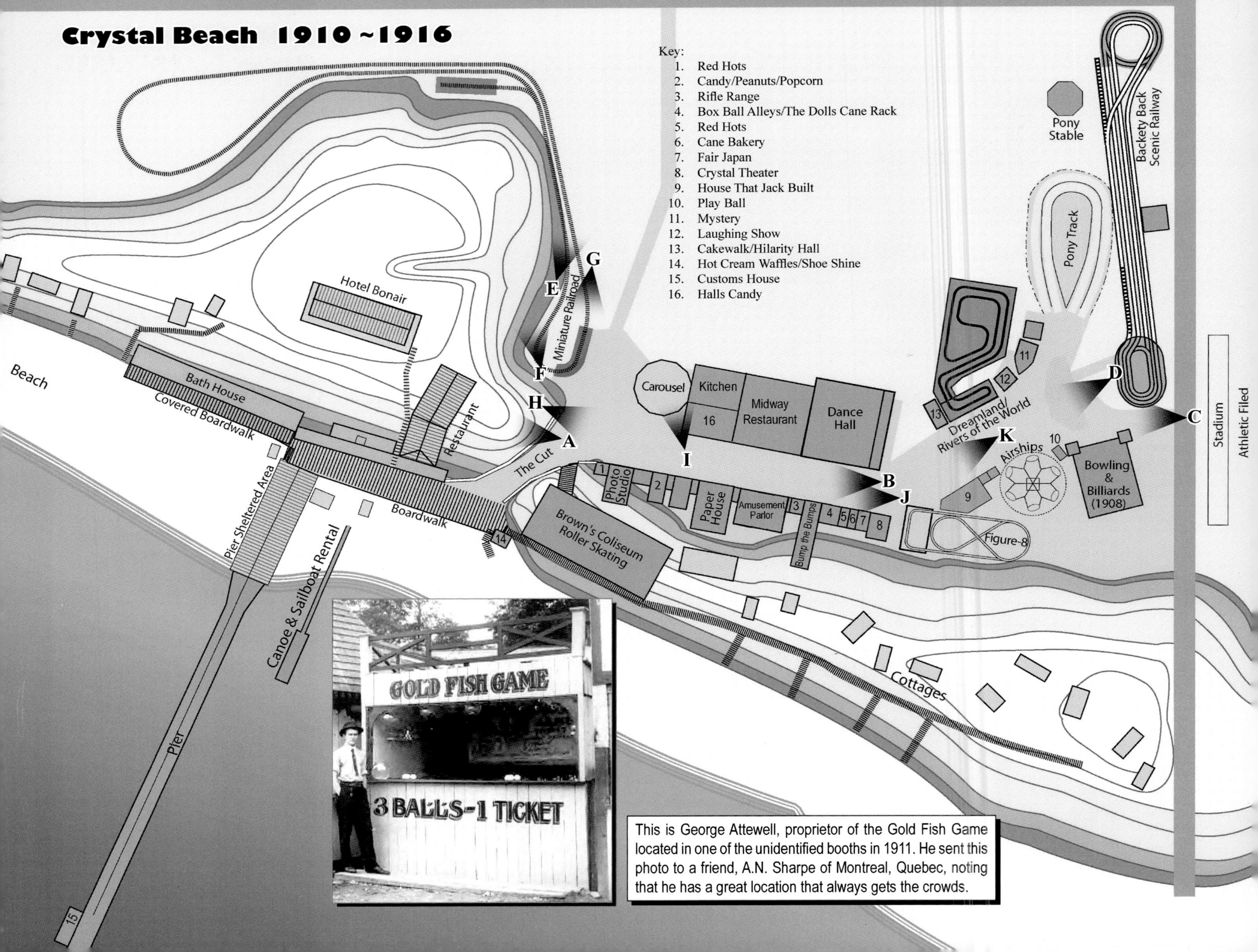

Crystal Beach 1910~1916

Key:
1. Red Hots
2. Candy/Peanuts/Popcorn
3. Rifle Range
4. Box Ball Alleys/The Dolls Cane Rack
5. Red Hots
6. Cane Bakery
7. Fair Japan
8. Crystal Theater
9. House That Jack Built
10. Play Ball
11. Mystery
12. Laughing Show
13. Cakewalk/Hilarity Hall
14. Hot Cream Waffles/Shoe Shine
15. Customs House
16. Halls Candy

Beach

Pony Stable

Backety Back Scenic Railway

Hotel Bonair

Pony Track

Miniature Railroad

G
E
F
H
A

Bath House

Covered Boardwalk

Restaurant

The Cut

Carousel

Kitchen

Midway Restaurant

Dance Hall

16

I

11

72

13

Dreamland/ Rivers of the World

D

C

Stadium

Athletic Filed

Boardwalk

Pier Sheltered Area

Canoe & Sailboat Rental

Pier

15

14

Brown's Coliseum Roller Skating

1 Photo Studio

2

Paper House

Amusement Parlor

3

Bump the Bumps

4 5 6 7 8

B J

K

Airships

9

10

Figure-8

Bowling & Billiards (1908)

Cottages

GOLD FISH GAME

3 BALLS-1 TICKET

This is George Attewell, proprietor of the Gold Fish Game located in one of the unidentified booths in 1911. He sent this photo to a friend, A.N. Sharpe of Montreal, Quebec, noting that he has a great location that always gets the crowds.

Niagara Falls, Ontario Public Library Collection.

Bowling Alleys   Cake Walk   Dreamland   The Laughing Show   Mystery   Backety-Back Scenic Railway

An interesting circa 1912 reverse angle image from the one on page 35 with Dreamland replacing Scenic Rivers. When the ride became Dreamland the scenes inside were probably a mix of fantasy and nightmare. Then it burned. Note the Mystery ship constructed to resemble the bow of a lake steamship freighter topped by the pilot house.

A WALK WEST ALONG THE MIDWAY 1910-1916

Cathy Herbert collection.

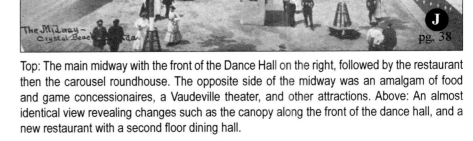

Top: An aerial view circa 1912 when Scenic Rivers was rethemed as Dreamland. Neighboring Dreamland is the giant face known as the Laughing Show. The image was probably shot from the station roof of the Backety-Back Railway. Above: Another view perhaps photographed from onboard the Ferris Wheel. In the foreground is Scenic Rivers, then the Dance Hall. The gap in between them would eventually be filled by the Giant Coaster station.

Top: The main midway with the front of the Dance Hall on the right, followed by the restaurant then the carousel roundhouse. The opposite side of the midway was an amalgam of food and game concessionaires, a Vaudeville theater, and other attractions. Above: An almost identical view revealing changes such as the canopy along the front of the dance hall, and a new restaurant with a second floor dining hall.

Fort Erie Historical Museum collection.

A tranquil night scene.

pg. 38

The Crystal Flyer station replaced the Supply House where summer residents purchased goods before merchants opened stores in the growing village.

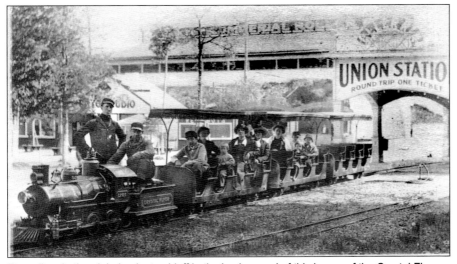

The roller skating rink dominates bluff in the background of this image of the Crystal Flyer.

During the late 19th Century, numerous railroads made the City of Buffalo a major railroad hub and their passenger stations peppered the city. Community leaders in 1889 proposed construction of the Union Station on the east side of Buffalo - it was planned to be a grand facility that centralized passenger rail services at one location. When the miniature railway debuted at Crystal Beach in 1909, twenty years had passed and the Union Station in Buffalo was still hotly debated. Naming the station of the Crystal Beach miniature railway as Buffalo's Union Station, prefaced with "At Last" was poking humor at what would become Buffalo's ongoing tradition of endless debate by its political leaders and special interest groups on any and all initiatives. A true "Union Station" was never built, although the New York Central Railroad did build a huge complex on the Union Station site known today as the Central Terminal.

Season opening announcements for the 1902 season note that

management purchased a number of canopied benches that were part of the 1901 Pan American Exposition. Romantic history notes that the miniature train at Crystal Beach came from the same exposition. If it did, it did made an 8-year detour and did not arrive at Crystal Beach until the 1909 season when references to the railway first appeared in Crystal Beach press (without references to the exposition). If it arrived in 1902, it is curious that announcements referenced a few canopied benches, but were mum on the far greater expenditure that the railway would have represented. Six miniature train lines operated at the Pan Am, all manufactured by McGarigle Machine Works of Niagara Falls, New York. However, the Cagney Brothers of New Jersey distributed and operated McCarigle miniature trains including all six that they installed and operated at the Pan Am.

The Crystal Flyer was an authentic miniature steam locomotive also built by McGarigle Machine Works of Niagara Falls, New York. The manufacturer is the only connection it has to the Pan Am trains. McGarigle built a second locomotive for the park around 1928. Charlie Butler owned and operated the concession until his death in 1935 then Lewis F. LeJeune purchased it. According to Lewis, the locomotives cost $10,000 each when new. He also notes that Engine 97 was the loco used at the Pan Am. Find a photo of one of the six locos at the Pan Am with a '97' on it then this Crystal Beach myth becomes fact. The mystery to solve then is where was the train between 1901 and 1909?

The steam locomotives operated through 1947. Though the rolling stock changed, the route through the grove remained the same.

The Crystal Flyer's twin locomotive, Cannon Ball, is taking a light load on the outbound leg of its loop. Note the picnic grove in the background shaded by a forest of trees. White paint on the tree trucks was used as an insecticide to keep ants and other insects from burrowing into the trees. It was also a common practice in some areas because people felt it was aesthetically pleasing.

The comical reference to Buffalo's Union Station disappeared with a station update, but the rolling stock remained the same.

Rounding the final curve entering the station

43

PTC Carousel 12

To park visitors, the Crystal Beach carousel was simply called the Merry-Go-Round but to amusement professionals, it was PTC #12 - the nomenclature used by the Philadelphia Toboggan Company to identify its 12th carousel. They built it during 1906. While there is no evidence to support its 1912 arrival in local press (there are no references to a new carousel added to the midway in 1912), there is other evidence.

Henry Auchy and Chester Albright founded the Philadelphia Toboggan Company (PTC) in 1904. Auchy also owned an amusement park in Philadelphia called Chestnut Hill Park which became known as "White City" because everything in it was painted white. PTC built their 12th carousel for Auchy's nearby park in 1906. Well-to-do neighbors felt the park was attracting the wrong class of people to the area and bought the park from Auchy with "an offer he could not refuse." The new owners sold the park's equipment in 1911, which would explain why PTC #12 did not arrive at Crystal Beach until 1912. PTC #12 went to Sea Breeze Park in Hartford, Connecticut before it made its final home at Crystal Beach. The dates of occupancy at Sea Breeze are elusive.

Fort Erie Historical Museum collection.

I
pg. 38

H
pg. 38

Above right: Clarence Teal delivers ice to midway concessionaires, circa 1915. In the background is the roundhouse with PTC #12 cloaked in shadow inside.

Right: Looking east down the midway with the carousel roundhouse on the left.

Previous page: PTC #12 was a colorful, smooth machine with some very unique animals including a rare hippo campus (horse with a fishtail) seen here. The outer row of animals were stationary. Most preferred riding the inner two rows of "jumpers."

The mountain goat was another unique animal of the menagerie on PTC12.

New, PTC #12 cost $9,000.

According to "Carousels of the Philadelphia Toboggan Company," PTC #12 had a diameter of 48 feet with three rows of animals in its menagerie. The outer row of animals were stationary, the inner two rows were "jumpers." There were 46 animals total. For those who preferred not to ride a mount, there where were two chariots placed 180 degrees from each other on the outside diameter - each chariot could seat 4. The total rider capacity of PTC #12 was 54.

PTC #12 underwent aesthetic alterations at various times during its 72 seasons. Upon its arrival, PTC #12 did not resemble the carousel in contemporary postcards and photos. The familiar décor of mirrors, neon lighting with story book murals and art-deco paint theme on its rounding boards replaced very intricate wood carving.

According to a PTC catalog, its inner framework and machinery were hidden from view by an artistic enclosure of oil paintings and decorations (see page 48). These oil paintings were supplanted with mirrors and neon lights. Originally, the overhead crankshafts that operated the jumpers were clearly visible before the alterations and riders could see up to the underside of the carousel building's roof. Hundreds of feet of exquisitely carved wood that adorned the perimeter and ornamented the overhead structural system were sacrificed for art deco. This radical change in appearance was made, for better or worse, to match the art-deco style face-lift the entire park received for the 1946 season. The advertised cost to "modernize" the look of PTC #12 was $10,000 - more than what the ride cost new.

The rounding boards received another modification during the late 1970s or early 1980s. The fluorescent tubes that partitioned each rounding board were replaced with a mirrored, four sectioned shield traced with lights. Colored incandescent light fixtures lined the bottom of each rounding board (see page 51). Some of the neon fixtures that had burned out or were damaged were never replaced.

PTC #12 was the sentimental favorite ride until it was dismantled, transported to Fort Wayne, Indiana and auctioned piecemeal in December 1984. Reportedly the auction grossed $500,000.

The decorative changes Crystal Beach made to PTC12 were so extensive, the only features that remained unchanged were the menagerie and the two chariots. The only photo of PTC12 known to exist before these changes is on the following page that reveals one chariot and the lion (below). The images to the right are from the 1984 Norton Auctioneers catalog.

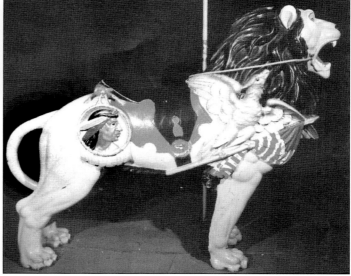

Philadelphia Toboggan Company archives courtesy of Philadelphia Toboggan Coasters.

PTC12 as it looked with its original ornamentation at its first home at White City Park in Philadelphia. The park, also known as Chestnut Hill Park, closed in 1911 and the machine was relocated to Crystal Beach where it operated from 1912 through 1984.

Cathy Herbert collection.

For better or worse, the post-war PTC12 was stripped of its original Victorian wood carvings and adornments and replaced with a theme that tied in with the art deco face lift the entire park received after World War II. Mirrors with neon lighting replaced the original artwork along the carousel's inside perimeter. Art deco painted rounding boards partitioned with fluorescent lights were fixed to its outer circumference. Images from fairy tales appeared on the rounding board panels in alternating pairs. Seen here are Mother Goose (left) and Hey Diddle Diddle (center).

The original round house for PTC12 at White City Park, Philadelphia.

Close-up of the nursery rhyme images on the rounding boards seen in the photo on the previous page.

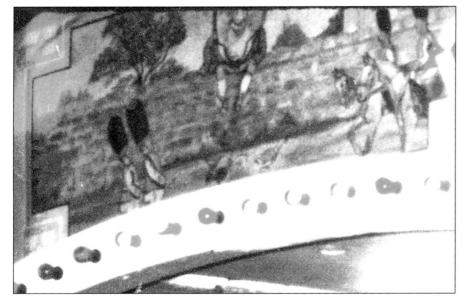

Enhanced and enlarged from the upper left corner image on the following page is another rounding board painted with Humpty Dumpty and all the king's horses and men gathering around Humpty Dumpty before his fall.

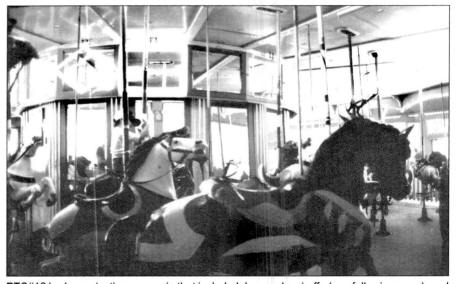

PTC#12 had an eclectic menagerie that included deer and a giraffe (see following page), and two dogs - one was a jumper (partially visible in the image on page 44) and a stationary St. Bernard (not pictured).

Above: This is an enlargement of a section of a photo from 1908. As faint as it is, It is the only known image that captures so much of the profile of the Figure-8, and the Traver Circle Swing with its oil-derrick tower. Other photos and postcards capture glimpses of these rides. Until this image, the best record of this coaster is the postcard on the following page.

BACKETY BACK SCENIC RAILWAY

Visitors to Crystal Beach during May and June 1908 would see the park's second roller coaster under construction - a mammoth, new Scenic Railway promised to be *"much bigger than the one at the Pan American Exposition, and considerably different in construction."*

Incandescent lights traced every arch and overhang of the coaster's ornate colonial-style station that was three stories tall, 72 feet long and 48 feet wide. Reportedly the entire ride required over 95,000 square feet of Georgia Pine and cost $50,000.

Designed and constructed by John H. Brown, the *Backety-Back Scenic Railway* was a second hand coaster when it arrived at Crystal Beach. Its first home was the Jamestown Exposition at Sewells Point, Virginia (now the Norfolk Naval Base) according to Crystal Beach newspaper announcements about the ride. The exposition was a

celebration of the 300th anniversary of the first permanent English settlement in America. The exposition, with its distinct military theme, operated from April to November 1907.

Exterior photos of the coaster in Robert Cartmell's book *"The Incredible Scream Machine A History of the Roller Coaster"* were not photographed at Crystal Beach although this is not immediately apparent until they are compared to photos of the roller coaster while at Crystal Beach. Analysis of these images are on the following page.

On July 4, 1908 the Backety-Back Scenic Railway made its Crystal Beach debut.

What made this coaster unusual was a series of two dead-end inclines that caused the trains to stop, reverse direction, then roll onto track on a lower level without any mechanical switching mechanisms.

A truly imaginative and simple technique invented and patented by John H. Brown permitted the coaster's trains to figuratively jump across a hole to a different track. A set of "extended" rollers on the trains would engage special side mounted rails that lifted the train over a gap in the track. Once across the gap, the bottom wheels would re-engage the main track, roll up the incline, stall and roll backwards then drop through the gap it had just crossed while going forward. The train rolled down approximately ten feet once through the gap and continued to roll backwards until it reached the other dead-end. Again, the train stalled, reversed direction to roll forward, drop through a gap down to another level of track and roll forward through the balance of the ride.

Patent diagrams on page 58 illustrate the simplicity of Brown's design (another description with illustrations are in the Appendix).

Approaching the gap in the track must have been disconcerting to first time riders – especially for those in the front seat (cont'd. pg. 59)

— THE L.A. THOMPSON SCENIC RAILWAY —
AND AQUARAMA
PAN-AMERICAN EXPOSITION

There was a LaMarcus Thompson Scenic Railway on the midway of the Buffalo Pan American Exposition in 1901. The inventor of the Backety-Back was undoubtedly inspired by its station design so much so that its a wonder Thompson did not sue John Brown. It is also possible, though speculative, that Brown could have designed the station for Thompson.

Robert Cartmell Collection. Courtesy American Coaster Enthusiasts.

A

B

This image shows the main lift hill and the second lift hill with its double-down element.

A   C   B

C

Aerial profile of the Backety-Back with the Giant Coaster in the foreground. Athletic fields at the top of the photo.

Above: This is an image of the Backety-Back from Cartmell's book. Note the framework indicated by the arrow (A). Such framing does not appear in Crystal Beach images like the postcard at top right. The photo above also does not have the house-like building seen in the postcard (B).

Inset: Enlarged from the right side of the image below is a coliseum-like building - the likes of which never existed at Crystal Beach. If it had existed at Crystal Beach, it would have been at (C) in the aerial image at right, and upper right - in the photo on the following page, it would be on the grounds where the track and bleachers appear in the upper left. There was no such construction in that location ever. Note the signage: "warpath" and "battle" is in fact advertising for the Jamestown Exposition concession "Battle of the Merrimac and Monitor."

Right: The porch railings lining the perimeter of the roof are solid - in any Crystal Beach image, this railing is very ornate with spacing. The scrub pines are not native to Southern Ontario. The wood planked grounds surrounding the coaster never existed at Crystal Beach.

Robert Cartmell Collection. Courtesy American Coaster Enthusiasts.

THE JOHN H. BROWN. PATENT

BACKETY-BACK SCENIC RAILWAY

John Bosco collection.

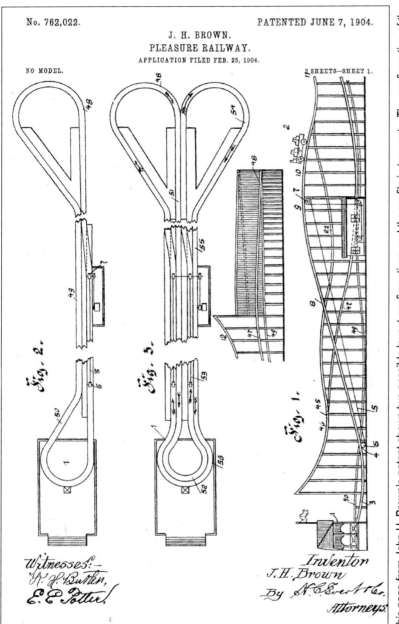

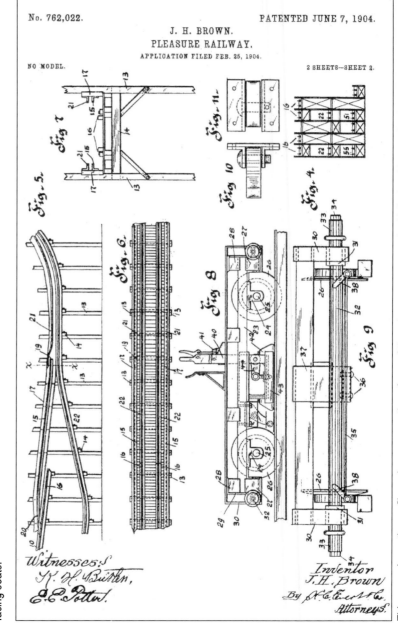

This page from John H. Brown's patent shows two possible layout configurations and the profile in two parts. The configuration of the Backety-Back at Crystal Beach was somewhat different. It was not the footprint he was patenting but the engineering for the roller coaster car wheel system and the special track design. Note in this image that Brown depicted the coaster with forward and backward-facing seats.

This page shows the profile and a cross section of one of the primary coaster truck with its breaking mechanism, the train-like weight-bearing wheels and the additional set of rollers that carried the train over the gap by sliding into the special slotted side rail that would allow the train, then to roll backwards without any mechanical switch. This sheet also profiles the track where the reversal occurred and a cross section illustrating the special slotted side-track.

where it looked as if the train would plummet to the ground below. Yet the train sailed across the gap as if by divine intervention.

There were no brakes to slow or stop the train anywhere along the coaster's layout or in the station. Like a true railroad, the brake was on the train and operated by a brakeman on board. He sat in the center between the two cars of the train and operated the brakes. In addition, he also operated a mechanism that clasped a cable that hauled the trains up the coaster's three lift hills* – another unique feature of the coaster.

The Backety-Back was a perennial favorite, particularly so for 17 year old Louise Koch and two of her friends who rode it numerous times on June 29, 1910. The girls shrieked and laughed through the forward-backward-forward sections of track from which the coaster's name was derived. After the second lift hill was a 520-degree tunneled helix that was the last part of the ride before the train returned to the station. The tunnel amplified the train's rumbling that nearly drowned out shrieks of the riders. When the train emerged from the tunnel, the seat holding Louise was empty.

*The main lift hill is seen here. The second and smaller lift hill is seen in the two images at the top of page 56. The third lift hill hauled the train to the second level of track (or third floor) of the station where inside it spiraled down to the loading and unloading areas on the first level of track on the second floor of the station. The third lift hill cable can be seen in the center of the track immediately to the left at the base of the first hill drop in the photo on page 54. The first floor was ground level with a staircase to the loading platform on the second floor.

Scenic Railway
Crystal Beach, Can.

Ride operators summoned Doctor Snyder from Ridgeway after they found Louise in the tunnel lying between the rails and barely alive. There was nothing Snyder could do for her. Carried on board the Americana on a stretcher, Louise died shortly after the steamer departed for Buffalo. A resident of Orchard Park, New York, Louise holds the inauspicious distinction of being the first fatality associated with an amusement device at Crystal Beach.

The circumstances that led to Louise's ejection from the train will remain a mystery without subsequent reports of any investigation - if one was conducted. In spite of this tragedy, the Backety-Back operated for 16 more years without another incident.

Following the 1926 season, *"some rides were removed because they outlived their usefulness."* This included the demolition of the Backety-Back.

Whether or not the Backety-Back outlived its usefulness is difficult to say. With the debut of the Cyclone in 1927, George Hall probably saw no need for three coasters in the park and removed the oldest one – leaving the Giant Coaster, built in 1917, and the Cyclone.

John Bosco collection.

RACKETY-BACK
SCENIC RAILWAY.
INVENTED AND CONSTRUCTED BY
JOHN H. BROWN
No.10 KENMAWR AVE. RANKIN, PA. U.S.A.

TICKETS
10¢
HOW MANY
RIDE
10¢
RIDE
10¢

ENTRANCE TO CARS.
HOLD YOUR OWN TICKET.

RIDE
10¢

e 10¢   BUY TICKETS

John Bosko collection.

Photographed from the corner of Erie and Ridgeway Roads, a very rare image of the Backety-Back under construction. The lower two levels of track will be tunnelled and the trains move from the left side of the image to the right. On the highest level of track the trains move from right to left. The lift hill is the background on the lower left.

X
pg 26

Harvey Holzworth collection.

The Cake Walk at Crystal Beach adjacent to Scenic Rivers of the World. The signs on the front of the Cake Walk from top left down: (1) One Dollars worth of laugh for a nickle. (2) Laugh now you can cry some other time. (3) HA-HA-HA The Cake-Walk. (4) They don't laugh at you, they laugh with you. One ticket. (5) A laugh with each step. (6) Everyone laughs, why not you? Its difficult to make out due to the lightness of the lettering, but on the side below Cake Walk is "Best of the Beach."

The walk through's monicker comes from the dance that was popular during the same era. Also known as the Brooklyn Cake Walk, it consisted of undulating bridges and gangways driven by cranks connected to an organ whose tempo increased with increasing speed of the ride.

Antics of those trying to negotiate the moving platforms was great entertainment for public viewing. The greater the laughter, the more people would gather around the device that enticed spectators to cough up the 5 cents to make the walk.

This ride was a new feature on the Crystal Beach midway from 1910 through at least 1912 where it appears next to Dreamland that debuted in 1912.

Cake Walks and similar stunts in large walk-through attractions are near extinction. But Cake Walks can still be found at European fun fairs.

Southern slaves mocked their high society masters by exaggerating their dignified promenading, low bowing, cane waving and hat doffing dance moves with high stepping and kicking while bending the torso severely backward. Some plantation owners would bake a cake on Sundays and invite neighbors over for a contest of slaves performing their "dance" not knowing they were being mocked. Different prizes were given including a cake and whoever won the contest would get the cake, giving birth to the phrase "that takes the cake" and the mocking dance became the *Cake Walk*.

The Cake Walk dance reached popular society through black minstrel shows of the 1800s. Although the phrase typically refers to a challenge that is easy to accomplish, the dance moves of the Cake Walk were elaborate and physically demanding. So was the Cake Walk walk-through attraction.

Above: The Cake Walk at Coney Island. Because there are no exterior trappings, its easier to see the out and back walkways. The diagrams from its patent illustrate the operation of this simple, but undoubtedly amusing device for its time.

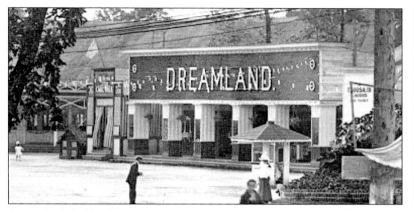

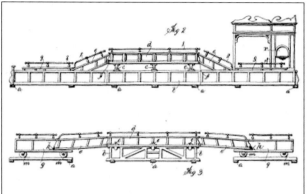

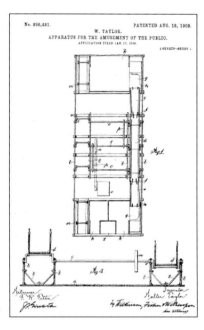

Just to the left side of Dreamland is the Cake Walk. Not exactly a maze, there were two moving walkways one from the entrance to back side of the machine, and one returning to the entrance. A very short walk, whether or not a patron got to pass through more than once is unknown, but based on the description of varying speeds, its probable they could pass multiple times as the speed increased.

2ND FERRIS WHEEL

THE HOUSE JACK BUILT

Right: This circa 1917 photo shows the second Ferris Wheel at Crystal Beach, which is considerably different from the one on the beach (page 18). This wheel has 10 passenger gondolas, the wheel on the beach had 8. This wheel's support structure is more complex as well.

The House That Jack Built was a walk-through attraction with a strange facade of Chess pieces, dice, the court cards from a deck of playing cards, and other odd trappings that do not seem to fit its Mother Goose name of the dog that worried the cat that killed the rat, that ate the malt that lay in the house that Jack built. "Jack" appeared as early as 1910 and lasted through 1926.

Fort Erie Historical Museum collection.

Photo by Mary Ann Kae

GIANT COASTER

Contrary to roller coaster data bases that note that the *Giant Coaster* debuted 1916, construction began on the coaster after the 1916 season and debuted on opening day 1917. Advertising noted that the new ride would be *"as safe as the rocking chair at home"* and that many of its descents *"are so abrupt they will no doubt, cause no end of 'ohs, ahs and dear me's.'"* For a number of years, the coaster was nameless, referred to merely as "The Coaster Ride" with an exaggerated length of 1 mile. Like the Figure-8, the Giant Coaster was of a design called "Side Friction" (see Appendix).

Details of the Giant Coaster are a mystery. Its presumed that Crystal Beach staff built the ride to blue prints supplied by its designer. Design credit is given to T. M. (Theodore Marshall) Harton but there is no official documentation known to exist that links the coaster to Harton. At the time of its construction, side friction technology was made obsolete by underfriction track (still used in wood coasters today). Harton was one of the last (if not the last) designer still building/designing side friction coasters when the Giant was erected so he is credited with the Giant. At the time, the T. M. Harton Company was well established in the amusement industry. Although the company lived on, Harton died in 1919 at the age of 56. The Giant may have been his last design. (The T. M. Harton Company built a side friction coaster for a Crystal Beach Park in Vermilion, Ohio in 1928 which may somehow feed the belief

that the Crystal Beach, Ontario Giant is Harton's.)

The lift hill was just under 58 feet tall. With approximately 2,600 feet of track, the Giant Coaster was far short of the advertised mile length. It was the only coaster at the park to have its track configuration modified. Originally, the diagonal stretch of track across the coaster's infield seen in contemporary images did not exist. The photos on page 72 illustrate the original and modified track configuration. The change came after the 1929 season when that area of the park, left vacant when the Backety-Back was removed, received a complete re-landscaping and beautification for the 1930 season. The copula at the top of the Giant's lift hill was removed at some point in time.

There are unsubstantiated claims that one of the trains came from a roller coaster called *Blue Streak* that operated at Erie Beach. There is no evidence to support this. In fact, the Blue Streak was still in operation at Erie Beach during the 1920s. The Giant had 3 trains and at one time during the 1940s the park named the trains as seen in the photo on page 74. Along with the Flash, there was a Blue (cont'd. pg. 71)

Left: The Giant Coaster eventually became a stepping stone from the tiny children's coaster in Kiddie Land to the Comet. Photographed in 1983, architecture historians could find a 3 dimensional Euclidean masterpiece of parallel and perpendicular lines in the coaster's lift hill whose side friction technology is almost extinct. Right: The loading platform as seen from the midway during the late 1970s.

A pg 77

The new "Coaster Ride" at Crystal Beach, nearing completion, one of the greatest of its kind ever built.

Buffalo Courier, May 13, 1917.

B pg 77

Getting the "Midway" Ready at Crystal Beach.

Newspaper images of the Giant Coaster under construction taken from microfilm. Above: Scraps of lumber are strewn at the base of the Giant's structure just before the opening of the 1917 season. Left: The Giant Coaster nears completion but the return run to the station still needs to be built.

Half way across the infield track just before entering the coaster's only left hand turn for the run back to the station.

A great 1920 aerial showing the Giant Coaster and the Backety-Back Scenic Railway. Note the cupola at the top of the Giant's lift hill and the protrusion of track that was eliminated by track that traversed the infield of the coaster. Note the original coaster station facade with its miniature cupolas to match the one on at the top of the lift hill.

Streak name plate on the blue painted train, and a third name yet to be discovered.

The Giant Coaster was not without incidents. On July 25, 1930, eight year old Margaret Brady was thrown from the coaster train she was riding. News accounts lack details of the accident. Her father sued the Buffalo and Crystal Beach Corporation for $11,000. Margaret spent 22 days in the hospital then missed five months of school while recuperating at home. Courts awarded Margaret's parents $1,200 for the medical expenses and additional $8,000 for injuries.

A 9 year old James Lacey was getting out of a train and somehow managed to fall off the platform onto the track in the station just as the train was put into motion. An alert ride operator quickly braked the train before it ran over James. He was treated for a bruise on his forehead and a scraped knee at the park's first aide station.

There is an unconfirmed account of an inebriated rider that suffered a fatal injury received while standing during a decent and impaled through the eye by a tie-board but this is most likely myth.

For a number of years the Giant Coaster had the distinction of being one of two side friction roller coasters remaining on the North American continent, and the only one still operating. After the 1984 season, the Giant Coaster became the oldest operating ride in the park after the PTC #12 was dismantled, shipped to Indiana and (cont'd. pg 75)

Photo by John B. deHass.

Rare images from the Giant Coaster lift hill. Left: The layout of the track before reprofiling. The third track from the left leads to the odd reversing elbow of track seen on the previous page. Below left: The same view in 1984. Below: Maintenance work on the second turn below the lift hill.

Buffalo Courier Express, April 10, 1952.

Fort Erie Historical Museum collection.

Above: The first hill and the second and fourth turns Giant Coaster glowing in the dark as seen from behind the Scenic Rivers of the World. Right: The original facade of the Giant Coaster station after a cloud burst. Far right: A train near the bottom of the first drop.

Fort Erie Historical Museum collection.

THE GIANT COASTER

A SPEEDY THRILLING SAFE RIDE

THE GIANT COASTER

Lower Lakes Marine
Historical Society.

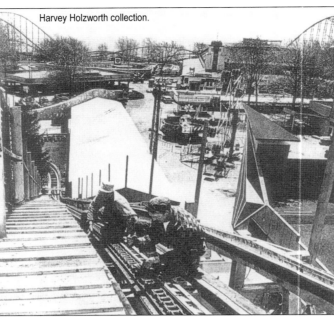

Harvey Holzworth collection.

Above: Return approach to the station in 1989.
Far left: A train in motion nears the bottom of the first hill.
Left: Maintenance men at work on the Giant's lift hill.

Niagara Falls, Ontario Public Library collection.

The art-deco station facade.

Photo by John B. deHaas.

Approaching the lift hill in 1984.

sold at auction.

A group of roller coaster enthusiasts purchased the Giant at the 1989 auction for $2,500. The sale gave the coaster a stay of execution in the hope that a park would come forward, dismantle and rebuild it. Unfortunately the day came when cranes attacked the Giant and reduced it to a massive pile of kindling in a few hours, which was its fate as a fire of suspicious origin reduced the pile of wood to ash before crews could bull doze it off the grounds.

Cathy Herbert collection.

Photo by John B. deHaas.

Clockwise from top right: Track work at the bottom of the first drop; returning to the station in 1951; a stark yellow and navy blue paint scheme; descending the first drop; view from the second drop; view from the infield showing some of the new unpainted lumber. Center: Approaching the lift hill.

Above: The Bug House is presumed to be another walk-through attraction filled with insect-themed stunts or scenes. At some point Bug House became Joyland (above right) perhaps a funny vs. crawly walk through attraction. The lifespan of both is unknown. These images are circa 1920.

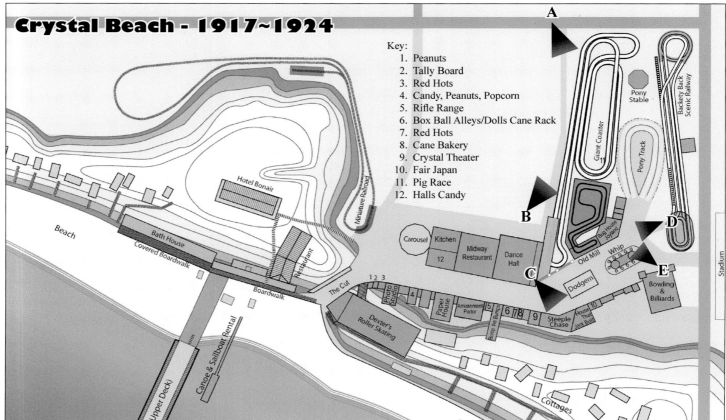

Crystal Beach - 1917~1924

Key:
1. Peanuts
2. Tally Board
3. Red Hots
4. Candy, Peanuts, Popcorn
5. Rifle Range
6. Box Ball Alleys/Dolls Cane Rack
7. Red Hots
8. Cane Bakery
9. Crystal Theater
10. Fair Japan
11. Pig Race
12. Halls Candy

Steeplechase remained on the midway at least through the 1929 season. Inset: Steeplechase under construction.

STEEPLECHASE

After demolition of the Figure-8 following the 1916 season, Steeplechase, another fun house, filled the vacancy.

A Steeplechase is a horse race with a number of horse and rider teams that negotiate a layout challenged with obstacles such as fences and ponds that horses leap over. Steeplechase at Crystal Beach may have earned its name because of the stunts inside that placed people in humorous and embarrassing physical situations - a Steeplechase where the human is the horse and obstacles take the form of turn tables, rotating cylinders, tilted rooms, vibrating staircases, and moving floors. According to press releases, *those who pass within its portals will no doubt have more mystifying experiences and more strange adventures than ever before therein* and *nearly every idea ever conceived for bewildering, perplexing, and amazing sensation-seekers is embodied in this wonderful castle. The adventures of Alice in Wonderland seem tame in comparison with the experiences that befall those who venture within the portals of this mystifying structure.* People *encountered many startling surprises as they made their way through its winding passages.*

Below: Looking west from the pier the *Sea Swing* waits for riders. Right: *Sea Swing* patent diagram.

SEA SWING

Sea Swings were fixtures at waterfront amusement parks across North America. Its appearance as a simple amusement ride is deceiving, but it was a somewhat complex device. According to its patent, the framework from which the slings were suspended could oscillate in a manner similar to that illustrated in the Razzle-Dazzle patent, dragging riders into and out of the water as it rotated. Also, according to its patent, the *Sea Swing* was also capable lifting and dropping its riders up and down as if they were tea bags.

The Sea Swing at Crystal Beach operated from approximately 1922 through 1938. The third of the rare amusements on the beach.

THE WHIP

The *Whip* was a simple device that appeared on the east side of the midway for the first time during the mid 1910s. Invented by William Mangels in 1914, it consisted of two large motor-driven discs, flush-mounted on the opposite ends of an oblong floor. The discs drove a cable that had a number of cars attached to it with spring-loaded flexible arms. The

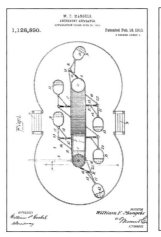

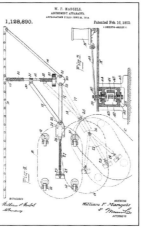

momentum of a car as it rounded each disc stretched the spring loaded arm. The springs then forced the arms back into position with a whipping action.

Crystal Beach patrons enjoyed being "whipped" seasonally through 1929. It never appeared in the line-up of rides after and presumed to have been removed before the 1930 season. The Whip had been relocated to a spot near the pier around 1925.

Cathy Herbert collection.

Aerial of the west end of the park near the pier. At the top are the Custer Cars, Aeroplane Swings and the Whip. The triangle shaped building is a check stand.

DODGEM

DODG-EM

CASH OR TICKETS | RIDE 10¢ | PAY ON THE WAY OUT

CASH OR TICKETS | RIDE 10¢ | PAY ON THE WAY OUT

Fort Erie Historical Museum collection.

The *Dodgem* was the first of Crystal Beach's bumper car rides. The exact year it appeared on the midway is uncertain, but newspaper references about it began appearing in 1924.

The Dodgem was a product of the Stoehrer and Pratt Dodgem Corporation whose first installation of the ride was at Salisbury Beach, Massachusetts in 1919. These early bumper cars had reverse steering where the riders had to turn the steering wheel in the opposite direction from the one they wanted to go - a feature that was eventually designed out as the ride evolved. It was the first amusement ride that the rider was in complete control of the motion. The ride operator controlled the electricity which flowed from the ceiling (usually metal fence or steel plates) through a contact bar to the motor in the car, then out through the floor and ground.

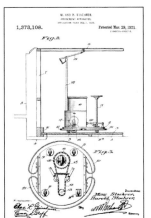

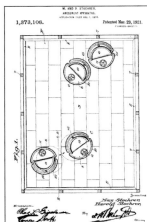

Top: Dodgem on the midway facing east. Backety-Back station in the background. Above: Two patent diagrams. Left: This is the interior of the Dodgem at nearby Erie Beach - the cars are probably identical to those on the Crystal Beach ride.

Chapter 3:
1924~1945

During the 1920s Thomas Newman was contemplating the future of his Cleveland and Buffalo Transit Company as its gross and net profits annually shrank. Expanding railroads and increasing use of the automobile were eroding the company's business lines. At the same time Newman had to have been concerned about the Lake Erie Excursion Company (LEEC) and the increasing talk of bridging the Niagara River between Buffalo and Fort Erie solely for automobiles. The *Canadiana* and *Americana* steamers were still the only practical way to reach Crystal Beach from Buffalo, but the bridge was an inevitability that would negatively impact the LEEC's steamer income once the bridge became reality.

Newman may have also been contemplating whether increasing use of automobiles could impact Crystal Beach Park income with or without the bridge. Amusement parks across North America numbered over 2,000 during the years after World War I but by 1921 their numbers began to decline. This decline was precipitated in part by the automobile whose increasing numbers gave more people the ability to travel independently and beyond the city limits where many of these early amusement parks existed. Park patronage declined and the parks closed in increasing numbers.

Reasons for the LEEC to not follow through with the 1919 expansion plans that included the construction of a new dance hall and leveling the sand bluff may never be known. It is clear, however, that someone at the LEEC recognized the potential of Crystal Beach to have considered these plans, but the LEEC officers were either unwilling or unable to exploit it. Since the takeover and modernization of the park starting in 1907, the major stockholders of the LEEC must have seen a substantial return on their investment by the early 1920s. With the C&B Line profits in decline and the future of the LEEC murky, it may have been the intention of the LEEC

stockholders to run the park into the ground. They were capitalists and industrialists whose core business was not the amusement industry. They spent considerable dollars on the concrete pier in 1921, but that probably was more out of necessity than want. When the first indications appeared that the LEEC was going to sell its assets late in 1923, the most recent capital improvement to the midway was the Giant Coaster, which opened six years earlier.

Crystal Beach Park flourished despite the fact it was antiquated by roaring 20s standards. The relatively new Giant Coaster was of a design style that was nearly obsolete when built. The existing dance hall with its numerous expansions and constant remodeling, was essentially the same structure built the by the CBSFC in 1896. The buildings on the midway and the beach were a substantial improvement in 1907 over what existed beforehand, but the quaintness of their piecemeal construction had faded. At the onset of the roaring 20s, their facades looked ramshackle and shack-like compared to new construction. The seclusion of the midway and grove created by the bluff worked for the park during its infancy, but 30 years later it was an obstruction to the lake breezes and the scenic view of the bay and Point Abino.

There is nothing to indicate that the LEEC actively marketed the sale of Crystal Beach assets, so the series of events that brought George Hall and the Lake Erie Excursion Company together to entertain the possibility of a transfer of ownership are lost to time. However, in a 1971 interview, Fillmore Hall indicated that some of the concessionaires (Charles Laube most likely one of them) discussed the complacency of the LEEC with improvement and expansion of park facilities and asked George Hall to be the spokesman for the group to approach the LEEC to discuss a sale of the park.

In 1923 the Toronto Star reported the $2 million sale of Crystal Beach scooping the Buffalo newspapers. The Star reported that the LEEC sold its assets to William G. Wilson, Charles A. Laube, J. Sweety [sic], and John M. Hoen. The sale, reportedly, was a surprise to some of the LEEC stockholders when they received notice of the sale and transfer of stock.

George C. Hall
President

Charles A. Laube
Vice President & Treasurer

Julius C. Degenhart
Secretary

Alexander Osborne
Director

Charles Diebold Jr.
Director

Edward E. Coatsworth
Director

M.J. McAlpine
General Manager

Carl W. Hayes
General Passenger Agent

Donald L. McKenna
Passenger Agent

T. F. Perry
Passenger Agent

George Hall formed the Buffalo and Crystal Beach Corporation (BCBC) to purchase the assets of the Lake Erie Excursion Company under a New York State charter on January 16, 1924. Then the formal negotiations for the sale Crystal Beach, inclusive of its U.S. assets began. On March 26, 1924 Thomas Newman and Morris Bradley of the Lake Erie Excursion Company and George Hall consummated the sale and executed the final papers that transferred ownership of Crystal Beach to the BCBC.

The directors of the BCBC included George Calvin Hall Sr., Charles A. Laube, Julius C. Degenhart, John H. Arnholt, Alexander Osborne, Edward E. Coatsworth, Charles Diebold Jr., George F. Hanny Jr., John M. Hoen, C. J. Irwin, Christ Laube, Walter Mattich, George S. Schultz, and John Sweeny – all from Buffalo. William G. Athoe, and William G. Wilson from Ridgeway, Ontario, and amusement man J. F. Gillman from New York City also sat on the board.

The directors appointed the following officers: George Hall, president; Charles A. Laube, vice president and treasurer; Julius C. Degenhart, secretary; Carl W. Hayes as general passenger agent and T. F. Perry and Donald L. McKenna as passenger agents. BCBC retained M. J. McAlpine from the LEEC to continue as general manager of Crystal Beach.

Hall realized that the park needed a thorough upgrading. Without new, modern attractions and facilities, Crystal Beach could easily follow the current trend of amusement parks to oblivion. Hall's conviction to expand and modernize the park is evident in his statement to the press after the sale. *"We hope to double the size of the summer colony,"* Hall stated, *"and will do it if service and attractive commuting rates* [of the steamers] *can bring it about. Also, we hope to convince a greater number than ever that Crystal Beach is the best place to spend vacations and weekends."* The least of Hall's vision was the development of a parking lot with space for 1,000 cars. For the parking lot, he drained the undeveloped field across Ridgeway Avenue adjacent to the athletic field's north side and filled it with cinders. The lot contained forty premium covered spaces, available for a fee. Anyone taking advantage of the premium parking could also have their automobile washed and filled with gas and oil.

Physical expansion of the park was the most ambitious aspect of Hall's vision that began, according to the press, immediately after the BCBC took ownership. Then Hall signed a contract for the construction of a $150,000 seawall to extend 1,000 feet eastward from the pier. Its base would be 100 feet out from the existing shoreline and stand 15 feet tall. When complete and back filled by leveling the sand bluff, the midway would expand by 5 acres.

Construction of the seawall progressed through the summer of 1924 and completed by the end of the season. Then all the structures on the bluff had to be demolished. The roller rink was the first building to go, followed by the thirty cottages. Before the bluff could be leveled to backfill the seawall, it had to be exfoliated. Men with saws and axes attacked the trees and horses with ropes dragged them away. To wash down the bluff, workers used the same hydraulic mining technique used to widen the Cut during 1907. Water under high pressure shot from a nozzle cut into the bluff and washed down the sandy aggregate that settled on the backside of the seawall.

The Schultz Brothers Company of Brantford, Ontario began the construction of a new dance hall immediately afterward. Their contract stipulated that all the concrete work be completed and ready for the erection of structural steel by February 1, 1925. Completed by opening day 1925, the dance hall boasted 37,125 square feet of floor area, and a polished hardwood dance floor of 20,625 sq. ft. Its outside dimensions were 165 feet by 225 feet and was 50 feet tall at its highest point at the center ventilation ziggurat (calculated from the scale noted on the blueprints). The design of the building employed a cantilever style roof system supported by the exterior joists. The system resembles the truss section the Peace Bridge over the Black Rock Canal. It permitted the entire dancing surface to be clear of supporting posts.

A

pg 87

EXTENSIVE IMPROVEMENTS UNDERWAY AT CRYSTAL BEACH Work has started on washing down the sand hill to the right of the boat landing as you arrive at the beach. Next summer you'll see a gigantic dance pavilion on this site and a beautiful cement promenade along the water front. Photos show the work progressing on removing the sand hill. (Baker)

This is the only known image captured from microfilm of the seawall fully constructed before significant backfilling had taken place. Most of the sand bluff is still in place as are some of the buildings and cottages. All would be gone in a matter of a few weeks. Construction of the seawall lasted throughout the summer of 1924 and the backfilling began at the close of the 1924 season.

Built of steel, concrete, glass and wood, the dance hall was an impressive structure that dominated the newly expanded midway. Sliding doors of glass and wood lattice surrounded the entire first floor. At balcony level, the dance hall was surrounded with windows that tilted outward. Fresh air made available when the doors and windows were open, coupled with the exceptionally high ceiling that vented through the roof, created a natural air conditioning system. As the hot air rose and exited through the ziggurat, it drew in the cool night air through the open sliding doors and balcony level windows.

Inside, the ceiling was decorated with metal lattice. The first bandstand was hexagonal and positioned in the center of the dance floor with a matching canopy hung from the ceiling. The canopy was concave to permit the sound to radiate outward. Electric sound amplification was years away.

The "front" of the dance hall faced the midway where two silver domed turrets rose above the roof top. Entrances to the men's and women's rest rooms in the basement were located at the front of the hall as well.

View looking towards new midway showing new concrete dining hall and old dance pavilion which will be roller rink.

Another view showing the removal of the hill.

Two views showing the new seawall and the 9 acres of new land, on which will be located the new dance hall.

Top left: Photographed from the top of the bluff that had not yet been washed away, shows a cleared out area where the new dance hall would eventually be built. Left: Looking east, a sluice channels away the sand and water being washed away. Above: West and east views after the levelling of the bluff is complete as teams of horses drag primitive graders to level the surface. Access sand would be dragged over to the new seawall and deposited in the lake.

Cathy Herbert collection.

Dance Hall under construction during the early spring of 1925.

"We are proud of our new ballroom, which is the largest and finest structure on this continent devoted exclusively to dancing," stated BCBC traffic manager Carl W. Hayes. Its alleged record breaking size is conjecture.

Demolition of the roller skating rink did not spell the end to roller skating on the midway. The old dance hall, already complete with a wood floor was the perfect replacement.

The BCBC improved their Buffalo dock facilities and leased the grounds adjacent to the terminal, graded it, covered it with cinders and opened a parking lot for 1,000 cars. Gasoline and oil was available made available at the Commercial Street facility.

At the onset of the 1925 season, George C. Hall noted, *"The new and greater Crystal Beach glories in its past which has furnished pleasure and recreation to countless thousands, but the chief thought of its ownership and management has to do with its present and future. Each year it will be made vastly better."*

Hall meant what he said. From 1925 through 1931, he developed the midway in ways that would make the grounds legendary.

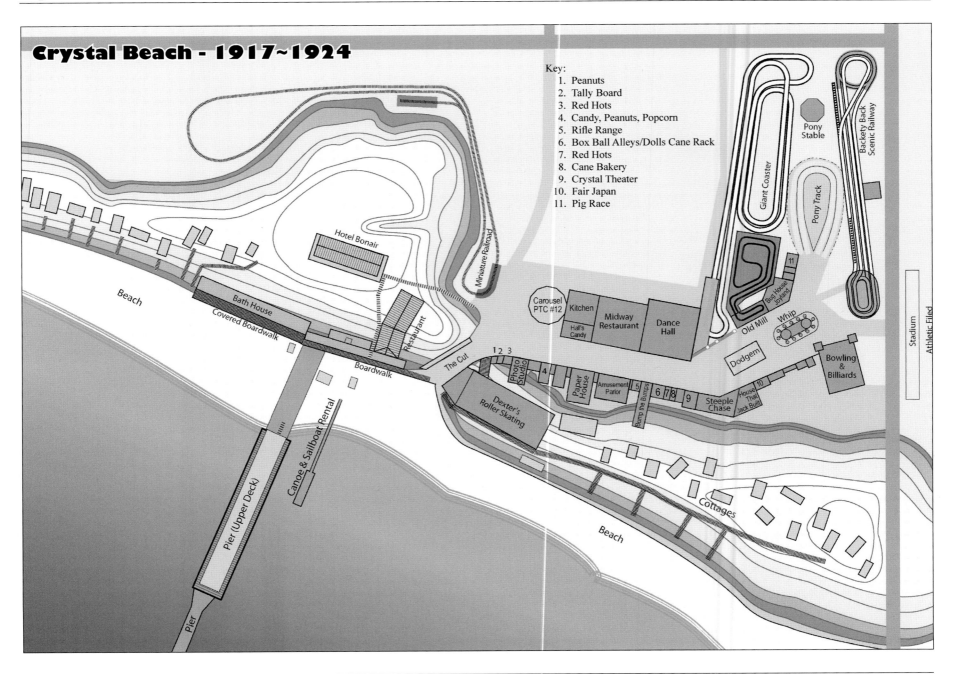

Crystal Beach - 1917~1924

Key:
1. Peanuts
2. Tally Board
3. Red Hots
4. Candy, Peanuts, Popcorn
5. Rifle Range
6. Box Ball Alleys/Dolls Cane Rack
7. Red Hots
8. Cane Bakery
9. Crystal Theater
10. Fair Japan
11. Pig Race

Beach

Hotel Bonair

Miniature Railroad

Bath House

Covered Boardwalk

Restaurant

Boardwalk

The Cut

Pier (Upper Deck)

Canoe & Sailboat Rental

Pier

Dexter's Roller Skating

Carousel PTC #12

Kitchen

Hall's Candy

Midway Restaurant

Dance Hall

Photo Studio

1 2 3

4

Paper House

Amusement Parlor

Bump the Bumps

5

6 7 8

9

Steeple Chase

House That Jack Built

10

Dodgem

Old Mill

Whip

Bug House Joyland

11

Giant Coaster

Pony Track

Pony Stable

Backety Back Scenic Railway

Bowling & Billiards

Cottages

Beach

Stadium

Athletic Filed

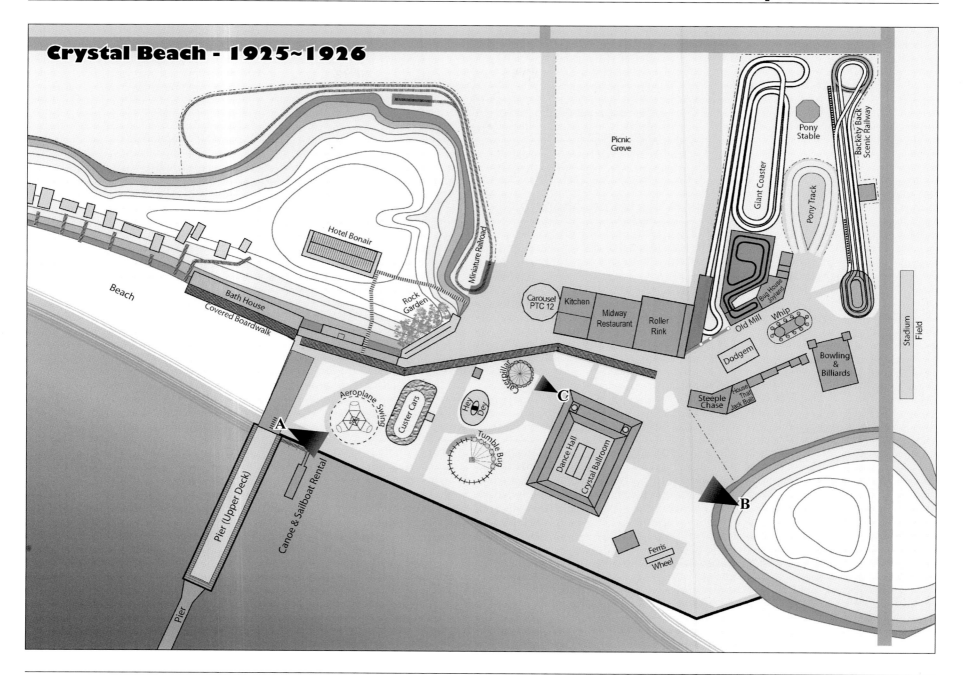

Crystal Beach - 1925~1926

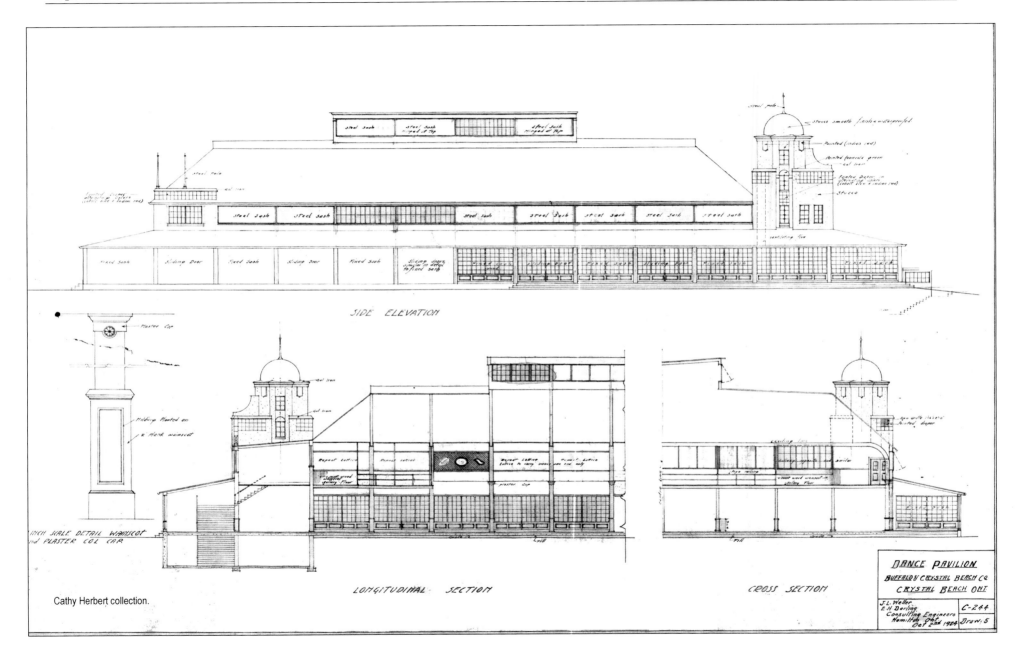

SIDE ELEVATION

LONGITUDINAL SECTION

CROSS SECTION

Cathy Herbert collection.

DANCE PAVILION
BUFFALO & CRYSTAL BEACH Co.
CRYSTAL BEACH ONT.

J.L. Weller
E.H. Darling
Consulting Engineers
Hamilton Ont.
Oct 2nd 1924

C-244
Draw. 5

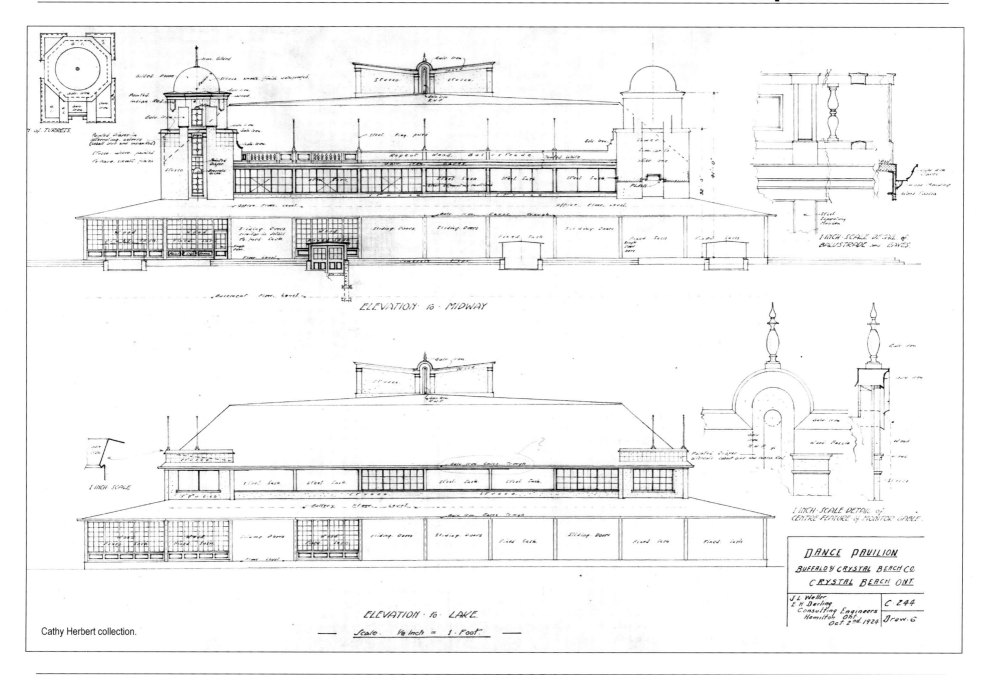

ELEVATION to MIDWAY

ELEVATION to LAKE.

Scale ⅛ Inch = 1 Foot.

DANCE PAVILION
BUFFALO & CRYSTAL BEACH CO.
CRYSTAL BEACH ONT.

J.L. Weller
E.H. Darling
Consulting Engineers
Hamilton Ont.
Oct. 2nd 1924

C-244

Draw. 6

Cathy Herbert collection.

ARCHITECTURAL SHEET METAL WORK

THE M S AND S C° LIMITED
METAL SHINGLE AND SIDING COMPANY
PRESTON — MONTREAL — TORONTO

BEAUTIFUL DANCING PAVILION AT CRYSTAL BEACH, ONT.
E. H. Darling, Hamilton, Engineer. An Unique Metal Ceiling of Lattice Design

A most interesting piece of sheet metal work is illustrated on this page. This lattice-work metal ceiling was conceived by the Engineer, E. H. Darling, with two objects in view. First he wished to conceal the structural steel work of the huge roof, without interfering with the ventilation. Second he wished to preserve the best possible acoustic qualities. As to how the first object was accomplished, these pictures speak for themselves. The acoustics of the pavilion are remarkable. Although the hall is 250 feet long it is possible to hear an ordinary conversation from end to end. This has been achieved by the lattice-work ceiling.

Close-up of a section of the lattice-work ceiling used in the Crystal Beach Dancing Pavilion.

[93]

Approximate profile of the sand bluff.
Approximate location of now buried shoreline,
15 to 20 feet below the new ground level.

Fort Erie Historical Museum collection.

B
pg 87

Above: The dance hall nears completion, circa April 1925. Inset: A page from the Metal Shingle and Siding Company that fabricated the interior lattice.

The *Caterpillar* arrived at Crystal Beach in 1924 and lasted through the 1964 season. Hyla Maynes invented the Caterpillar and sold manufacturing licenses to Traver Engineering, Allen Herschell, and Spillman Engineering. Each paid Maynes a royalty for each unit produced. The Caterpillar, a continuous train of two-passenger cars, sped around a circular, undulating (hilly) track, and once up to speed, a canvas canopy would unfurl over the cars to enclose them.

According to the patent, *"...a canopy ... which may, during the ride, alternately be opened up to expose ... passengers in the cars, and closed upon the cars ... to feel that they are traveling within a tunnel, thus affording a new and unexpected element... The passengers are not warned as to when the canopy will be closed nor ... opened."* There were options available that *"when the canopy is down...sudden blasts of air may blow into the cars...strange lights may flicker on the canopy walls."* Whether Crystal Beach had any of these options remains to be discovered.

The ride was operated at a fast speed and when the canopy closed, the train resembled a rapidly moving green caterpillar.

Closely associated with the Caterpillar is the *Lindy Loop* a ride named after aviation pioneer Eric Lindbergh. It was a Caterpillar with alternate rider carriages. A park could buy a Lindy Loop, but if it had a Caterpillar, they could purchase a Lindy Loop conversion kit.

Each carriage on the Lindy Loop rolled back and forth on tightly arched rails that followed the undulating circular track. The rails were blocked so the carriages could not roll 360 degrees. Each carriage had its own canopy mounted to the rail tips giving each the look of a sleigh. (Cont'd. pg. 93)

CATERPILLAR & LINDY LOOP

pg 87

Above: The author's grandfather, mother, and grandmother, Chester, Geraldine and Sophie Radominski at Crystal Beach in 1941. Behind them is the Caterpillar in motion with the canopy nearly closed.

Records from the Traver Engineering Company were destroyed after the company went bankrupt during the Great Depression. Cathy Herbert acquired Caterpillar blueprints from Crystal Beach with the Traver Engineering title block implying they supplied the Crystal Beach Caterpillar. This print of the Crystal Beach Caterpillar is one of the few surviving Traver documents. The bottom inset is an enlargement of the print's title block and the insets at right are two patent illustrations.

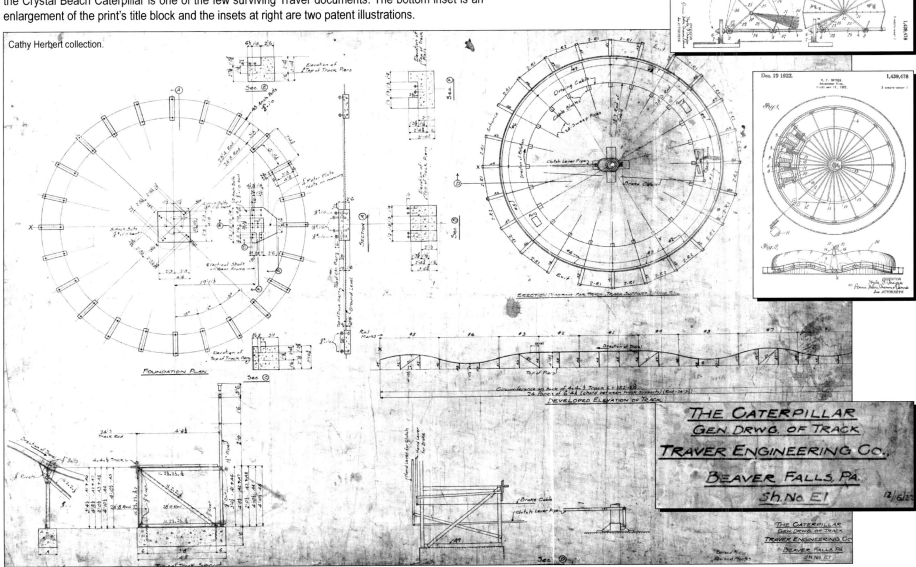

Cathy Herbert collection.

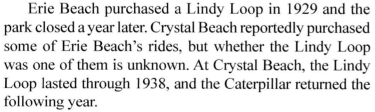

Lower Lakes Marine Historical Society collection.

Lower Lakes Marine Historical Society collection

Erie Beach purchased a Lindy Loop in 1929 and the park closed a year later. Crystal Beach reportedly purchased some of Erie Beach's rides, but whether the Lindy Loop was one of them is unknown. At Crystal Beach, the Lindy Loop lasted through 1938, and the Caterpillar returned the following year.

Top left: The Lindy Loop at Crystal Beach on the site of the Caterpillar. Image enlarged from a post card. Top right: Close-up of a Lindy Loop at an unidentified park. Above left and center: Preparing the Caterpillar for another season. Right: Young riders on the Crystal Beach Caterpillar on an apparently chilly day. Right bottom: Ladies looking like British Royals as the canopy unfurls.

AEROPLANE
SWING

A minor change to Traver's original Circle Swing converted it to the *Aeroplane Swing*. The change required swapping out the six ornate gondolas with three carriages that resembled biplanes. Traver even had the biplane carriages patented.

The Aeroplane Swing debuted on the Crystal Beach midway in 1925. The original Traver Circle Swing disappeared from Crystal Beach advertisements around 1910 and assumed it was scrapped rather than dismantled and stored to be rebuilt after 15 years with biplane gondolas.

The Aeroplane Swing did not last long. For the 1937 season, the biplanes, suspending cables and booms were removed and the tower was festooned with red, white and blue neon lights with a rotating cluster at the top. The Aeroplane Swing became the *Coronation Tower* for the 1937 season - a tribute to Prince Albert and his then recent coronation.

Coronation Tower by day.

Coronation Tower by night.

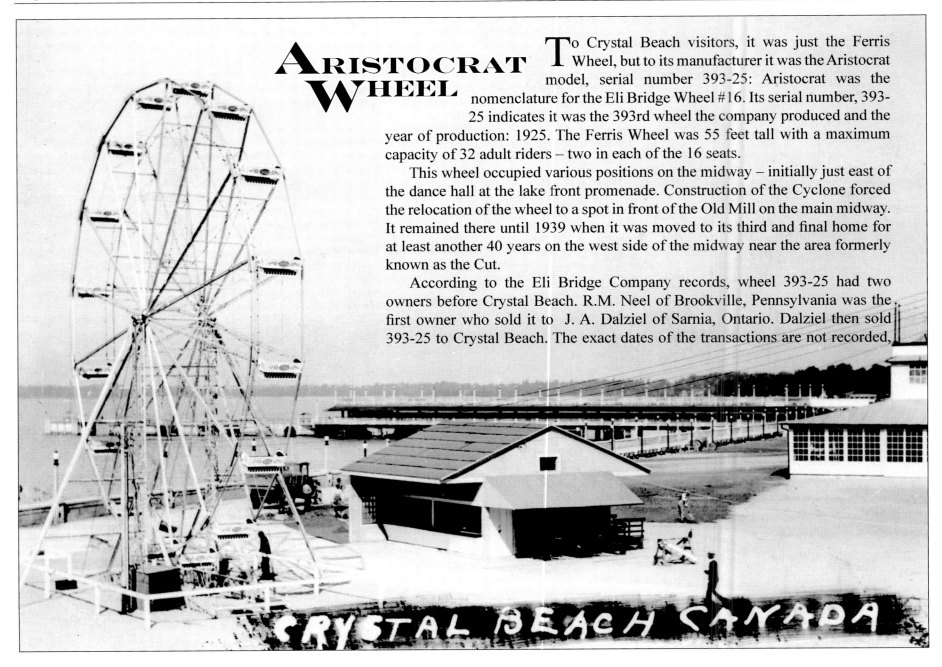

ARISTOCRAT WHEEL

To Crystal Beach visitors, it was just the Ferris Wheel, but to its manufacturer it was the Aristocrat model, serial number 393-25: Aristocrat was the nomenclature for the Eli Bridge Wheel #16. Its serial number, 393-25 indicates it was the 393rd wheel the company produced and the year of production: 1925. The Ferris Wheel was 55 feet tall with a maximum capacity of 32 adult riders – two in each of the 16 seats.

This wheel occupied various positions on the midway – initially just east of the dance hall at the lake front promenade. Construction of the Cyclone forced the relocation of the wheel to a spot in front of the Old Mill on the main midway. It remained there until 1939 when it was moved to its third and final home for at least another 40 years on the west side of the midway near the area formerly known as the Cut.

According to the Eli Bridge Company records, wheel 393-25 had two owners before Crystal Beach. R.M. Neel of Brookville, Pennsylvania was the first owner who sold it to J. A. Dalziel of Sarnia, Ontario. Dalziel then sold 393-25 to Crystal Beach. The exact dates of the transactions are not recorded, only that they all occurred in 1925 - the same year the wheel debuted at Crystal Beach. Why there were so many transactions in less than a year will never be known however, its possible these people purchased the wheel with the intent to operate it as a concession. Speculation aside, Crystal Beach became the third owner of wheel 393-25 in 1925.

On August 10, 1936, Marjory Weber and her sister Gloria were on the Ferris Wheel. At the end of their ride, the ride operator raised the unloading platform to meet the footrest of their chair and opened the restraining bar. The girls stood up to exit but then tumbled onto the unloading platform when the wheel began to rotate prematurely. Before the operator could stop the wheel, Marjorie became pinned between the unloading platform and the footrest of the next seat to be unloaded as it rotated down. She sustained back and hip injuries. Gloria suffered bruises to her chin and cheek from her tumble.

Marjorie sued Crystal Beach for her injuries, and sought a sum of $3,000. Her father also sued the park for $200 to cover medical and incidental expenses. A jury found Crystal Beach negligent in the matter, siting a faulty brake on the Ferris Wheel. County Judge A.D. Standbury of St. Catharines, Ontario awarded Marjorie $1,500 dollars, and $150 to her father on June 18, 1937.

The wheel was moved to the location seen in the images on this page in 1939 and it remained there until permanently dismantled. There was no Ferris Wheel in the park during 1983 implying 393-25 was removed after the 1982 season, however its last operating year is circa 1980, having lasted through the 1970s. The reason for its removal remains unknown, but its age may have precipitated prohibitively high insurance and maintenance costs that forced its removal during the park's financially troubled 1980s.

Richard Schwegler collection.

Previous page: The largest Ferris Wheel at Crystal Beach first appeared on the east side of the expanded midway in 1925 with a fantastic view of the bay. Above: 1960s view from the Comet entrance. Below: As seen from the Comet circa 1950.

Cathy Herbert collection.

CUSTER CARS

Harvey Holzworth collection.

Forerunner to go-carts, *Custer Cars*, appropriately named by its inventor Levitt Luzern Custer, were battery powered, single rider cars that came to the Crystal Beach midway in 1925. They traversed an oval stock car-like track lined on the inside and outside perimeter with bumpers. Elongated, spring loaded bumpers guarded the front and rear of each car.

L. L. Custer manufactured the cars through the Custer Specialty Company of Dayton, Ohio. He also licensed their manufacture to a number of companies that included Traver Engineering and Spillman Engineering – both companies advertised Custer Cars for sale in Billboard – a monthly entertainment journal. According to Traver Engineering advertisements, a Custer Car installation cost between $4,000 to $6,000 contingent on the length of track and the number of cars purchased. The supplier of Custer Cars at Crystal Beach is unknown. They were removed after the 1934 season.

Above: Custer Car track under construction in 1925, the mounting posts on the inner and outer perimeter of the track in place. Below, an unknown rider on Custer Car number 1 in 1926.

Cathy Herbert collection.

TumBleBug

BUG

NO RIDERS IN
BATHING SUITS

ADMISSION
3
TICKETS

ACME

Perhaps one of the most popular of all the early amusement devices, the *Tumble Bug*, (or the Bug) consisted of six circular tubs linked together that traveled on a circular, undulated rail. Motors between each tub turned iron wheels to drive the tubs along the rail. The motors received power through the central axis.

The *Bug* traveled in a counter-clockwise rotation and each rider got a slightly different sensation because they faced a different direction in the tub.

Cathy Herbert collection.

ONE OF THE 100 AMUSEMENT DEVICES AT CRYSTAL BEACH

Invented and patented by Harry Traver and manufactured by Traver Engineering, there were four-tub, six-tub, and eight-tub models. The eight-tub model was arranged so that there were two sets of four tubs arranged 180 degrees apart. There is no evidence that an eight tub was constructed. In 1927, a 48 passenger (6 car), 100 foot diameter Tumble Bug cost $12,500.

The first reference to the Tumble Bug at Crystal Beach appeared in the press during 1926. It was removed during the mid 1960s.

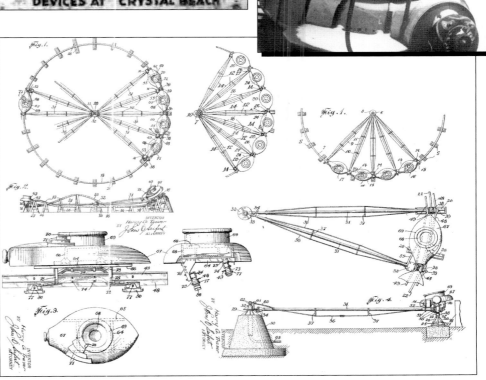

Previous page: The Tumble Bug at the loading platform. Note the red-painted dance hall turret in the background - confirming the color seen in some colorized postcards. Top right: Tumble Bug in winter. Above: Post card of the Tumble Bug in operation - the Ferris Wheel in the background over the dance hall roof dates this image circa 1925. Right: Patent diagrams for the Tumble Bug that include the four, six and eight tub configuration. Following page: Exceptional photograph of the Tumble Bug and the Comet from the top of the Ferris Wheel.

HEYDEY

This fun ride from Spillman Engineering Corp., of North Tonawanda, New York was added to the park's midway ride offerings in 1926. Spillman advertised the *Hey Dey* in Billboard as *"Latest and greatest novelty ride."* It consisted of approximately 10 to 12 cars that traveled an oval path on an undulated wood deck. The path of the cars was covered with heavy gage, polished sheet metal to protect the wood deck underneath and reduce friction.

The cars had a front and back seat capable of seating a total of four. Constructed of wood and iron, the cars were extremely heavy. The front of each car pivoted on its front wheel assembly that resembled the "truck" of wheels underneath a railroad car. Large casters at the rear corners allowed the rear of each car to orbit clockwise or counter clockwise around its front wheel assembly.

As the cars rounded the curves on either end of the oval track, the back of the cars would swing outward in a manner similar to those on the Whip. Unlike the Whip, there was no mechanism to stop the whipping action so the rear of each car went into a fast orbit about the front truck. Riders usually sat in the back of the

copyright 1979 / Michael J. Losi

Right: A solid wood roof replaced the canvas canopy when the park got an art-deco face lift after World War II. The six letters H-E-Y-D-E-Y were reflective silver sequins. Following page: The Hey Dey when it debuted in 1926.

Rick Doan collection.

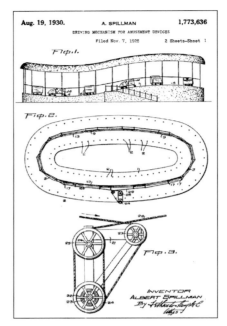

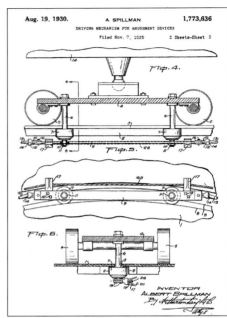

Above: This image captures the very large casters mounted on the rear of each car. Top right: Hey Dey patent drawing showing its undulating platform in the elevation. Bottom right: Hey Dey in spring stripped of canopy and cars that are in winter storage.

cars experience the greatest whipping action - their weight increased the displacement and rotational speed. The cars often spun so rapidly, they continued to spin after they stopped moving around the track.

All the mechanics that moved the cars were out of site under the deck. The cars were all attached to a cable that kept them a measured distance apart, but close enough that riders were provided the illusion that the back end of one car could smack the back end of the car in front or behind it. Also attached to this cable were grips that a drive cable clamped into.

Bob Hall was vague when asked about the Hey Dey's removal, noting only that getting the ride started at the onset of each season got to be troublesome and only Jack Roth knew how to finesse it. It remained a part of the midway through 1979 or 1980.

Lower Lakes Marine Historical Society collection.

Fort Erie Historical Museum collection.

Cyclone

Prior to the opening of the *Cyclone*, the press reported that George Hall had *"visited leading pleasure parks throughout the country, and culled for the Cyclone, the most desirable features of roller coasters to be found. At the same time, features undesirable, from experience with old coasters, were eliminated."*

The extent of Hall's travels is unknown, but he did visit the Philadelphia Sesquicentennial Exhibition in 1926 with his son Fillmore. On the midway of the exhibition was a roller coaster named Cyclone. It had a steel structure and laminated wood track. The first drop gently spiraled downward from the 60-foot tall lift hill, and the 2,000 feet of track was a tangled configuration of hills and curves that were banked up to 65 degrees.

The designer and owner of this roller coaster was Harry G. Traver (pronounced Tray-ver). Hall was familiar with Traver, at least in reputation. There were two of Traver's rides on the Crystal Beach midway, possibly two more that Traver built under license from their inventors.

One of the features of the Philly Sesquicentennial Cyclone that had to appeal to Hall was its steel structure. Steel was an unproven structural material for building roller coasters, but Hall certainly thought, or was convinced by Traver, that a roller coaster with a steel frame increased its durability thereby reducing maintenance expense. Hall was indeed familiar with the damage winter storms produced at the park - especially to the wood structures. Steel therefore, Traver would exhort, was the ideal building

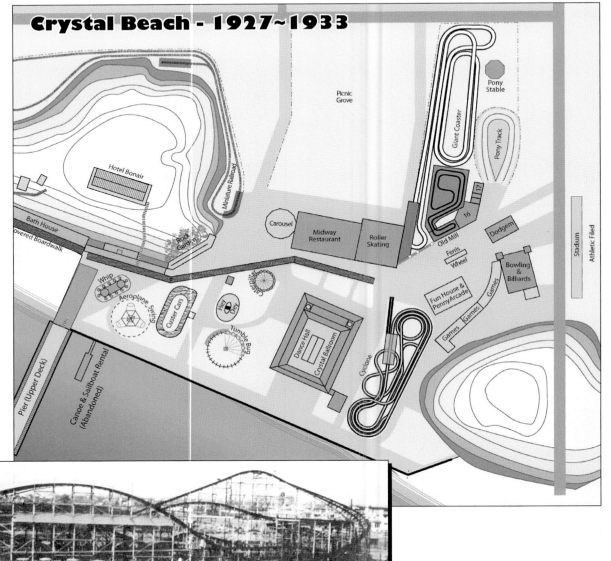

Crystal Beach - 1927~1933

Previous page: Waves pound the seawall during a winter storm with the Cyclone looming in the background. Left: The Philadelphia Sesquicentennial Cyclone.

material for a roller coaster given the location of Crystal Beach.

At some point during their conversation, Hall told Traver he wanted something *"twice as big, twice as fast, and twice as thrilling"* than the Philly Sesquicentennial Cyclone. Traver came to Crystal Beach that fall with plans for his "Giant Safety Cyclone," a ferocious mutant of his Philadelphia Sesquicentennial Cyclone that packed speed and terror into every inch of its compact layout. Its unlikely that George Hall culled any design elements for inclusion in the Cyclone as the aforementioned announcement claims - there was nothing in existence near the ferocity of the Cyclone to "cull from." Whether Hall's request was the impetus behind Traver's Cyclone is not likely. Traver probably already had the design – he just needed a buyer. (However, he had not filed his patent until 1928, after the Cyclone had been in operation.)

As the 1927 season approached, George Hall said in an announcement, *"The Cyclone Coaster represents the last thought in that form of amusement. It has, among other things, a sheer descent of 100 feet* [a slight exaggeration – it was 96 feet tall]. *Riding on it will give one all the thrills, but not any of the danger of stunt airplaning."*

Crystal Beach reported that construction on the Cyclone was complete and it would be ready for the Memorial Day weekend opening. However, a month would pass before the Cyclone opened to the public.

The delay may have been caused by alleged design problems that prevented the trains from rising over the crest of the second hill after the first spiral plunge. Whatever Harry Traver, Peter Cowan – the builder of the Cyclone's steel structure, and Crystal Beach management initially attempted to resolve this problem before the opening of the park is unknown. On June 5, Crystal Beach backed off its earlier claim that construction of the Cyclone was complete, and noted that it was rapidly approaching completion. Assuming remedial work was underway to get the coaster operating, the Cyclone was absent from all subsequent Crystal Beach newspaper

Traver dismantled his Philadelphia Cyclone after the Exposition closed. He erected it again in Chicago for the Century of Progress. This is what George Hall saw in 1926 - a small compact roller coaster with mildly banked turns roughly 60 feet tall. Below: What George Hall got.

Cathy Herbert collection.

advertisements until July 1927.

According to Peter Cowan, construction superintendent for Standard Steel of Welland, Ontario, the second hill was lowered by 18 inches for the trains to clear it.

A foot and a half does not seem significant, but disassembling layers of laminated wood on curved and twisted track is complex. The laminations are staggered to avoid seams running from the top of the track to the bottom and each board is typically twelve feet in length or longer. These layers of wood are held together by thousands of bolts and nails. There is no telling the length of track that required dismantling in order to decrease the height of the second hill, but it could have easily amounted to a hundred feet or more to maintain a smooth track profile. (Ed Hall, commenting on the coaster decades later, noted that replacing a few feet of rotted boards under the rails often required dismantling forty feet of track. He called the Cyclone a maintenance nightmare.) After dismantling the track, steel had to be cut from the structure and holes drilled to reposition the track ledgers (ties that hold the track to the structure) a minimum of 18 inches. Rebuilding the track required the bending and twisting wood because the top of the second hill was a tight 90-degree curve.

This composite image shows the entire length of the Cyclone with its ground-level figure-8. Note the start of the figure-8 with the sudden bank and sharp turn just after a drop.

The Cyclone received its final tests on July 1, 1927 and unceremoniously opened to the public on July 4, 1927. A statement made by George Hall decades later that 75,000 stormed the ride and toppled the fence around it to get a closer look is more than an a slight exaggeration. At the time of the Cyclone's debut, Crystal Beach operated two boats with a capacity of 3,500 each. If the steamers operated at maximum, a boat could leave Buffalo every hour. It would take almost 24 hours to get such a multitude to the park. Attendance over a holiday weekend may have totaled 75,000 – but never on a single day.

The Cyclone was an imposing structure. It instilled vertigo just gazing upon it. Its name could not have been more appropriate. The track was a knot of sharp twisting drops with few, very short straight sections of track. All the curves were extremely banked – some nearly vertical. The track banking on the first spiral plunge from 96 feet increased gradually with every foot downward from zero degrees at the top of the hill to its maximum banking of eighty degrees to horizontal at ground level. The second drop was exceptionally steep (estimated at 52 degrees) and the third element - the double helix, was extremely banked with drops that appear, in some images, to be nearly vertical although they were not. Undoubtedly the most intense portion of the ride followed. The train plunged down a steep drop into the sharp and steeply banked right turn of the figure eight element. After this extreme right turn, the train found a few feet of level track then entered a left hand turn that was as equally severe as the right turn. The figure eight allegedly inflicted the most injuries to Cyclone riders. First time riders were particularly vulnerable when caught off guard by the abrupt right turn after the drop into the element. An occasional rider would black out from the intense g-forces generated as the train sped through the low-profile knot of track with its 75-degree banked turns and abrupt directional changes. Elbows thrust into the side of a riding partner produced bruised and cracked ribs. For many Crystal Beach patrons, one ride on the Cyclone was one too many. Legend indicates such injuries were frequent, but they were probably not as frequent as implied, however severe bruising was probably experienced by people on every ride.

Legend maintains the park kept a nurse in the station to attend to those who fainted or sustained injuries. In 1984, Ed Cowley of the American Coaster Enthusiasts solicited rider recollections from anyone on the Niagara Frontier who rode the Cyclone. Not a single submission noted a conspicuous nurse at the unloading platform. During a 2000 interview, when asked if the park really kept a nurse on the Cyclone's unloading platform, Bob Hall (grandson of George C. Hall and son of Edward Hall) stated *"My father said there was. However, the park had to keep a nurse on the grounds, and the first aid station was 'near' the Cyclone."*

George Kunz tells of his experience riding the Cyclone with a date who had passed out during the ride. Kunz notes that ride attendants revived his date with smelling salts - not a nurse.

There should have been some mention of "Nurse Cyclone" in 1938 (circa) in an unconfirmed account of a freak accident that cost Warren Anger his life. Warren, a grounds keeper, was raking under the Cyclone's structure. A train thundered toward him while he raked under the track of the approaching train. At a moment of unfortunate timing he unknowingly raised the pole of the rake into the track work at the instant the train began to pass overhead. The force of the train shattered the wood handle and somehow a large piece of it lodged in his chest and lungs. Warren died in transit to Buffalo General Hospital. There was no mention of a nurse attending to Warren while he lay in the grass gasping for breath.

Enlarged from the photo on the previous page, the expressions on the riders faces and the position of their bodies reveal the intensity of the Cyclone. One of the riders in the first seat of the last car appears to be getting an elbow to the jaw.

If there ever was a time for "Nurse Cyclone" to be in the press it should have been in the recap of opening day 1938 that focused on Amos Wiedrich's last ride on the Cyclone.

At 10:00 PM on opening day 1938, Amos was reportedly taking his fourth consecutive ride. The chain slowly hauled the train to the top of the lift hill, then it accelerated down the twisted plunge of the first drop, negotiated the near 90-degree bank at ground level then climbed the steep, swooping, and twisted incline up the second hill.

Robert J. Kelly stood at the coaster's safety fence, and like so many other people, preferred to watch the Cyclone rather than ride it. The train was barely visible – enveloped by the night and cast in shadows from the tracer lights that lined the track profile. Kelly's feet felt the ground tremble when the train swooped by at 60 mph at the bottom of

In this photo, the lift hill looms in the background. In front of it is the sharp 90 degree turn of the second hill - where Wiedrich fell.

the first drop. His eyes followed the train as it climbed the twisted track to the top of the second hill.

The Cyclone was notorious for separating personal belongings from riders including lose change, eye glasses, hats, buttons from shirts, wallets, and even dentures and hair pieces. So, Robert Kelly did not think anything unusual when he saw a jacket fall from the train when it was at or near the top of the second hill. He did not realize at first, that the jacket was inhabited. Then he heard the screams - screams that were not the same as those typically evoked by the ride – but screams that indicated that something was seriously wrong.

According to the description of the accident, Amos Wiedrich fell from the top or near the top of the second hill, and landed somewhere on the tracks below. With any luck, he died from the fall.

There were no emergency brakes anywhere on the Cyclone's track so it was impossible to stop the train. It must have been a nightmare for the front seat riders to see a body lying on the track. They would have felt the jolt when the train hit the body and heard bones snapping as it dragged the body 200 feet before stalling. The wheels decapitated

Wiedrich and cobbled his legs and after the train stalled, the torso fell to the ground. He was 23 years old.

Not that there would have been anything she could have done for Wiedrich, but Nurse Cyclone could have assisted traumatized riders that had to walk down a catwalk from the stalled train. She was absent from all newspaper accounts. Attorneys for the plaintiffs would have found her history of treating Cyclone riders useful.

Following a coroner's inquest during which several witnesses testified that the safety bar of Amos's seat opened, Attorney George Lurie announced the intention to sue for $100,000 on behalf of Amos's family. The suit charged Crystal Beach Company Ltd., and Concessions Amusement Co. (a wholly owned subsidiary of Crystal Beach which operated the Cyclone) with negligence concerning Amos's death.

A court hearing took place on November 29, 1939. Witnesses to the accident gave testimony:

Vincent Hertel, who was on the ride with Wiedrich, testified that the safety bar popped open at the top of an incline. He stated that before the fatal ride, an attendant in the station checked the safety bar, and it appeared to be locked.

Robert Castater of Buffalo told the court that earlier (cont'd. pg. 116)

The diving trackage of the double helix.

It is amazing that the wood could be bent and twisted so severely without snapping. In the foreground is the backside of the banked track of the figure-8's first curve. Trains exit the figure-8 on the track to the left of the photo where it rises from under the station and twists uphill.

Cathy Herbert collection.

in the day, he rode the Cyclone twice, and both times, he sat in the same seat Wiedrich was in during the fatal ride. Both times the safety bar had come loose at the top of the second incline. He told the court that he notified the ride attendants. Their response, Castater claimed, was that it was impossible for the safety bar to open.

John Pyc of Depew, New York was in the seat behind Wiedrich. Pyc claimed that at the same instant Wiedrich was ejected from the car, he [Pyc] was thrust forward and managed to reach out and push Vincent Hertel back into his seat.

Constable Elmer Hoath of Fort Erie told the court that he tested all ten of the safety bars and three of them had come loose.

The negligence suit asked for $25,000 instead of the $100,000 earlier announced. On December 4, 1939 the court found Concessions Amusement Company negligent. The amount awarded Wiedrich's estate is laughable by today's standards and was substantially less than $25,000 asked for in the suit. The judge calculated the award based upon the expected income of Wiedrich over a five-year period, and awarded his estate a paltry $3,000.

Close-up of the bottom of the first drop.

A nearly empty train descends the first drop in this 1939 image.

Without references to the Cyclone nurse in any period published material or in recollections of riders years later (except for the Hall family who had a vested interest to maintain the legend), the question remains: Did Crystal Beach management really keep a nurse at the Cyclone's unloading platform? Probably not. Undoubtedly, some people incurred bruised and cracked ribs, and a dislocated shoulder, but these injuries require emergency room treatment, not a bandage and Bactine. Its possible that the severity of the Cyclone induced fainting, but again, not to any degree that would justify staffing the ride with a nurse to administer smelling salt on occasion. People were not fond of the Cyclone – a fact confirmed by low ridership. A nurse on the unloading platform would only have discouraged potential riders – making the Cyclone a greater financial liability and reinforce the fear of those already too scared to ride and deter those who otherwise may have dared the ride – at least once. The above argument does not prove conclusively that Nurse Cyclone is fiction, though it makes a strong circumstantial case. However, the reader can decide whether or not she existed.

After 20 seasons of operation, the Cyclone had become too great of a financial drain. At the end of the 1946 season, Crystal Beach management announced it was time for the Cyclone to go.

Retrospectively, the Cyclone was headache before it opened. The delay of the ride's 1927 debut not only resulted in additional construction cost it also translated into lost revenues. The rework is also indicative of high maintenance expense yet to come.

In Joe Heflin's insightful article on the Traver Cyclones, Ed Hall claimed that the weight of the trains was a major [maintenance] problem. Further, wood on the inner layers underneath the rails would rot because of water seepage. High maintenance costs would not necessarily have brought the coaster down if it were profitable. However, as maintenance costs increased and ridership decreased, the Cyclone was in an untenable financial position.

Lack of patronage and maintenance expense brought an early demise to the other two identical Cyclones, neither of which saw ten years of service. Traver's Cyclone at Palisades Park in New Jersey operated for eight years. "Lightning," the third Cyclone at Revere Beach, Massachusetts saw only seven years.

Peter Cowan, in charge of the Cyclone's construction in 1926 was responsible for its demolition twenty years later, which began shortly after Labor Day, 1946.

Park superintendent Jacob Nagel estimated that the Cyclone was comprised of 250 tons of structural steel, 20,000 board feet of lumber, and tons of nails and spikes. During the demolition, he stated that plans were underway for construction of a new modern coaster along the lake front, but it would not be ready until the 1948 season.

Of the Cyclone triplets, the Crystal Beach Cyclone was the first erected and far outlasted its younger identical siblings. For these reasons, the Crystal Beach Cyclone is the one that achieved legendary status. It survived long enough for it to live in the memories of millions of Crystal Beach visitors who passed down stories of its ferocity for generations. Decades later, posthumous interest in the Cyclone by roller coaster enthusiasts precipitated a book about its designer, Harry Traver, and raised him from amusement history obscurity to an icon.

The Cyclone's superstructure lays stacked, waiting to be reconstituted as the Comet. To the left is the Fun House. In the background an arcade game and maintenance shed.

Lower Lakes Marine Historical Society collection.

Incompatible with the Comet's track design, Crystal Beach put the Cyclone's trains up for sale. Its unknown if the trains were ever sold.   Billboard March 15, 1947.

MISSOURI MULE

Crystal Beach was doing considerable business with the Traver Engineering having acquired the Cyclone, the Auto Racer (pg. 122), Tumble Bug and Caterpillar. Another of his inventions, new to the 1929 Crystal Beach midway, was the *Missouri Mule*. George Hall may have also seen this device at the 1926 Philadelphia Exposition where it made its debut. An onboard operator controlled the twelve passenger carriage like an automobile including its most thrilling feature, the trigger that made the car bounce like a bucking bronco. The Missouri Mule was not listed as a midway feature after 1933.

Courtesy Richard Munch and the American Coaster Enthusiasts.

HARRY BURNETT'S CIRCUS

Fort Erie Historical Museum collection.

Advertised to have cost $15,000 the *Circus* debuted in 1930 and was owned and operated by Harry Burnett. The type of attraction the Circus was is uncertain. Placards suggest that it was freak side-show that invited visitors to meet "Bozo the Wildman", "Ivan the Terrible Turk," and "Madame Fifi." Visitors could watch as "Bosco Eats em Alive."

The last reference found for the Circus was 1937. However, it may have operated through 1939 when *Spook Alley* debuted in 1940, occupying the same building.

With a repainted façade, the slide mounted to the outside of the building is a strong indicator that Spook Alley was an actual walk-through attraction with mazes and mechanical stunts. Spook Alley remained a midway attraction through 1943, and possibly 1944.

FUN HOUSE

The *Fun House* replaced the Steeplechase and The House That Jack Built. Its debut was overshadowed literally and figuratively by the Cyclone as it stood behind the new coaster's double helix.

Built at a reported cost of $50,000, the Fun House was a combination arcade on the first floor and obstacle walk-through on the second and third floor. If it contained the advertised 100 new amusement features, most of them had to be the arcade games that populated the ground floor.

Stunts inside the Fun House included a slide that began on the third floor, swooped outside then back in where it deposited people in

a large wood bowl approximately 8 feet high with highly waxed walls that made escaping it a challenge. Other stunts within the walk-thru included a horizontal rotating barrel that had to be walked through, dark tunnels, distorting mirrors and blowers.

Management, every few years, reported that they upgraded, changed or placed new stunts in the dark rides and walk-throughs. Wanting them to be a surprise for their guests, they never elaborated on the changes. One of the new Fun House stunts for 1938 that they did not keep secret was addition of a Magic Carpet 1938. The carpet device may have come from Spillman Engineering in North Tonawanda. Albert Spillman filed for a patent on October 8, 1937 for a device *"to provide a downwardly inclined endless belt which is carried over driving rollers...and which belt is provided to receive*

passengers...in a seated position...with a plurality of humps which extend...underneath the belt...to provide the passengers with a mirth-provoking shock." Spillman, in his description, could have chosen a different word instead of "shock" as there was nothing shocking about the carpet.

There was a 10 cent admission fee to the Fun House. Operationally, the owners lost revenue as the trip through it did not end with an exit to the outside. Once inside the building, kids could make the trip through the mazes as often as desired until they left the building.

Eldon and Marion Knapp purchased the aged concession in 1944 then began to develop plans for a new fun house and an arcade that could be operated independently from each other. The magic carpet inside the Fun House may have been removed after the 1945 season

and reinstalled in the Knapp's new fun house that opened in1946, and appropriately named after it.

Its presumed that the first floor arcade of the Fun House continued to operate when the Magic Carpet fun house opened. After the 1948 season, construction of a new arcade began with the demolition of the "old" Fun House. The new arcade was ready for the 1949 season and remained in operation for the next 40 years.

These three images show the changing face and hat that marked the entrance and exit to the Fun House. On the previous page left side: The shadow of the Cyclone is cast onto the side of the Fun House. Immediately left: The round painted sign above the left side of the brim notes that there are "Barrels that Whirl."

AUTO RACER SPEEDWAY

Above: The Auto Racer circa 1935 enlarged from the image below where it can be seen on the left. There are no known photos of the entire ride, only sections of it captured in images of other subjects. The image reveals a car beginning to cross the bridge, and one on the outer track having just passed under it. Right: Not-to-scale track layout of the Auto Racer.

Fort Erie Historical Museum collection.

In 1929 another ride from the mind of Harry Traver – the *Auto Racer* appeared on the midway. It consisted of a number of electric powered autos supplied by an electric rail that ran along the length of the roadway on its left side. A contact arm that trailed each auto was secured to the electric rail to power the motor in the rear of each two-passenger car. There was no locking mechanism holding the autos to the roadway, but horizontal wood guard rails prevented the autos from careening off. The roadway was sufficiently wide that autos could be steered freely without making contact with the wood guard rails.

The Auto Racer occupied two different sites during its existence. At the first site, halfway between the dock and the dance hall, the track configuration consisted of a series of concentric ovals. Where track sections lay side-by-side, the cars appeared to be racing.

Changes to the midway circa 1941 moved the ride along side the miniature railroad where it was re-christened the *Auto Speedway*. The track configuration changed to consist of a long straight stretch of track, a 360 degree turn near the miniature golf course, followed by a return run to the loading platform.

Installation of Saw Mill River brought an end to the Auto Speedway

Left: An advertisement notes that the park modernized the Auto Speedway in 1947 but it did not elaborate how. There was not much to this simple ride to modernize, however the loading platform received its art deco façade that spring seen here under construction.

Lower Lakes Marine Historical Society collection.

Richard Schwegler collection.

Above: A car returns to the station. Right: The out-and back serpentine layout of the Auto Speedway hugs the miniature golf course - 14 of 18 greens are visible in this aerial.

Fort Erie Historical Museum collection.

BANKRUPTCY & RECOVERY

The impact of the Great Depression that followed the Crash of 1929 had not impacted Crystal Beach immediately and management continued to pour money into the park. The grounds where the Backety-Back Railway stood were landscaped for 1930, and a new formal entrance made to the park at the intersection of Erie and Ridgeway Road. It consisted of an elaborate, lighted gateway, paved walkways lined with flowers, benches and lamp posts. Sod was laid elsewhere. It was probably at this time that the track footprint of the Giant Coaster had been modified at an uncertain cost. A new $15,000 attraction, "The Circus," debuted and owned by Harry Burnett. The Old Mill that existed for the past few decades had been removed, and a new one reconstructed in its place at a cost of $30,000.

Tom Thumb Golf, with operations at 84 John Street in Toronto manufactured miniature golf installations and announced that they had an order from Crystal Beach, implying that the park's first miniature golf course arrived that summer.

The Great Depression eventually hit the amusement industry hard. Locally, Erie Beach closed permanently and immediately after the Labor Day weekend, 1930. However it had not gone bankrupt. Crystal Beach mythology maintains that the management of both parks discussed the future and concluded that following the crash, the local economy could not support both parks. The stronger of the two parks, Crystal Beach, would remain, Erie Beach would close in favor of residential development. Crystal Beach purchased a number of the park's assets (and assumed some of its liabilities) under the condition that the Erie Beach grounds could never again be used for the purposes of amusement.

Sensitive to the declining economy the Buffalo Evening News printed discount coupons for the *Canadiana* starting in 1931. This helped to maintain park attendance levels, however, the purse strings of park patrons were tight.

By the end of 1931, the Buffalo and Crystal Beach Corporation (BCBC) was unable to make interest payments on its loans, or pay dividends to stock holders. The board of directors, after a March 1932

Some of the greens of Crystal Beach's miniature golf course in 1946.

Another shot of the greens, circa 1950. Auto Speedway track in the background.

Harry S. Hall

meeting, recognized that the corporation would have to restructure its capital and debt structure. In order to accomplish this, the company had to declare bankruptcy. The board authorized Charles Diebold Jr., and Edward E. Coatsworth to file papers for voluntary bankruptcy, and did so on April 7, 1932. A few weeks later, Diebold filed a declaration of assets and liabilities compiled by George Hall.

Two of the largest claims against the company included the M & T Trust Company for $128,000 and the Erie Beach Company for $47,500. A detailed list is in the Appendix. (The debt to Erie Beach gives credence to the aforementioned deal with Erie Beach that prohibited its use for amusement purposes.) An asset that the BCBC owned outright was Concessions Amusement Company under which Crystal Beach operated the park rides that it owned, including the Cyclone. Hall valued "Concessions" at $100,000. (Many other rides, primarily the portable ones, were privately owned concessions. As the years passed, Conklin Shows of Brantford, Ontario populated the midway with an increasing number of rides).

After Diebold filed the bankruptcy declaration, he told the press that the beach would operate as usual. *"It is one of the finest sand beaches in the country."* He also added that the park would also operate, however, before any action could be taken to prepare the park for the 1932 season, the court would have to appoint a trustee. On April 23, 1932, that appointment was made - Joseph W. Becker of Gurney, Overturf and Becker Realtors.

Becker acted as manager of Crystal Beach while the park was in receivership. He hired Harry S. Hall as assistant manager who became responsible for the park operations. Harry was no relation to George Hall.

Becker announced that opening day of the 1932 season would be May 28 and fares for the Canadiana were reduced from 50 to 35 cents for adults and from 25 to 15 cents for children. Its difficult to assess when Crystal Beach returned to the management of George Hall with a restructured company. Press coverage of the 1933 season refer to "The Management", "Managers" or "Executives." of Crystal Beach rather than the names.

Three companies emerged after the BCBC reorganized. The Crystal Beach Transit Company owned and operated the *Canadiana*. The Crystal Beach Company operated the park. The DHL Company was the holding company for the operation, taking the last name initials of Charles **D**iebold, George **H**all, and Charles **L**aube.

A rock garden was made out of the last vestiges of The Cut. At its base, was a raised cement sun deck approximately four feet above the midway grounds. Wood benches were placed on the deck and cement stair cases lined the left and right side of the garden.

Harry S. Hall remained with the reorganized Crystal Beach company as its general manager. Harry, in 1936, seen the increased attendance at the park as a measure of recovery from the great depression, *"And good times are no longer around the corner, they are here. People don't come to the beach to buy coal, they come to buy a good time and they take the enjoyment home with them. The large sized crowds and their willingness to spend money on beach pleasures indicates the barometer is well on its way back to the top again."* At the end of the 1936 season, Hall estimated that attendance ran close to 2 million; 285,000 came aboard the Canadiana and at least 5 times as many via automobile. Harry reported that improvements were already underway for 1937 that included indirect lighting of all gardens in the park.

Jacob H. Nagel
Superintendant
starting c1937

Fort Erie Historical Museum collection.

LAFF IN THE DORK

Photo by Mary Ann Kae

LAFF IN THE DARK

Although the park was only a few years out of bankruptcy, George Hall continued his policy to constantly upgrade the rides and attractions – with an apparent caveat to spend as little money as possible. A true dark ride, *Laff in the Dark* (LITD) was installed in a building that housed bowling alleys and billiard tables built in 1908.

Before installation could begin, the bowling alleys were removed and reinstalled in the basement of the dance hall.

LITD consisted of a number of 2-passenger cars that traversed a track full of hairpin turns in total darkness. The motion of the cars activated relays, tripped switches, or in other ways completed the circuits that illuminated scary scenes, or put into motion stunts designed to startle, and scare riders. Other stunts gave riders the "willies" with things heard and felt but not seen. (cont'd. pg. 130)

Laff in the Dark exterior, circa 1980. Above right: The Asian motif of the loading platform and the multi-colored cars. Right: Laffing Sal had a spot front and center in this image.

127

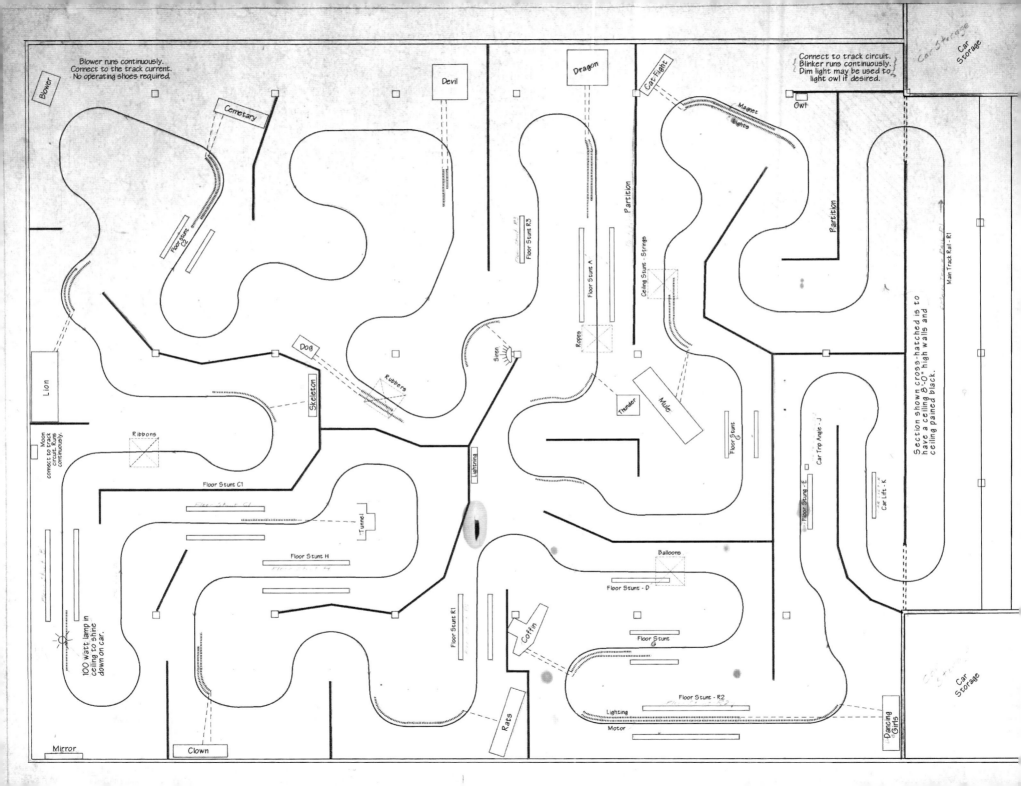

Blower runs continuously. Connect to the track current. No operating shoes required.

Connect to track circuit. Blinker runs continuously. Dim light may be used to light owl if desired.

Car Storage

Car Storage

Blower

Cemetary

Devil

Dragon

Car Flight

Owl

Magnet Lights

Partition

Floor Stunt C2

Floor Stunt R3

Floor Stunt A

Ceiling Stunt - Strings

Partition

Main Track Rail - R1

Lion

Dog

Ropes

Siren

Skeleton

Rubbers

Thunder

Mule

Floor Stunt G

Car Trip Angle - J

Moon connect to track circuit. Runs continuously.

Ribbons

Floor Stunt C1

Lightning

Floor Stung - E

Car Lift - K

Section shown cross-hatched is to have a ceiling 8'-0" high walls and ceiling pained black.

Tunnel

Floor Stunt H

Balloons

Floor Stunt - D

Car Storage

100 watt lamp in ceiling to shine down on car.

Floor Stunt R1

Coffin

Floor Stunt

Floor Stunt - R2

Rats

Lighting

Motor

Dancing Girls

Mirror

Clown

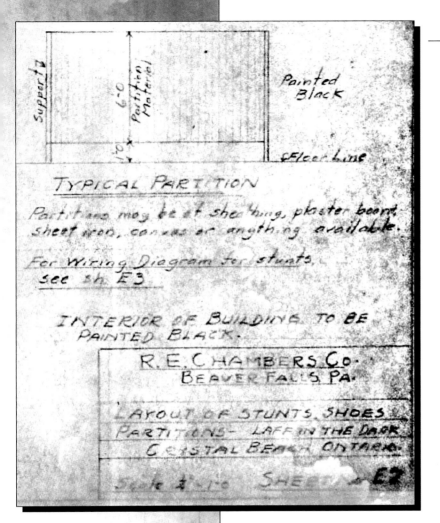

Support "

6'0"

Partition Material

4'0"

Painted Black

Floor Line

TYPICAL PARTITION

Partitions may be of sheathing, plaster board, sheet iron, canvas or anything available.

For Wiring Diagram for stunts, see sh. E3

INTERIOR OF BUILDING TO BE PAINTED BLACK.

R.E. CHAMBERS Co. BEAVER FALLS PA.

LAYOUT OF STUNTS SHOES PARTITIONS— LAFF IN THE DARK CRISTAL BEACH ONTARIO

Scale ⅜"=1'-0"   SHEET E2

Above: image showing construction of the building in 1908 that would eventually house Laff in the Dark. Below: Laff in the Dark building circa 1910.

BOWLING ALLEYS AND POOL ROOM

Left: Digitally enhanced floor plan of Laff in the Dark showing the location of the stunts. Above: Enlarged title block from the print.

129

Photo by Rick Doan.

Photo by Richard Schwegler.

Installing LITD in an existing structure was a smart use of existing assets. Minor alterations were required such as permanently sealing the open air windows and installing fans and vents for fresh air. (In spite of the ventilation, the smell of ozone was thick inside.)

Correspondence regarding the installation of LITD reflects how cost conscious park management had become since emerging from bankruptcy:

From General Manager Harry S. Hall to park Superintendant Jacob Nagel: *"Can the cars from the old Dodgem be used in our LITD ride as the Euclid Beach cars operating now in their LITD were formally Dodgem*

cars. If we can use them it will save us a lot of money." September 23, 1935.

From R. E. Chambers (LITD Manufacturer) to Harry S. Hall: *"I am working on the LITD proposition from another angle,"* and asks Hall to price a motor from Canadian General Electric or Westinghouse. *"We may be able to work out another scheme to save you a substantial amount."* October 5, 1935.

From Hall to Nagel: *"Kindly keep your help down to the least possible number. I think with so much carpentry work to be done that two carpenters might take the place of three or four ordinary men. I know you will have to have several men take the*

Top left: A rare interior shot shows one of the many hairpin turns that the cars seemed to accelerate around. It also shows the "Jazz Track" that would rock the car as they traversed forward. Left center: As the car passed by this locomotive, Jazz Track was appropriately placed to give the sensation that the riders were crossing railroad track. Bottom left: Publicity photo of the dragon in the Laff in the Dark at Rye Playland from the 1930s. It clearly shows the simplicity of the stunts. Amusing for adults but effective for scaring the beejeezus out of children not fond of the dark when the dragon suddenly illuminated with eyes flashing and ears rocking. Lower right: Bottom center: The dragon at Crystal Beach during the late 1980s. After more than 50 years, the layers of paint was probably all that was holding it together. Bottom right: Another shot of the loading platform art.

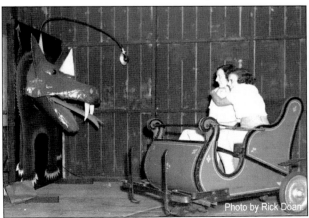

Photo by Rick Doan.

Above: Laffing Sal left and Laffing Sam right on display at a PTC trade show booth.

bowling alleys from one building to the other [dance hall], *but you should be able to cut down the force after that.*" November 12 1935

Chambers to Hall (apparently after Hall rejected Chamber's suggestion of bringing in a Chambers employee on site): "*The laying of the track is a very important item and we believe it would be well for you to have one of our men supervise the job.*" November 25, 1935.

An exasperated Chambers to Hall: "*It is very necessary that all of the curves be bent perfectly and that there are no kinks in the track, especially in the curves as this would tend to throw the cars off the track.*"

In addition to hairpin turns, sections of the layout consisted of "Jazz Track" – ripples built into the track to rock the cars left and right, up and down, or up and down on one side as the car moved forward - one of the stunts felt but not seen.

At the time of its installation, LITD advertisements described it as "*A thrilling experience that takes you through creepy subterranean passages where hobgoblins and other startling apparitions pop out at you at every turn.*"

Within the left and right hand corners of LITD's Japanese Pagoda facade were mechanical characters that gave a hint to the surprises inside. One was "Charm'in Charles" a skeleton playing a piano.

Charm'in Charles was a product of Funni-Frite Industries of Lancaster, Ohio. According to the sales flyer from Funni-Rite, Charm'in Charles "*rocks back and forth, turns his head from side to side, his jaw moves realistically as though singing along with the song. His hands travel up and down the keyboard and he stomps his foot with enthusiasm.*" Without sound equipment, Charles cost $830, $950 with sound.

The other mechanical figure was "The Laffing Man" who became part of LITD's exterior as part Crystal Beach's golden jubilee in 1940. According to Harry S. Hall, the Laffing Man was "*a well dressed robot and doesn't talk. He just "Laffs" great peals of hearty, merry, infectious laughter.*" Either Hall was confused and Laffing Sal was the automaton ordered, or Laffing Sal replaced the Laffing Man at some unknown year. The Philadelphia Toboggan Company manufactured animated and talking figures for dark rides and fun houses including "Laffing Sal" and her partner "Laffing Sam" that could have preceded her at the Laff in the Dark at Crystal Beach. PTC's Sal cost $415 dollars, her head, arms and body moved and swayed in harmony with a laughing record. Her dress, if purchased separately, was $22.50.

LITD was invented by Harry Traver in 1930 and his patent application was filed on November 14, 1930. However, Traver Engineering went bankrupt in 1932. R. E. Chambers purchased all assets and patents of Traver Engineering that same year.

Traver describes the original stunts in the patent including the Jazz Track - the sequences of strategically placed bumps. There were noise producing devices such as a clapper to produce a loud sudden bang in the dark; another device was to simulate the sound of clashing cymbals. Another auditory prank was to place a device called a ratchet onto the track that would produce a sound like that of a roller coaster train being pulled up the lift hill as the car passed over it.

One of Traver's illusory stunts was a sudden flash of lightning followed immediately by a clap of thunder. Traver intended to simulate the lightning by arcing electricity between two conductors. Wagging sheet metal suspended from the ceiling would produce thunder.

Another illusory effect was the strategic placement of a mirror, and a spotlight at a hairpin turn. The spotlight, triggered by the car and aimed at it just before it entered a hairpin turn would give the impression of a sudden head-on collision as riders glimpsed a car heading directly toward them. The strategically placed spotlight would provide sufficient glare so the riders would have difficulty recognizing themselves in the mirror at the moment the light flashed on.

The "Falling Statue" was another illusion designed to evoke fear of an imminent collision. The car would trigger a spotlight on a statue, and as the car was about to pass, the statue would fall in front of the car on seemingly real track. At that point, the light would go out and the car would swerve on the real track around the fallen statue.

Traver also planned a dragon to move toward a car while its electric eyes flashed and a device in its mouth spewed sparks.

The simplest device, extremely effective and to this day is guaranteed to make skin crawl is a stunt Traver called it "The Tickler."

From the ceiling, strands of fiber hung to create the tactile feeling of cobwebs on the face in total darkness.

There was also the bucking mule and the shaking skeletons, and sudden blasts of air.

Next are perhaps two of Traver's most devious stunts, exposing his sadistic side manifest in the Cyclone. He proposed that a "plate" (meaning dummy or fake) be created of a LITD car. Strategically placed, this plate would be struck by a real car in motion. The rigged plate, immediately upon collision, would tumble with the associated noise of a derailing car, sparks, and screaming riders.

In Traver's words taken from the patent, the following had to be the most devious. If it ever existed on a prototype or actual installation, it had to be the most unnerving:

"To impart a thrill to patrons the cars are arranged with a backward tiltable seat by providing ... a releaseable support to the seat ... to be released to permit of backward tilting movement of the seat and impart to the patrons the sensation of falling backward out of the car."

The simpler stunts described in Traver's patent – the Tickler,

Left: Two young men riding in Laff in the Dark at the end of the ride, returning to the loading platform. Right: Prior to the addition of the peaked roof facade, circa 1970.

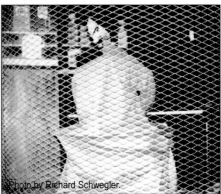

Photo by Richard Schwegler.

Photo by Richard Schwegler.

Photo by Richard Schwegler.

Photo by Richard Schwegler.

Laffing Sal occupied a window in the left side pagoda. Above: Charm'in Charles at the piano and as seen in is alcove on the right side of the Laff in the Dark building.

Jazz Track, the Clapper, the bucking mule and the shaking skeletons were part of the stunt package installed at Crystal Beach. To what extent the more complicated stunts described in the patent came to fruition in park installations remains to be determined. Certainly, some of these stunts may have proved to be too difficult to produce for the technology of the time, too expensive and perhaps too dangerous – such as the arcing electricity and the backward tilting seat.

Laff in the Dark operated flawlessly until August 12, 1987. A car carrying two teenagers sliced through the insulation of a cable that electrified the rail that supplied power to the cars. The cable shorted, the car stalled and sparks spewed over the car, striking the ceiling and burning the insulation. A car following behind them carrying the brothers of the teens, collided with the stalled car and tipped it over.

The teens found their way out by walking closely along the wall to an emergency exit. The ride operator had turned the lights on inside the building, cut the power to the track, and guided about a dozen riders out of the ride. The smoke that billowed out of the building stopped when the power was cut. After firefighters inspected the ride, it was repaired and put back into operation for the remaining years of the park's history.

LITD was the precursor of today's high tech illusion rides found at the Disney, Universal, and MGM theme parks in Florida and California.

Sales flier for Charm'in Charles.
Philadelphia Toboggan Co. collection courtesy Philadelphia Toboggan Coasters.

NEW From FUNNI-FRITE

CHARM'IN CHARLES

(ALIAS KNEES)

THE PERFECT DARK RIDE OR WALK-THRU FRONT ANIMATION

SIZE:
50" Wide
42" Deep
48" High

If you've been looking for something out of the ordinary to add bally-hoo to the front of your dark ride or walk-thru, consider this undernourished lad. He will entertain your guests for years, and they will always look again for him upon their return to your amusement area, as he sits at his old honky-tonk upright piano and bangs out old favorites. Built into his body are six different animations. He rocks back and forth, turns his head from side to side, occasionally he looks out toward his admirers, while his jaw is moving realistically as though singing along with the song. His hands travel up and down on the keyboard and he stomps his foot to the rhythm with real enthusiasm. CHARLES is delivered to you dressed in a red night shirt

and cap. The piano and the stool are finished in rich tones of walnut, and on top sits an imitation candle which flickers with realism. This display unit comes complete with our continuous magnetic tape playback which has five different songs installed in the cartridge, or you can use your own sound equipment.

NOTE: If our playback is installed for delivery, it is also electrically connected to the hand and foot animation so that CHARLES will cease playing for ten seconds between selections while he surveys the situation and your patrons. After the pause he begins again to stomp his foot and the honky-tonk rolls from the upright.

No. 98   CHARM'IN CHARLES AT THE UPRIGHT (NO SOUND EQUIPMENT INSTALLED)................. $830.00
No. 98-S CHARM'IN CHARLES WITH SOUND EQUIPMENT INSTALLED AS DESCRIBED ABOVE......... $950.00
1/3 DEPOSIT WITH ORDER (ALL PRICES F.O.B. LANCASTER, OHIO)

Funni-Frite Industries
LANCASTER, OHIO 43130

1300 EAST MAIN STREET

PHONE 614-654-3294

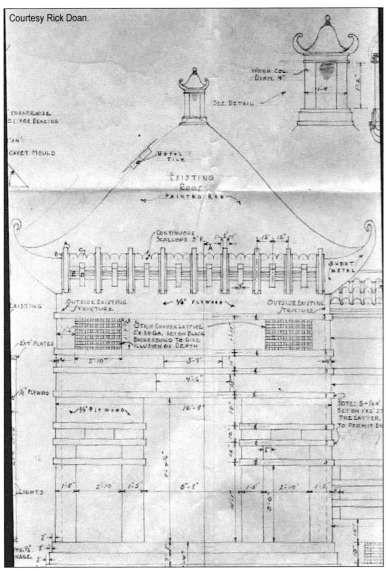

Courtesy Rick Doan.

Above: Partial elevation detailing the facade of the left side pagoda. Not all of details in the print came to fruition. The slight curvature to the roof was not incorporated. The lanterns would have made interesting architectural detail to the peaks of the pagodas but it was a detail the park apparently felt it could go without.

Right from top down: Original Traver patent diagram stunts for Laff in the Dark: Derailed car plate (Fig. 25), mirror (Fig. 27), kicking mule (Fig. 26), the tickler (Fig. 28), Falling Statue (Fig. 29), clapping cymbals (Fig. 30), lightning maker (Fig. 31F) followed by thunder (Fig. 31E), the dragon (Fig.32) Patent diagram for the Laff in the Dark cars showing the tilting backward seat.

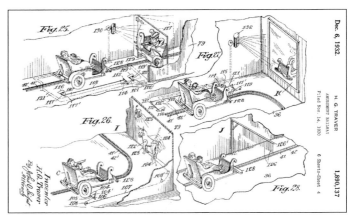

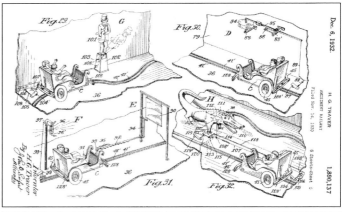

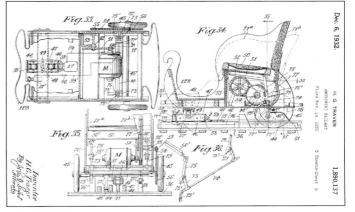

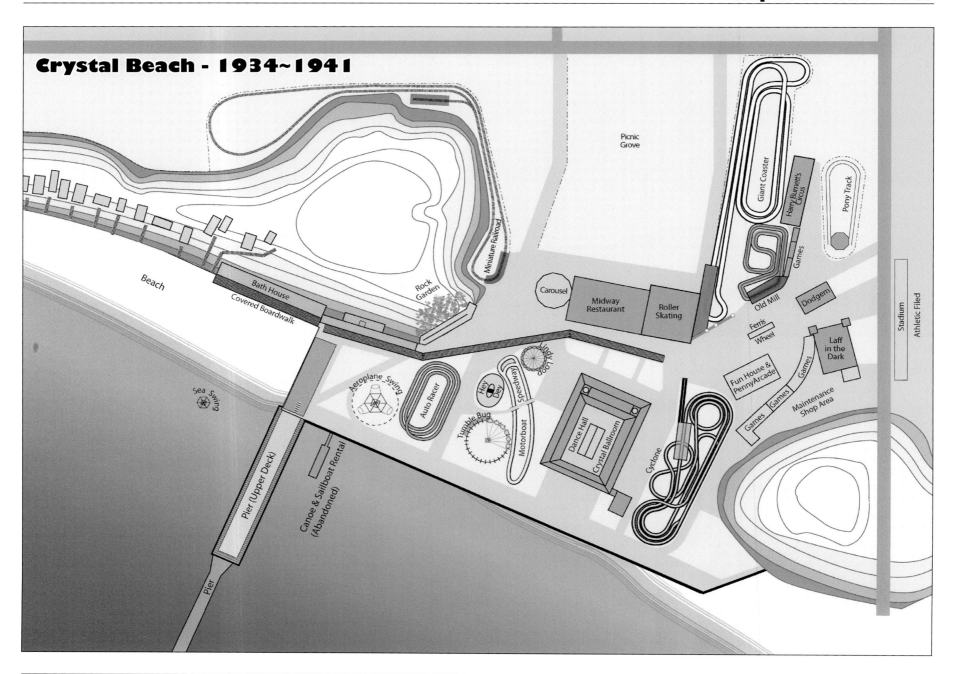

Crystal Beach - 1934~1941

Picnic Grove

Beach

Bath House

Covered Boardwalk

Rock Garden

Miniature Railroad

Giant Coaster

Harry Burnett's Circus

Pony Track

Games

Old Mill

Dodgem

Carousel

Midway Restaurant

Roller Skating

Ferris Wheel

Laff in the Dark

Fun House & Penny Arcade

Games

Games

Games

Maintenance Shop Area

Sea Swing

Aeroplane Swing

Auto Racer

Lindy Loop

Hey Dey

Speedway

Tumble Bug

Motorboat

Dance Hall

Crystal Ballroom

Cyclone

Stadium

Athletic Filed

Pier (Upper Deck)

Canoe & Sailboat Rental (Abandoned)

Pier

MOTORBOAT SPEEDWAY

Fort Erie Historical Museum collection.

CRYSTAL BEACH ONT.

Top: Postcard of the Motorboat Speedway from the loading area, Above: The far end of the canal was anchored by a lighthouse. Tumblebug in the background. Right: Ladies cruising the high seas.

The park spent $10,000 for the *Motorboat Speedway*, new for 1933. Called the Power Boats in the press, it consisted of a cement lined oval-shaped canal. Each gasoline-powered boat had the capacity for two people and had to be steered through the canal. It operated through 1945.

ACROPLANE

Lee Eyerly was an aviator and pilot trainer and set up a pilot training school in Salem, Oregon. There, he developed the forerunner to the modern flight simulator for his flying school in 1931. It was powered with a 15 horsepower electric motor and a real aircraft propeller. And like an airplane, the simulator had working elevators, ailerons and a rudder. Mounted on a huge bracket, the "trainer" plane could be positioned to climb, dive, loop and roll like an airplane. The Secretary of the State Board of Aeronautics, Art McKenzie, saw the potential for an amusement ride in the simulator

and brought Eyerly more orders than he could fill. So Eyerly set up a production line, which turned into a factory that turned out 50 Acroplanes at $1200 to $1400 each. The *Acroplane* soon became a staple at carnivals and fairs across North America. However, with a low rider capacity of one its longevity on amusement park and county fair midways was short. It was at Crystal Beach only during 1934 and called the *Aeropractor*.

The ride was marked a turning point for Eyerly as he shifted focus from the aviation industry to the amusement ride industry.

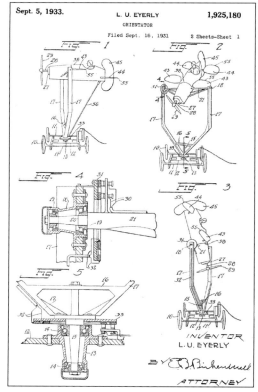

Right: Patent diagrams for the Eyerly's pilot trainer he first called the Orientator. Center and far right: The Acroplane climbing and diving on the grounds of Eyerly Aircraft in Salem, Oregon. Difficult to see in the images are wings and tail flaps. Acroplane riders had complete control of the machine that responded to their movements of the flap pedals and stick.

OCTOPUS

Eyerly filed a patent application for this ride in 1936. One these metal cephalopods became part of the Crystal Beach midway in 1938. Appropriately, the ride had eight sweeps upon which free-spinning tubs were mounted that carried two riders each.

The description of the *Octopus* released by Crystal Beach at the onset of the 1938 season was colorful.

"The Octopus will occupy a prominent berth on the midway, and will be in the form of a giant devil fish with all the appurtenances of one of those monsters from the deep.

"In the interior of the Octopus, spacious cars will operate. Patrons

Harvey Holzworth collection.

riding in these are promised no end of thrills as they journey through the 'tummy' of the devil fish and in and out of its tentacles, the movement of the cars having been designed to give the illusion that the creature is alive."

This ride was a midway fixture through 1952.

Cathy Herbert collection.

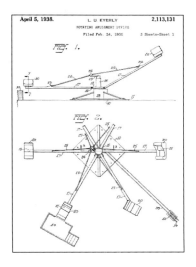

Above: Octopus at Crystal Beach circa 1950. Right: Eyerly's patent illustration for the Octopus helps illustrate the motion and mechanics of the ride.

Roll -o- Plane

The next generation *Acroplane* was the *Roll-o-Plane*. Unlike the Acroplane, the Roll-o-Plane did not provide riders with any motion control.

Passengers boarded a pair of bullet-shaped cylinders mounted on the opposite ends of a vertical axis. The opposite pairs of cylinders spun in synchronicity back and forth to keep the riders from going upside down.

The main axle rotated in both directions to give all the riders a forward and backward perspective.

Another operational option of the ride, (sometimes not engaged during busy times to shorten the ride) was a motor that slowly tilted the vertically rotating boom until it rotated horizontally.

The Roll-o-Plane was the new feature for 1943 and would come and go during the ensuing years, and was described as a "new" ride each time it reappeared after a few years absence.

Fort Erie Historical Museum collection.

Above: The Roll-o-Plane in 1944. Above right: Repositioned in 1946. Right: A different model Roll-o-Plane in front of what was then the hall for the "I Got It" game, circa 1963. Giant Coaster in the right background.

Fort Erie Historical Museum collection.

Photo by Mary Ann Kae.

MAGIC CARPET PALACE

Built on the site of the Backety-Back Scenic Railway station, the 1946 season announcement informed readers that the new fun house had the dimensions of 75' x 150' with striking Turkish-style architecture of balconies, graceful columns and arched entrances.

Named *Magic Carpet*, inside were rooms that contained stunts and illusions interconnected by a labyrinth of pitch dark corridors. People negotiated their way through the lightless 3-feet wide hallways by feeling the walls. Along some of these darkened corridors were windows that opened to scenes designed to startle, scare or otherwise amuse. These scenes came to sudden light and life when someone stepped on an activation pad in floor just before the window. During the late 1960s and early 1970s scenes included a flower girl sitting on a round cushion – the cushion rotated to reveal the flower girl's backside that was a witch or an ogre. There was a menacing gorilla that swung at you from a vine. A ghoulish scene contained a skeleton set 15 or 20 feet back whose head suddenly detached and hurtled toward the onlooker.

Where the maze was illuminated or open to outside light, it became an obstacle course. There were slides, (cont'd. pg. 145)

copyright1979 / Michael J. Losi

Photo by Rick Doan.

Above: Looking down from the top of the slide. These was a mate to this slide behind the wall with the open window frames on the left. To the right of this slide was a staircase for anyone uncomfortable using the slide.

Photo by Rick Doan.

The maze of the tilted room looking from its entrance to its exit seen in the center of the photo.

Photo by Rick Doan.

Three of the distorting mirrors in the hall of mirrors.

MYSTERY SEAT

Left: This photo reveals the art in architecture in the exterior of the Magic Carpet. In the center, the arrow points to the shocking Mystery Seat. One of the women is being blasted by an air jet in the floor. Inset: Looks like the Mystery Seat gave grandma a jolt and a young father picks up his daughter off the seat.

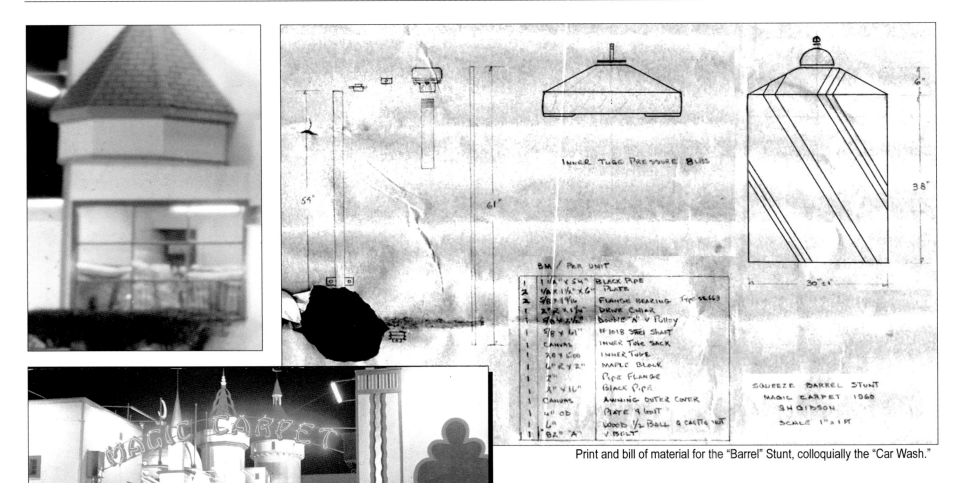

INNER TUBE PRESSURE 8LBS

SQUEEZE BARREL STUNT
MAGIC CARPET 1960
S.H. GIBSON
SCALE 1" = 1 FT

BM / PER UNIT

1	1 1/2" X 54"	BLACK PIPE
2	1/8 X 1 1/2" X 6"	PLATE
2	5/8 X 1 9/16	FLANGE BEARING TYPE SE663
1	2" R X 1 1/4"	DRIVE COLLAR
1	5/8 X 3 1/2"	DOUBLE "A" V PULLEY
1	5/8 X 61"	# 1018 STEEL SHAFT
1	CANVAS	INNER TUBE SACK
1	20 X 5.00	INNER TUBE
1	4" R X 2"	MAPLE BLOCK
1	2"	PIPE FLANGE
1	2" X 16"	BLACK PIPE
1	CANVAS	AWNING OUTER COVER
1	4" OD	PLATE & BOLT
1	4"	WOOD 1/2 BALL & CASTLE NUT
1	82" "A"	V BOLT

Print and bill of material for the "Barrel" Stunt, colloquially the "Car Wash."

Left: Enlarged from the image below is a glimpse into the "Car Wash" distorted from enlargement and reflections on the glass. At the back wall is a dark entryway that led to the room with the falling wall of crates and barrels.

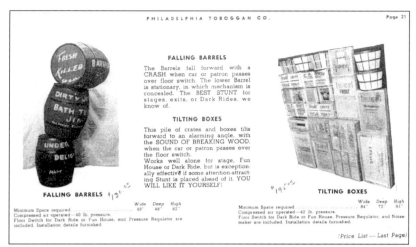

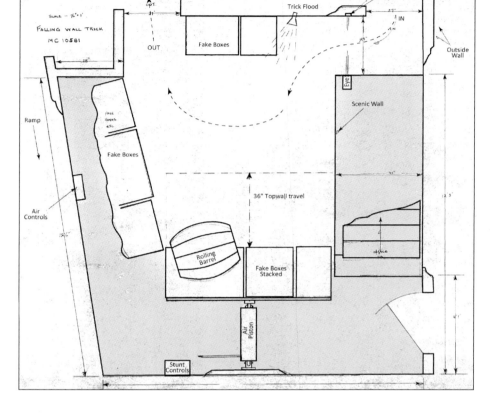

Above left: Advertisements for falling barrels and a tilting wall of boxes from a Philadelphia Toboggan Company catalog. They may have supplied the stunt for the room in the Magic Carpet. Left: Digitally enhanced site plan from the original layout print for the room with the tilting wall of crates and barrels in the Magic Carpet.

and wobbly lily pads that had to be traversed – anyone who lost their balance got a wet foot.

The tilted room was a maze within the maze. Pitched on a diagonal – low at one corner, high at the opposite corner, the tilted room was lined with hand rails to create a maze that merely weaved back and forth. It was a simple yet effective and momentarily created the sensation that, once back on a level floor, that too was tilted.

Other rooms included the hall of distorting mirrors, and a room with a wall lined with crates and barrels that tipped and threatened to topple onto those passing through. The first room after the entrance was the "Car Wash" with slowly revolving striped canvas bumpers that resembled the vertical spinning brushes one might find at a car wash. Patrons would have to push their way through these bumpers that were approximately four feet tall, two feet wide and a foot apart.

The rooms and stunts were changed periodically, so whether any of these were the original stunts is uncertain, the exception being the tilted room.

Teens float down the Magic Carpet as part of a feature on Crystal Beach in the Buffalo Courier Express Sunday Magazine in 1967.

Philadelphia Toboggan Co. collection, courtesy Philadelphia Toboggan Coasters.

From its opening and into the 1960s, at one of the balconies was the "Mystery Seat." A bench where patrons were encouraged to sit and rest before pressing on. The keister of the unsuspecting received a very mild electric shock. Assumed a health hazard and a liability, it was removed.

Where the maze was exposed to the inner courtyard a "controller" could watch the progress of the people and blast them with air from jets built into the floor.

The Magic Carpet culminated with the ride's namesake. The carpet was not a carpet at all but a wide loop of thick rubber – like a giant rubber band that was put in motion by large rollers. Patrons sat on the carpet, which propelled them downward to the ground level exit from an entry platform one floor up. The carpet sagged somewhat between the rollers that moved it and created the illusion of waves as if it was a real carpet flying through the air. The carpet was motionless until turned on by an attendant.

As previously noted, this "carpet" may have been the same carpet installed in its predecessor, the Fun House. The patent diagrams in the Spillman Engineering patent look exactly like the carpet in the Magic Carpet. The Philadelphia Toboggan Company was yet another source for "Magic Carpets."

The building had a few minor modifications through the years. The bay window area to the left of the entrance was removed. Also, the entrance into the hall of distorted mirrors was also modified and can be seen in the photos. What precipitated these modifications is lost to time.

After the 1971 season, the Knapps sold the Magic Carpet to the park. The carpet was taken out and the attraction was renamed *Magic Palace*. New stunts filled the space occupied by the carpet and the machinery that propelled it. One of these was a corridor that was painted black with a succession of door frames spaced at regular intervals. The frames were painted with fluorescent paint in such a manner that they gave the illusion that the floor was tilted.

Following this corridor was a "Jail" - a room lined with mirrors that contained a maze created by jail bars for walls. A strobe light created more confusion in the room. Although the new stunts were well crafted, they were a poor substitute for the Magic Carpet.

As time wore on, the stunts in the Magic Palace suffered from a lack of care and maintenance. The car-wash bumpers were removed and the room left with nothing in it; the wall of crates and barrels no longer tilted when passed. The lily pads were covered over, and the slides were barricaded.

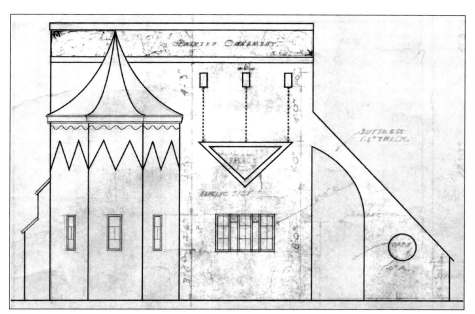

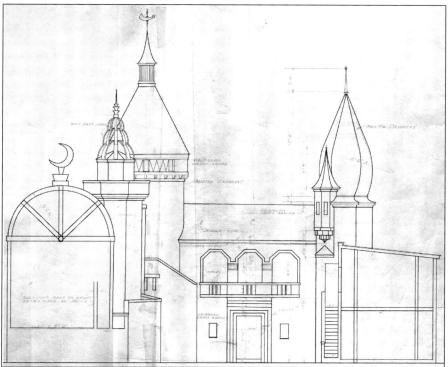

At completion, not everything in these elevations came to fruition. The buttress drawn as part of the Magic Carpet's left-front facade never was built (above), nor was there ever a hanging sign. The drawing supports the contention that the Magic Carpet had an older twin somewhere in California. Note the sign name for the walk-through is Blue Beard's Palace. Missing from the Magic Carpet's right side facade are the windows on either side of the exit, the decorative window in the center near the roof, and the two tall decorative pencil-like columns as seen at right.

The Magic Carpet under construction and nearing completion during the spring of 1946. Compare this image to others in this section and note the change to the bay window on the left and the curving staircase near the center that were later removed.

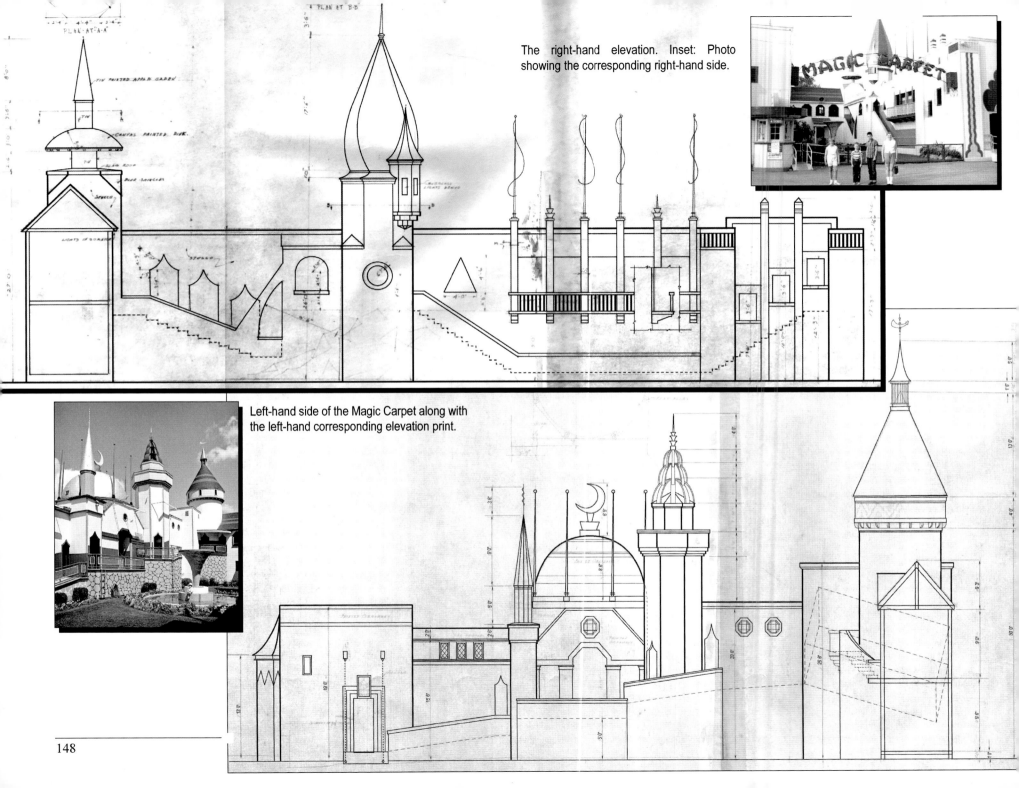

The right-hand elevation. Inset: Photo showing the corresponding right-hand side.

Left-hand side of the Magic Carpet along with the left-hand corresponding elevation print.

"Patty" Conklin (standing) with ride inventor Norman Bartlett.

Fillmore Hall became general manager in 1948.

Earlier noted, some of the midway attractions, including the Magic Carpet and the Miniature Railroad were owned and operated by concessionaires from whom Crystal Beach received a percentage of the gross receipts. Many of the portable rides that appeared on the midway were supplied by Conklin Shows of Brantford, Ontario, near Hamilton. This decades-long relationship began with James Wesley "Patty" Conklin shortly after World War II. For most of its existence, Crystal Beach's Kiddie Land was populated with rides that were entirely from Conklin's inventory. On the main midway, portable rides would appear, stay for a season or longer, then be replaced with other portable rides. Switching out rides kept the midway fresh with at least one new attraction every year at no expense to the park.

According to Jim Conklin, there was a standard financial arrangement used for supplying rides to amusement parks on a seasonal basis. Sixty-five percent of the gross receipts represented by the tickets that a Conklin ride took in were Conklin's, the balance stayed with Crystal Beach. Jim Conklin trained for the travelling carnival business by working the games at Crystal Beach that were part of Conklin's annual staging on the midway – including Bingo housed in the building along side the Giant

Coaster added in 1956.

Following World War II, there was an era of prosperity from the industrialization and technological advancements that were a by-product of it. The art deco style of the post war era was a reflection of the great expectations for the future that science and technology would bring. It impacted the designs of everything from household appliances to automobiles. It influenced art, architecture and advertising. Crystal Beach did not escape the art deco influence as another transitional phase at the park began with the 1946 season. Except for paint, most, if not all of the buildings and structures in the park had not changed since their installation, including the Giant Coaster, which opened in 1917. Beginning in 1946, and through the next few years, the building facades and ride entrances would be remodeled with art deco designs, bright rainbow colors, and neon and fluorescent lighting. Not even the carousel escaped the transformation.

The face lift would not be complete until the 1948 season with the completion of the Comet. Fillmore L. Hall, son of George Hall, became the general manager of Crystal Beach in 1948. This change in management may mark the start of the buy-out of other Crystal Beach stock holders by the Hall family.

The Fun House was demolished after the 1948 season, and on its site, at a reported cost of $70,000, a new penny arcade opened. The Amusement Construction Company of Brantford, Ontario built the new arcade that featured a 50-foot tower marquee illuminated at night. Its façade was a perfect fit with the midway's new art-deco theme.

Fillmore Hall implemented some cost-cutting measures in 1950. He had the entire midway paved except for areas regularly landscaped. The picnic grove was the only area not landscaped that was spared blacktop. According to Hall, *"It will not only make walking easier, but it will eliminate dust and make cleaning easier."* He explained that each night after closing, 25 men would comb the grounds washing the park from stem to stern to get the dust and dirt off everything for the next day. The new paving would eliminate most of the dust and everything could be hosed in a few hours rather than taking all night.

To promote the highest sanitary conditions, Hall noted that the midway restaurant had been remodeled to facilitate food handling and all food would be served on paper plates eliminating the need to wash dishes. These changes in food service perhaps indicates the Charles Laube terminated his long affiliation with the park and the tableware Laube used was most likely taken to Buffalo for use in his restaurants there. Disposable tableware was the easiest and cheapest replacement.

John Rebstock opened Crystal Beach on Sundays beginning in 1895. From March 8, 1906 and for nearly 50 years, activity as the park was limited when Canada passed the Lord's Day Act forbidding Sunday work, travel, sports and commercial entertainment. In 1950, an amendment to this Act allowed "sport parks" to open from 1:30 to 6:30 PM on Sundays. The Crystal Beach Property Owner's Association went on record favoring the amendment on June 13, 1950. Earlier, the Ontario Legislature amended the act to allow municipalities to hold local referendums to set the ban aside. Before the referendum could be voted upon in Crystal Beach, a petition had to be signed by ten percent of the residents. George Hall Sr. personally circulated the petition. The Ridgeway Property Owners' Association, The Crystal Beach Athletic Club, and the Crystal Beach Fire Department were also in favor of the referendum, much to the angst of the local clergymen. Residents voted on June 26, passing the referendum 278 to 150. Fillmore Hall said the amusement park would immediately begin Sunday operation - all amusement devises and bathing facilities would be open. The law specifically banned dancing, bingo, and shooting galleries, but permitted bowling, baseball, tennis, golf,

This glass and neon entrance replaced the one below.

arcades, roller rinks, bathing, concerts, amusement rides, athletic events and games of skill.

The entrance to the park at Derby Road had been remodeled in 1951 and sported new glass-block pylons that were back-illuminated with neon lights.

Ontario government started a crack down on bootleggers and gamblers in 1952. Elden Knapp, operator of Crystal Beach's Penny Arcade found himself a target of a raid by the Anti Gambling Squad of the Provincial Police working out of Toronto. They confiscated thirty amusement games valued at $125,000 during a raid on June 18, 1952. Magistrate Roberts, upon review of the evidence said, *"...these machines consist of mixed games of skill and chance, with chance predominating."* Because the outcome of the games was determined more by chance, Roberts decided that they could be used for gambling which was a violation of the criminal code. Therefore, Elden and his three employees Patrick Daley, Cecil Dean, and Charles Hollet were found in violation of the law and each fined $25 plus court costs. Presumably Knapp appealed – the arcade never did close. While there was no formal gambling in the park, Roberts was apparently unaware that people bet on everything.

The restrictions on gambling must have been relaxed to some extend to allow Bingo. In 1956 management erected a new $55,000 hall along side the lift hill of Giant Coaster just for Bingo. To permit easy access to it, the park's roller rink housed in the building that served as the dance hall until 1925 was demolished a few years earlier.

Violence in the park marred the 1956 season on opening day when racial tensions created by the social inequities of the time erupted at the park. Riots at the park and onboard the *Canadiana* made news headlines from coast to coast and precipitated investigations by the FBI.

The earliest reports of violence were from onboard the *Canadiana* on its 12:15 PM run out of Buffalo. Alledgedly one of three U.S. servicemen on board made a racial slur that ignited a fight that the steamer's crew managed to break up. Once at Crystal Beach the fight resumed on the pier. One of the servicemen jumped into the water to escape. Someone later saw an individual being carried off the *Canadiana* – presumably injured during the fighting on board. Before the evening riot on board the steamer, the park and the Village of Crystal Beach were plagued by roving gangs that assaulted pedestrians and park patrons.

The Penny Arcade, built on the site of the 1927 Fun House, cost $70,000 and opened in 1949.

A major incident in the picnic grove set the course of events for the balance of the day when two teens, one black and one white, started fighting. Before the Ontario Provincial Police (OPP) could break them up, both managed to inflict injuries to each other. The police escorted them to the park's first aid station, then located at the corner of Erie and Derby Roads at the village entrance to the park. While the boys were being treated for their wounds, a mob of black and white teens gathered outside. Inside, Vincent Palladino's wounds required more sophisticated treatment, so the nurse called for an ambulance. Outside First Aid the crowd grew to approximately 400.

Witnesses noted that as Palladino was carried to the ambulance black teens nearby started heckling him. In the crowd were Tony

John H. "Jack" Roth was appointed superintendent of the park in 1954. The facade of the Bingo Hall was Art Deco extreme seen here in 1961.

Pinto and Leo DiGiulio. When they tried to find out what happened, threatening words were exchanged then the melee began. Witnesses reported that bottles were flying everywhere, some people reported that they had seen knives. Three of the park's special police and two OPP where unable to contain the fighting and called for back-up.

Charles LaMarca said he walking near the park entrance on Erie Road when someone hit him on the head with a steel-handled umbrella. (He later received four stitches at Buffalo Columbus Hospital.)

One woman reported that she was trapped and wedged in between all the fighting when it erupted – and was pushed, shoved and stepped on.

DiGiulio and Peter Giglia, managed to escape the brawl. Farther into the midway witnesses saw them attack a black man, Jarvis Jones, who was at the park with his wife and 13-month old daughter. Jones received a severe blow to the head and suffered facial lacerations. He was later admitted to Millard Fillmore Hospital in Buffalo.

Ride operators of the Auto Speedway stated that two men were fighting in the middle of the track.

Forty OPP were dispatched from Ridgeway, Fort Erie, Niagara Falls and Port Colborne.

Five black and four white young men were arrested and taken to the OPP station in the village. Seven knives were confiscated. An estimated 125 black youths converged on the station and demanded the release of the five black men. Some young men and women formed smaller gangs and moved into the midway. Shortly afterward, Police began receiving reports of assaults on the midway.

A fight broke out at the Old Mill, which closed for the balance of the day. Black teen girls punched a 35-year old white woman near the Bingo Hall around 8 PM. The OPP chased a girl through the park. She ran onto the Caterpillar, jumped off its platform but could not escape the police. Smaller gangs and young adults and teens assaulted people walking along Erie Road in the village.

On June 13, 1956, of the nine arrested, eight were scheduled for trial, and seven of them appeared in court. Absent from the trial was Michael Guzzio who forfeited his $250 bail; the judge issued a warrant for his arrest. Two black teens had the charges against them dismissed. Five of the young men were convicted of creating a public disturbance by fighting and fined $250. Two were charged with carrying weapons and fined $300.

Fortunately Crystal Beach was well maintained and patronized, and through the dedication of the Hall family, the park continued to be the primary summer destination for families, company picnics, and outings for schools and social groups for decades to come.

Other parks that sustained such traumas did not survive. One of them is Olympic Park in Irvington, New Jersey. Early in May 1965, youths rampaged throughout the park, wrecking amusement equipment, and stealing prizes and other merchandise. The youths were ejected from the park, but they continued their rampage in the surrounding residential areas. The resulting publicity kept people away from the park all season and the park closed permanently after the summer.

Chicago's Riverview Park became a magnet for racial and gang conflicts, vandalism and robbery during the 1960s, which precipitated its closing at the end of the 1967 season.

Violence of another kind ravaged part of Crystal Beach after the 1957 season. On September 8, the athletic field stadium burned. The fire originated in an adjacent pony barn. The damage was put at $25,000. The stadium was rebuilt for the 1958 season.

Cathy Herbert collection.

Flames engulf the stadium.

1
pg. 161

The caption for this Associated Press Wirephoto read: A policeman holds a girl as teenagers look on during disorders at Crystal Beach Amusement Park. The Crystal Beach riots remain a subject of study by sociologists.

Crystal Beach - 1942~1946

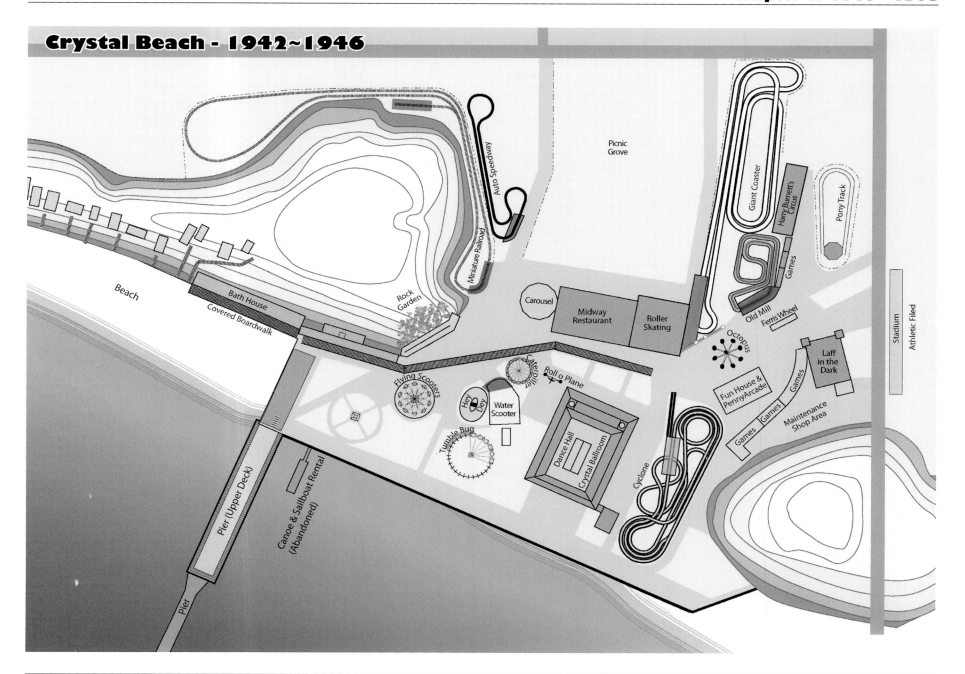

FLYING SCOOTERS

Exaggeration was nothing new to Crystal Beach press releases and the 1942 season opening announcement had a whopper that claimed the latest addition to the midway, the *Flying Scooters*, traveled at 45 miles per hour in a 300 foot wide circle. In reality, it was perhaps 3 miles per hour in a 100 foot circle. One feature about the ride that was not exaggerated was the fact that riders were able to sail, dive, or climb at will by controlling a fin in the front of each scooter.

Bisch-Rocco of Chicago manufactured this ride; invented and patented by Alvin Bisch.

Flying Scooters remained on the midway at least through 1960. During these years it occupied a site near the dock and the area left of the Giant Coaster station.

This version of the Circle Swing is the third incarnation of Traver's original. The tower was raised 12 feet and the frame sheathed with a futuristic art deco facade. As the world started to enter the space age, stainless steel Flash Gordon style rocketships replaced the biplanes. To board the *Rocketships*, riders had to climb a flight of stairs within the tower's frame to the second floor loading platform.

Rocketships landed at Crystal Beach in 1947 on the former Dodgem site, and according to the press release cost $20,000. Each of three ships was 25 feet long with four seating positions, each could fit two people. Reportedly, the tower was 80 feet tall and illuminated.

On appearance alone, Rocketships fit perfectly with the new art deco facades the buildings received earlier.

ROCKETSHIPS

Lower Lakes Marine Historical Society collection.

The Rocketships in motion. Left: A close-up of one of the ships with an Old Mill windmill and the Giant Coaster lift hill in the background. Above: As the ride appeared from the near the Magic Carpet.

- there was no other area of the park with sufficient space to accommodate its length

Noted earlier, incorporating the Cyclone's structure reduced material expenses. According to James T. Mitchell, its structure accounted for 60% of the steel in the Comet. Re-erecting as much of the Cyclone as possible without re-engineering saved additional money. Consequently, the lift hill of the Comet, with exception of the wood track, was the exact lift hill of the Cyclone. Its believed that the incline to the Comet's first turn is the incline to the Cyclone's double helix. The Cyclone's station was re-erected but masked behind a stylish art deco façade. Additional savings were realized when park management opted not to purchase preformed structural steel to complete the structure. They purchased flat iron stock and formed it locally.

Cathy Herbert collection.

Cathy Herbert collection.

Cathy Herbert collection.

Above right: A workman climbing the structure of the first turn as the internal bracing is erected. Compare to the image on the following page in the lower right corner with the internal bracing erected.

Construction began immediately after the 1947 season to the design by Herb Schmeck, president of PTC. John Allen, also of PTC, had the responsibility for all of the Comet's machinery, brakes, and a major portion of the station's design. A Buffalo Evening News article credits James T. Mitchell, an employee of Crystal Beach, with the Comet's design. The article noted that he was one of only five men internationally known for their roller coaster construction expertise.

In reality, Mitchell did supervise the construction of the Comet. Indeed, his twenty years of experience maintaining the Cyclone made

him the perfect candidate for the job. Prior to his Crystal Beach tenure, Mitchell was employed by Traver Engineering and probably worked on earlier Traver coasters. Roller coaster databases do not credit Mitchell for the design of any roller coasters. This does not diminish his contributions to the Comet which was guiding the carpenters building the track. John Allen credits Schmeck with (cont'd. pg. 163)

Cathy Herbert collection.

Comet as Monkey Bars

On the Comet, one day, the crew noticed a monkey walking on the catwalk that escaped from a local home. They [Comet ride operators] eventually cornered it under the platform and the owner came to pick it up.

"Lone Man on Long Walk is Searching for Danger." Buffalo Evening News, 7/17/63

Left: May 1948 view of the Comet nearly completed. The courtyard waits post construction cleaning and landscaping. The Tumble Bug is in the left foreground.

Record Player & Record Holder

Danny Neaverth, long time Buffalo disk jockey at WKBW radio, holds the record for the most consecutive rides on the Comet – 210 times.

"They Keep Coming Back to a Ride That Scares Them Out of Their Wits." Niagara Falls Review - Fort Erie Review. June 15, 1974. Fort Erie Historical Museum clippings file.

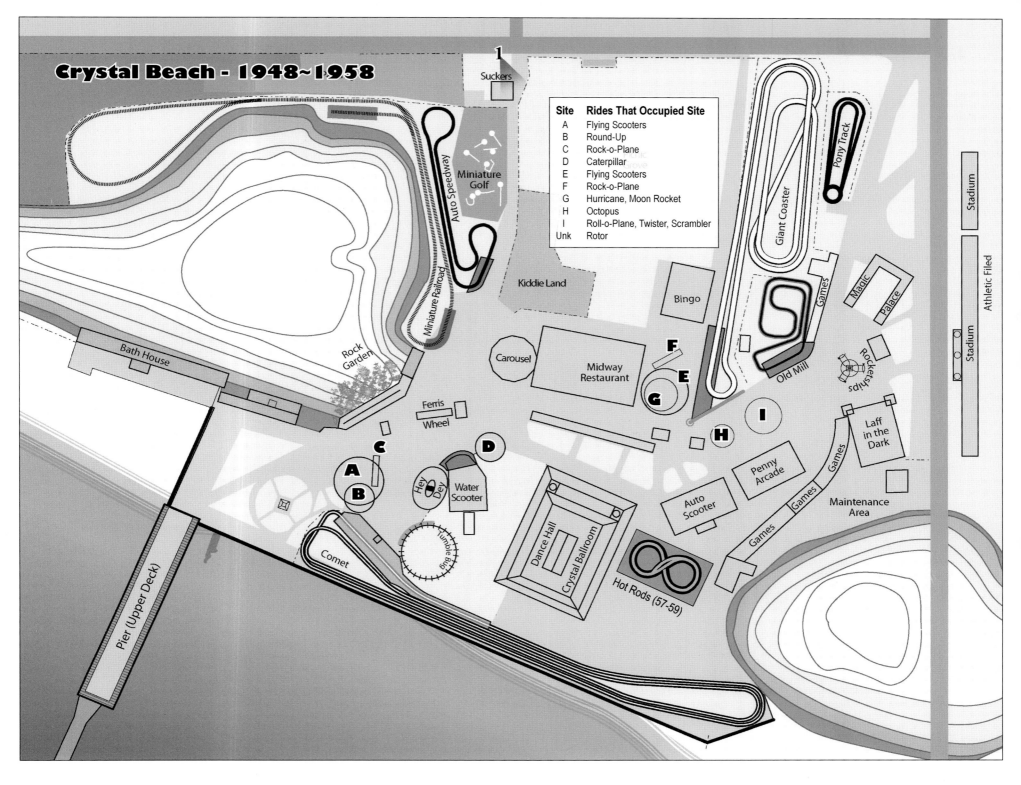

Crystal Beach - 1948~1958

Site	Rides That Occupied Site
A	Flying Scooters
B	Round-Up
C	Rock-o-Plane
D	Caterpillar
E	Flying Scooters
F	Rock-o-Plane
G	Hurricane, Moon Rocket
H	Octopus
I	Roll-o-Plane, Twister, Scrambler
Unk	Rotor

Suckers

Auto Speedway

Miniature Golf

Miniature Railroad

Kiddie Land

Rock Garden

Bath House

Carousel

Bingo

Midway Restaurant

Giant Coaster

Pony Track

Games

Magic Palace

Old Mill

Rocketships

Ferris Wheel

Hey Dey

Water Scooter

Comet

Tumble Bug

Dance Hall

Crystal Ballroom

Hot Rods (57-59)

Auto Scooter

Penny Arcade

Games

Games

Games

Games

Laff in the Dark

Maintenance Area

Pier (Upper Deck)

Stadium

Stadium

Athletic Filed

A B C D E F G H I 1

Cathy Herbert collection.

As the Comet nears completion, the worker sitting on the rail of the second hill near the center of the photo as thousands of bolts behind him and up the hill to sink. The wires for the tracer lights hangs and waits placement. On the ground and paralleling the track is new guard fence marked by the evenly spaced of leftover earth from the fence post holes.

the Comet's design, so does a Wall Street Journal article about the amusement industry which at the time of publication, noted that the last major installation of the Philadelphia Toboggan Company was at Crystal Beach, Ontario.

Louis Scapillato, a carpenter, recaps his experience building the Comet's track and indicates Mitchell was not the designer:

"Early in February 1948, I had just finished a course in cabinet making in Hamilton...

"I happened to be in the unemployment office, registering for benefits or a job, whichever came first. At the same time a man called Mr. Mitchell, 'Jim' as we would later know him, was in there looking for carpenters to work on the new 'Comet' being installed at Crystal Beach.

"I was immediately hired along with some others. I think I can still name the ones who were to be with me until the completion of the Comet. There was, Gord Clifford, Pete Marr, John Noonan, Willard McIntyre, Harry Marshman and one man who I can't-recall his last name, Harley was his first. Duke Teal, we always called him Duke, was to be our foreman, a very mechanically minded guy, worked at a slow pace but very wisely. He guided us through it all. There was also on site an engineer from Pennsylvania, U.S.A. I think he was instrumental in the plan and design of the Comet.

"It was very cold that February, but we survived it to it's completion. The steel workers had completed a the structural work to be done. Now we had to complete it. This included the track, the hand rails, the cat walk, around the complete ride."

If Louis's recall is correct, then the engineer from Pennsylvania was Herb Schmeck.

The structural work on the Comet was completed by January 1948 and most of the ledgers that would support the track were in place.

Promotions during its construction claimed that the trains would approach speeds up to 100 miles per hour. Under ideal operating conditions the speed of the trains may top out at 65 mph. The first test runs took place on May 11, 1948, well in advance of the park's opening on Decoration Day.

According to Scapillato, testing the Comet began with cycling a single car from the four-car train through the track. Sitting in the car during its first trip was Louis, James Mitchell, Duke Teal, and the "Engineer." The car plummeted down the first hill, sailed over the following hill, but failed to breach the crest of the third hill on the far-east side at the first turn around. "Dogs" underneath the car grabbed onto the ratchets in the center of the track, which prevented it from rolling backwards. The four men had to exit the car and push it the balance of the way up the hill. Once it was rolling again, the men jumped back in. The car stalled again on the incline of the second turn just above the station.

This "breaking-in" of the train and track was repeated countless times until a single car completed a circuit without stalling, indicating the tight spots in the track were adequately worked out and would not stall an entire train. Then the entire train was cycled numerous times. (This breaking-in and testing was an annual preseason ritual.)

The initial estimate to build the Comet was $125,000. Costs ran approximately $75,000 over the original estimate. George Hall sighted rising labor and equipment costs for the difference. Louis Scapillato and his colleagues were in part responsible for the increased labor costs:

"I must also mention that we were hired at a rate of $1.00 per hour. Work was going along very well, and getting higher off the ground. At approximately fifty feet, we began thinking about the danger of climbing and handling equipment. So we decided it was time for an increase in pay, (known as danger pay). We talked

Photo by John. B. deHaas

A train plunges down the hill immediately behind the station during the American Coaster Enthusiasts convention during 1984.

to Mr. Mitchell, our supervisor, and he wasn't too keen on giving us a raise. Finally, he okayed it. We also mentioned that after so many feet, as we progressed, we should have more money. He shook that off, and we came to a conclusion, finally. However, we ended up at about $1.80 an hour, before reaching 96 feet."

The Comet's station was a work of art. By day its art deco facade was a splash of red, yellow, and sky blue paint. By night it was awash with neon lights with red neon art deco comets. It was a sharp contrast to the stark, utilitarian Cyclone station hidden underneath.

Sand-flies, mosquitoes and other flying insects swarmed the tracer lights at night. Speeding past them at 60 mph, riders were pelted by the insects – stinging their eyes, splattering on their faces, and going down the throats of screamers. Front seat riders received the brunt of the pelting. To alleviate the problem a framed screen was mounted

to the front of each train. The screens did not eliminate the insect problem entirely, but it helped. The year the screens were fashioned is uncertain, but they disappeared when the Comet received a new set of trains during the early 1960s.

In 1970 the lift hill received 220 feet of new lift hill chain.

The Comet operated flawlessly until a minor accident on June 16, 1974 that sent two riders to the hospital.

On the station approach was a trim brake that slowed the trains. Those familiar with the Comet will recall this is the section of the track before the unloading platform that was roofed and sheltered.

According to Bob Hall there was excessive moisture on the trim brake that day which reduced friction and allowed the trains to enter the station faster than usual. This in itself was not uncommon, but it required the brakeman in the station to be alert and apply the station brake early in the braking process. On this run, the brakeman failed to apply enough pressure early on. The train's speed was reduced, but the first car rolled off the brake, then the second. Although the brakeman applied more pressure to the brake the forward momentum of the first two cars pulled the third car off the brake and then the fourth. The train filled with people rolled forward to the loading platform where a second train had seated riders and others boarding. The speed of the incoming train at the time of impact was slow enough not to damage either train, but it did inflict minor injuries to some riders.

Richard Derr of Buffalo was one of the riders in the train that failed to stop and said that he just banged his shins. Vicky and Christine Langley of Welland were taken to Douglas Memorial Hospital for x-rays for possible head and back injuries - they were in the rear of the train stopped at the loading area.

Tragedy came to a Comet fan on June 21, 1975. Kieran Glynn, 26, of Stevensville, Ontario and a friend, Gene Harasay, were riding the coaster, seated in the very last seat. From this spot, riders can feel extreme whipping action as the train exits curves or rounds the top of a hill. Glynn decided to sit on the top of the seat back, rather than in the seat as the train entered the last horseshoe turn before the home stretch to the station. Exiting this turn is where riders feel the most intense lateral Gs (force to the left or right) on the coaster.

Photo by John. B. deHaas

"We were going around the bend when I saw him sort of crunched up, half crouched and half sitting" Harasay recalled of the accident.

"I looked over the other side and then I looked back and he was falling out of the car... I don't know what he was trying to do. I had no idea he was going to try to sit up [on top of the seat back]."

As the train completed the last turn, Glynn and Harasay were subjected to intense forces that slammed them to their right. Glynn, sitting on the back of the last seat, rather than in the train, was thrown off and flung into the steel superstructure that braced the first curve that was high above. Glynn died instantly. His body ricochetted of the frame then fell onto the catwalk. Bob Hall said that when he first spotted the body he had to turn away. The torso was hanging from the catwalk, bent backwards with the head toward the ground.

The park continued to operate the Comet, feeling confident that Glynn's death was not the result of a malfunctioning train and indeed, after an investigation, the Comet was cleared and found to be in perfect working order.

By the mid 1980s, the new owners were desperate for something new on the midway, but money was tight, so there was no possibility of any major new attractions. The need for this new attraction was

Photo by John. B. deHaas

Left: The sheltered trim brake (inner parallel tracks) area before the station. Note the rivet holes in the iron supporting the roof - other structural elements were fastened at these holes here when the iron was in the Cyclone. Above: View from the loading station in 1984.

imaginatively filled by reversing the first two cars of the Comet's four-car trains so that riders could ride the Comet forward or backward, which reinvented the coaster.

The novelty of riding backwards undoubtedly was a major factor that contributed to the attendance increase of 1985. Soon afterward the novelty wore off, and by the middle of the following season, it was clear that riders preferred to face forward. The rear, or forward facing last two cars, where often filled. The backward facing front of the train often made the ride circuit with many empty seats. Riders would wait on the platform for a front-facing seat rather than ride backwards. Management either did not notice this preference or no longer cared. One of the three trains remained unaltered and could have been engaged rather than spend money to change the other trains back to their original mechanical configuration.

Members of the Western New York Roller Coaster Club (WNYCC) had special privileges with the Comet, which made the

Photo by Cathy Herbert

Cathy Herbert collection

Left: At one time, the sand flies and mosquitoes swarmed the Comet's tracer lights at night that park maintenance fashioned a protective screen to shield the eyes of front seat riders from being blinded when hurtling through a swarm at night. The screen also kept to a minimum, the number of flies ingested by screamers. The screen remained on the front seat into the mid 1960s when the original trains were replaced with the three sets that ran until 1989. Far left: Facing west from the top of the first turn around just before the plunge.

coaster especially endearing to the club's local members. Every spring, Comet superintendant Sam Aquilina invited WNYCC members to help break-in the Comet's trains before each season's opening. These roller coaster enthusiasts became human sand bags, beasts of burden, and painters to help the park prepare the Comet for the summer after nine months in hibernation. These annual rituals mirrored Louis Scapillato's memories of breaking in the ride for the first time. WNYCC called these spring events "Comet Break-ins." Nobody on the planet was closer to the Comet or enjoyed it more than the members of WNYCC during the late 1980s.

From 1981 to 1987, CTV television aired a "reality" series called "Thrill of a Lifetime." The show's premise: fulfill fantasies of participants. Fantasies ranged from meeting celebrities to special reunions or action/adventure thrills. Each fantasy was an actual request made by a viewer that had written, phoned or walked into the "Thrill" offices to ask for his or her thrill of a lifetime.

Roller coaster enthusiast Michael Horwood, then of Brampton, Ontario was one lucky viewer and had his wish granted: to ride the Comet through a mound of shaving cream. Thrill of a Lifetime crews filmed the event on July 19, 1982. With shaving cream ingredients in buckets, and a cylinder of propellant, the bottom of the drop from the first turn-around was the location for the shaving cream mound. Michael and his wife Celia boarded a train, and in no time the train climbed the top of the first turnaround, then dropped at about 50 mph into a mound of shaving cream that exploded on impact.

"It was like going through a cloud," noted Celia during a follow-up interview.

Their episode aired on CTV during October 1982.

When the assets of Crystal Beach were auctioned in October 1989, the Comet sold for $210,000 (original construction cost $200,000) after a bidding war between Darien Lake and Charles Wood - then owner of the Great Escape Theme Park and Fantasy Island. It was a record price for a used wood roller coaster. This speaks volumes for the quality of the ride and the thrills it provided. After 41 years of operation, the Comet remained in the top 5 wood roller coasters in the world.

The resurrected Comet debuted at the Great Escape during the Memorial Day weekend of 1994. Except for new track, new trains, a white paint job, and a redesigned more efficient station, the rebuilt Comet remained true to its original design.

The open sky and the wide expanse of Lake Erie behind the Comet during its Crystal Beach tenure created optical illusions vanquished by the foothills of the Adirondack Mountains just south of Lake George. From the ground at Crystal Beach, the Comet's lift hill against the open sky seemed taller than at Great Escape where an

Photo by John. B. deHaas

Photo by John. B. deHaas

Adirondack foot hill cast a shadow on the coaster. From the top of the lift hill, the illusion of plunging into the lake is gone. Also, the height of the Comet while on ride at Crystal Beach seemed taller because the water surface was an additional fifteen feet below the base of the seawall.

Illusions aside, as of 2010, in spite of the dozens of wood coasters that have been built since 1989, the Comet still ranks among the top 25 in Amusement Today's annual survey. It is also the only surviving unique OEM (original equipment manufactured) ride from Crystal Beach Park.

Photo by John. B. deHaas

In 1972, the International Association of Amusement Parks and Attractions, sponsored 22-year-old James Payer to travel the continent from coast to coast to ride roller coasters to promote amusement parks. This publicity stunt garnered priceless media attention for the parks Payer visited, including Crystal Beach. Thirteen years later, Crystal Beach would use the image of Payer to promote the Comet in 1985 when the park reversed the first two cars on each train so the Comet could be experienced riding backwards.

Left: A maintenance man takes the easy way to the top in 1984.

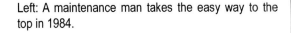

Comet Break-in t-shirt of the
Western New York Coaster Club.

Photos from Mike and Celia Horwood's "Thrill of a Lifetime." From top left down: Building the mound of shaving cream. Impact. The train explodes the mound. Above: "Creamed."

Photographed from the brink of the first plunge at Crystal Beach (right) and at its new home at the Great Escape near Lake George, N.Y. (far right). The Comet appears diminished but its an illusion.

View from the top in 1980.

View from the top in 1994.

Schmeck's artistry engendered in the Comet was accentuated by dramatic Lake Erie sunsets.

Cathy Herbert collection.

Photo by Thomas Martin Smith

Photo by Steve Urbanowicz.

CONTINENTAL LIMITED

Like PTC #12 and its original Victorian trappings, the steam locomotives and their carriages clashed with the park's art-deco makeover – at least in the eyes of Crystal Beach management.

"They're getting old," noted Lewis LeJeune at the close of the 1947 season, *"so the park company wants me to put in a new type, modern streamliner."* LeJeune had been the proprietor of the railroad concession since 1935.

Eighty-six feet long, the first 22 feet of the train (the front diesel locomotive and following car) each contained a 22 horsepower diesel engine.

Named the *Continental Limited*, it pulled four 12-passenger cars. The package cost $22,000 and presumably operated on the existing track gage. According to Billboard, the Miniature Railroad Train Co. of Addison, Illinois manufactured the rolling stock.

TWISTER

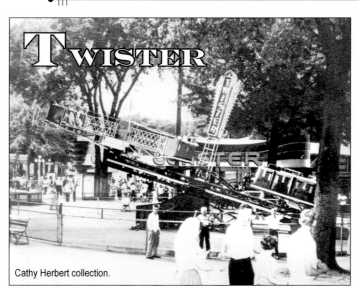

Cathy Herbert collection.

Twister near the Giant Coaster station circa 1955.

Twister in the Comet courtyard circa 1957.

Little background about *Twister* exists in the U.S. patent files or elsewhere, however, the patent for a ride that most closely resembles the action of the Twister is the Tempest. The motion of these rides resembles that of a taffy-pulling machine.

Twister occupied various locations on the Crystal Beach midway from 1954 through 1959.

Auto Scooter

A Lusse Brothers *Auto Scooter* became part of the Crystal Beach midway in 1947. Press releases noted that the $50,000 Auto Scooter would be housed in a building 125 feet by 65 feet.

In 1964, the original Lusse cars were replaced with 25 modern Lusse vehicles that cost $2,000 each. During the late 1970s or early 1980s, the 1964 models were replaced with cars manufactured by Soli that were not as fast as the Lusse cars and the steering mechanisms of the Soli cars were not as sensitive. This set-up remained through the remainder of the park's years.

Lower Lakes Marine Historical Society collection.

The Auto Scooter building nearing completion during the spring of 1947.

This image taken in 1968 appeared in a Buffalo Courier Express photo essay on Crystal Beach in 1969 shows the new Lusse model cars purchased in 1964.

Starting in 1977 the Auto Scooter II operated simultaneously with the Auto Scooter. This was not the most well thought out ride addition since a bumper car ride already existed. Compounding this poor choice of ride was its placement on the midway – next to the loading station of the Giant Coaster and directly across from the Auto Scooter.

Cars on Auto Scooter II were allowed to travel in any direction. Bumper car gridlock was frequent.

The Auto Scooter from a post card, 1947.

MOON ROCKET & OLYMPIC BOBS

The lighted sign that was part of the backdrop of every installation indicated the ride name was "Rocket" although the company marketed it as *Moon Rocket*. Crystal Beach press releases also referred to it as Moon Rocket which made numerous appearances in different ride sites. William J. Wendler, one of the founders of the Allan Herschell Company (AHC), patented the ride in 1939.

Moon Rocket merely chased itself in a circle, but it was able to operate at fast speeds because there were no hills on the track and riders sat one-behind-the-other rather than two across.

Edward Zebulske and Spillman Engineering of North Tonawanda, New York introduced a variant to Wendler's design enabling the cars to tip slightly toward the center of the ride. Spillman named their version Silver Streak. On the surface, the rides were so similar that AHC may have considered patent infringement, but it became moot when AHC purchased Spillman in 1945. Afterward, AHC either discontinued Spillman's version or incorporated the variant as a Moon Rocket option.

Moon Rocket is similar to the *Olympic Bobs* from Chance Rides. Olympic Bobs riders sat 16 cars split into two trains of 8 cars that travel a circular track. Half of the track is horizontal to the ground - the other half is tilted upward. The only exceptional element about this ride is speed. Because the cars were slightly tilted toward the center they could move at a faster speed than the Moon Rocket. A blast from an air horn announced the start of each ride.

A direct competitor of the Olympic Bobs is as the *Bayern Kurve*, from Anton Schwarzkopf. Nearly identical to the *Olympic Bobs*, right down to the illuminated pine trees and rising sun, however it had one long train that stretched over two-thirds of the track.

Olympic Bobs appeared at Crystal Beach during 1964 and 1965.

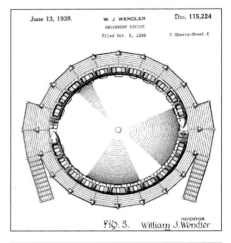

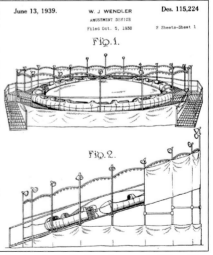

A Moon Rocket in a candy-striped theme in 1972. Right: Patent diagrams illustrating a top view and the front and side elevations. Note on the top view the two trains that each cover half the ride.

174

Lower Lakes Marine Historical Society..

Top: The Rocket in 1950 being assembled. Above: The fully assembled ride as seen from on front of the Giant Coaster station.

Courtesy Chance Rides.

Top: The Moon Rocket at Crystal Beach in 1950 from a right angle to the perspective at bottom left. Center: Olympic Bobs at an unidentified location. Left: Bayern Kurve at Kennywood Park near Pittsburgh.

HURRICANE ~ SATURN 6

Norman Bartlett is credited for inventing this ride that appeared on midways starting in 1948. The image on page 149 captured Bartlett sitting in a *Hurricane* at Belmont Park in Montreal, Quebec in 1948. Oddly, the original patent belongs to Tracy B. Tyler who filed it in 1948. Tyler may have worked for Bartlett or sold him the design. Allan Hershell Company manufactured the ride starting in the 1950s. All the Hurricanes built resemble Tyler's patent illustrations. Bartlett filed his patent during the late 1960s that included "improvements" on Tyler's design, but there is no evidence that a Hurricane was built to this patent with its odd protruding hinges and braces.

The early Hurricanes had overly sensitive hydraulic systems that failed with the slightest impurity.

Clyde Mulligan bought the design rights and reconfigured the Hurricane for quick set up trailer mounting, and renamed the ride *Saturn-6*.

Cropped from a photo whose subject was not the Hurricane, and partially blocked from a tree, is a record of the Hurricane at Crystal Beach in 1953.

Early model Hurricanes had 8 sweeps like this one at Coney Island circa 1948.

Courtesy Greg Gibbs

A Saturn 6 unit.

An early Saturn-6 unit labeled Hurricane shows how far above the horizontal the arms swing upward.

Monicker aside, the ride had six 35-foot long arms (original Hurricanes had eight arms) attached to a 40 foot tall tower. At the base of each arm was a fixed car that could seat up to four. The ride starts at a slow spin propelling the arms outward due to centrifugal force as it accelerated. At maximum speed, the arms were about 20 degrees shy from being in line with the top of the tower. The operator then "pumped" the arms using the hydraulics to swing the arms higher so that the cars were over the top of the tower by 10 degrees. After the pump, gravity returned the arms down to their centrifugally-forced inclination. The operator repeated the pump throughout the ride.

Anyone who has ridden an original Hurricane (or Saturn 6) will attest to the ride superiority over modern versions. The fixed cars gave the riders the sensation of being slightly up-side down when the arms were at maximum during the pump. Modern versions have their passenger compartments hinged to keep the riders at or near horizontal.

The first Hurricane to hit Crystal Beach was for only one season in 1952. Twenty years would pass for the Hurricane to return in 1972 and again in 1974 in the Saturn-6 versions.

National Foundation for Carnival Heritage, Kinsley, Kansas, in partnership with the Kinsley Library

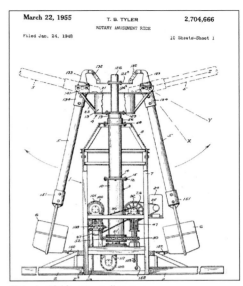

Tyler's 1948 patent diagram.

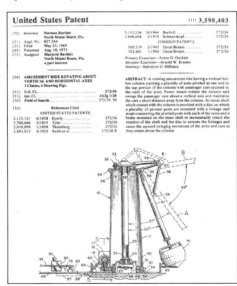

Bartlett's improvement had odd protruding hinges.

LOOPER

A Norman Bartlett ride originally built by Allan Hershell Co. and then by Chance Manufacturing. The original Loopers consisted of approximately ten circular tubs, that moved in a circle. Each two-passenger tub contained foot pedals that could be used to engage a clutch that caused the tub to roll over. The *Looper* was a fixture on the Crystal Beach midway from 1952 through approximately 1977.

ROTOR

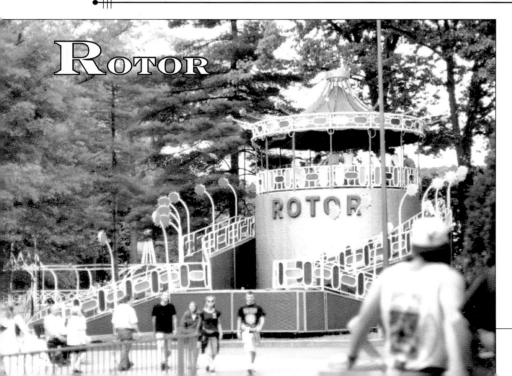

Invented by Ernest W. Hoffmeister of Hamburg, Germany around 1948, the *Rotor* is a rotating cylinder that uses centrifugal force to pin its occupants to the inside cylinder wall. At optimum speed the operator (observing from above) lowered the floor while the riders remain pinned to the wall. As the cylinder gradually slowed to a stop, riders slowly slid down the wall to land on the lowered floor.

A unique feature of the Rotor was a viewing platform at the top of the cylinder where prospective riders, or just the curious, could observe the ride and the riders. Because the cylinder was approximately 20 feet tall, it was impossible to see from ground level.

Conklin placed a Rotor at Crystal Beach in 1956 that remained part of the ride offerings through the remainder of the 1950s. Its exact location is uncertain. The Rotor returned during the early 1970s and occupied the site just to the left of the Comet station.

A Rotor, like this one at Great Escape (1995), was at Crystal Beach during the 1970s.

Rock - o - Plane

Everly Aircraft's take on the Ferris Wheel was to make it a hybrid. Riders, enclosed in steel mesh pods, could sit and enjoy the ride like any other Ferris Wheel, or modify their ride experience by operating a locking mechanism inside the car. The lock mechanism could be manipulated so that riders could hold the pod in position or make it tumble.

Above: Photo of the backsides of a Rock-o-Plane and a Round-Up that occupied an area of the midway that the Wild Mouse would later occupy. Top right: Although this image is not terribly sharp and also of the ride's back side, it is significant in the fact that the photographer was standing in the picnic grove looking toward the midway. The Rock-o-Plane stands on the site of old dance hall/roller rink and the 1956 Bingo Hall had not yet been built. Right: The Rock-o-Plane in operation with the cars in various degrees of tumble. The background shows the still thickly wooded grove before the construction of the Bingo Hall. Far right: A Rock-o-Plane in 1968, behind it, the Bingo hall.

SCRAMBLER

OLD MILL

that made the crossing on the July 4, 1962 were heading for the Crystal Beach area. According to park officials, the estimated crowd in the park at mid-afternoon that day was at 21,000 (how they were able to arrive at this attendance number when the park had an open gate and a pay-as-you-go policy remains a mystery, though it may be based upon industry standards applied to the day's receipts.) A month later, the park reported another large crowd of 19,300. Labor Day attendance reportedly was up 10 percent over 1961, with 20,800 visitors. Average Sunday attendance ranged from 13,000 to 18,000.

Perhaps the most popular promotional device the park ever employed began in 1964. WKBW Radio in conjunction with Loblaws Supermarkets initiated the annual academic achievement award. Elementary and high school students were eligible for free amusement ride tickets based on academic performance recorded in their report cards. Simultaneously with this promotion, every Tuesday and Thursday in July and August were Loblaw Days at the park. With every $3.00 in grocery purchases, the customer would receive a coupon redeemable for 60 cents worth of tickets for 40 cents.

In spite of these efforts to keep attendance up, in 1968 management announced that the park would open at noon Monday through Saturday instead of the customary 11:00 AM. Sunday hours would remain unchanged and open at the customary 1:30 PM, saving a significant amount in hourly wages.

Also, by 1968, George Hall Sr. was 84 years old and had been in a wheelchair since at least 1956. He had had a role in the park for 58 years (if the 1910 start as a concessionaire is accurate), and had been directly involved with its ownership, growth and development for 44 years. Except for military service, Fillmore and Ed worked at the park since their teen years. Its not surprising that in

George Hall Sr. photographed in 1956 during a confab of the 1956 riot.

1968, George Hall began to consider selling the park.

Colin T. Robertson was a developer and owned a number of business enterprises in Broward County, Florida during the early 1960s that included Ocean World, a television station (Channel 51), a yacht marina and the Rudi Shipyard, all in Fort Lauderdale. He also purchased 100 acres of land in Dania Beach, south of Fort Lauderdale and opened "Pirates World" – an amusement park that opened in 1967. The park was themed with pirate statues and ships and among the park's 15 rides were a roller coaster (Wild Mouse style), and a log flume, a Trabant, a tunnel of love and an autoride. The centerpiece of the park was the famous Coney Island Grand National Steeplechase, moved to Pirates' World from Brooklyn. Entertainment included staged pirate fights and rock concerts. Robertson's company, Recreation Corporation of America (RCOA),

CONGRATULATIONS!

Your child's academic achievement this year can earn . . .

FREE

TICKETS AT CRYSTAL BEACH

For each final grade of 'A' (91-100) you will get 6 tickets. For each final grade of 'B' (80-90), you will get 4 tickets.

LOBLAW-STAR and WKBW are jointly co-operating in rewarding your children's academic achievements with FREE TICKETS for rides at CRYSTAL BEACH. Bring report cards showing final exam grade results to your LOBLAW-STAR manager for certificate. FREE TICKETS are good for rides on the days shown on the certificate.

Bring The Entire Family And Save! Tuesdays And Thursdays Are . . .
LOBLAW-STAR FUN DAYS AT CRYSTAL BEACH

Every Tuesday and Thursday through August 25th are LOBLAW-STAR "Fun Days" at Crystal Beach. With each $3.00 in purchases you will receive ONE customer's discount coupon which can be exchanged for 60c worth of Crystal Beach Amusement Tickets upon payment of 40c when presented any Tuesday or Thursday at the Loblaw-Star exchange booth on the Midway or in front of the Dance Hall at Crystal Beach Amusement Park.

operated Pirates' World.

In 1969, the Halls entered into negotiations with Robertson to merge the Crystal Beach Company with RCOA. Apparently both firms entered into an agreement where the Fort Lauderdale Company would spend up to $1 million on upgrades and expansion at Crystal Beach. As part of the sale, the stockholders of Crystal Beach would receive $3 million in debentures – convertible into cash or common stock of the RCOA. The Crystal Beach Company would become a wholly owned subsidiary of RCOA that would continue to operate the park. George Hall Sr. would become an honorary member of the RCOA board. George Jr. and Edward would become directors of RCOA. Fillmore would remain the general manager of Crystal Beach.

Both companies predicted a smooth and quick merger, Robertson claiming that two-thirds of RCOA's stockholders had already approved the transaction, and assured that he would exercise the option to merge. George Hall stated, *"There will be no problem completing the deal."*

Robertson's last day to exercise the option to consummate the deal was September 12, 1969, but Hall expected the merger to be completed by June or July.

Images of Pirates' World. Top: Press release photo of the Cable Car - would a similar one have fit at Crystal Beach? Right: Antique Cars - Crystal Beach had a similar ride on wood planked track along the dance hall.

RCOA's planned improvements announced to be in place by 1970 included a Cable Car system that would carry passengers over the entire midway, and construction of a log flume.

In the meantime, Fillmore Hall said that business was so brisk, $30,000 was spent to erect 5 picnic shelters in the grove that could accommodate up to 3,000. It forced the sacrifice a number of trees in the grove, but it made seating more efficient. Part of the monies spent for the 1969 season included creating a bus parking lot at the corner of Ridge and Erie Roads behind the Magic Carpet and alongside the Giant Coaster to accommodate increased of charter bus services.

September 12 had arrived, but Crystal Beach and RCOA had not had contact with each other in over thirty days. Neither party would comment about the merger collapse, however Robertson said that the two companies parted for "mutual reasons." Robertson then announced that his company was planning a theme park near Buffalo based on the city's early history.

Bob Hall, son of Edward Hall worked for Robertson as manager of Pirates' World. He indicated that Robertson was more of a promoter and was not familiar with the operations of an amusement park - especially the seasonal nature of Crystal Beach compared to Florida's year-long venues. Bob did not know the exact reason the merger was never consummated, but knowing Robertson, Bob suspected that he [Robertson] could not get the backing to complete the sale although he led others to believe it was in the bag. This very well may be true. By 1973, Pirates' World operated in bankruptcy. The financial troubles of Pirates' World were further complicated when buildings in the park failed to meet building codes. Pirates' World closed in 1975.

Crystal Beach was beginning to feeling the pinch of declining attendance and increasing maintenance and operating costs. At the onset of the 1970 season, Crystal Beach would not open on Mondays.

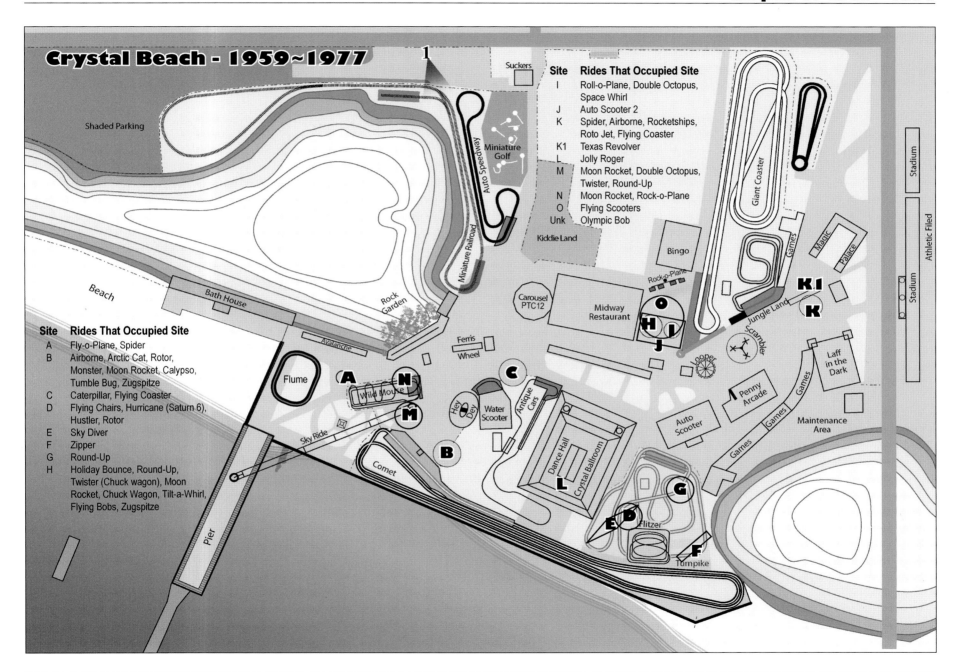

Crystal Beach - 1959~1977

Shaded Parking

Suckers

Site	Rides That Occupied Site
I	Roll-o-Plane, Double Octopus, Space Whirl
J	Auto Scooter 2
K	Spider, Airborne, Rocketships, Roto Jet, Flying Coaster
K1	Texas Revolver
L	Jolly Roger
M	Moon Rocket, Double Octopus, Twister, Round-Up
N	Moon Rocket, Rock-o-Plane
O	Flying Scooters
Unk	Olympic Bob

Miniature Golf

Auto Speedway

Miniature Railroad

Kiddie Land

Giant Coaster

Magic Palace

Bingo

Rock-o-Plane

Carousel PTC12

Midway Restaurant

Jungle Land

Scrambler

K1

K

Beach

Bath House

Rock Garden

Avalanche

Ferris Wheel

Looper

Laff in the Dark

Site	Rides That Occupied Site
A	Fly-o-Plane, Spider
B	Airborne, Arctic Cat, Rotor, Monster, Moon Rocket, Calypso, Tumble Bug, Zugspitze
C	Caterpillar, Flying Coaster
D	Flying Chairs, Hurricane (Saturn 6), Hustler, Rotor
E	Sky Diver
F	Zipper
G	Round-Up
H	Holiday Bounce, Round-Up, Twister (Chuck wagon), Moon Rocket, Chuck Wagon, Tilt-a-Whirl, Flying Bobs, Zugspitze

Flume

A N

Wild Mouse

M

Hey Dey

Water Scooter

Antique Cars

C

B

Penny Arcade

Auto Scooter

Games

Games

Games

Maintenance Area

Sky Ride

Comet

Dance Hall

Crystal Ballroom

L

E D

Flitzer

G

F

Turnpike

Pier

H J O I

Stadium

Athletic Filed

Cathy Herbert collection.

Above: Hot Rods exterior. Below: The interior near the second level loading area.

Cathy Herbert collection.

HOT RODS & TURNPIKE

The Hot Rods ride was the portable precursor to the permanent Turnpike installation. It consisted of a dismantlable structure housing an over and under figure-8 style track that was wide enough for the gas-powered cars to pass each other. *Hot Rods* occupied the site where the Turnpike entrance would later be found on grounds that had been unoccupied since 1947. Hot Rods was a part of the midway from 1957 through 1959.

Above: Turnpike loading area. Following page: Turnpike entrance and overhead drive-by from a postcard. First inset: The Turnpike under construction. Second inset: High altitude aerial showing the Turnpike layout.

At a reported cost of $78,000, Crystal Beach installed the *Turnpike* that debuted in 1961 on the grounds once occupied by the Cyclone. Each of the cars that operated on the Turnpike were imported from Germany at a cost of $1,280 each and manufactured by Streifthau. The track weaved about itself and with an elevated section that ran on top of the loading platform that was *"a replica of a Thruway toll entrance."*

The cars were gasoline powered, and like automobiles, had an operating throttle and brake. The 2,700 foot-long track was a combination of cement and asphalt. Drivers were able to control the movement of the cars as they traversed the seven-foot wide track. This popular ride was removed after the 1970 or the 1971 season.

TURNPIKE

ROTO JET

Lower Lakes Marine Historical Society collection.

Roto Jet was the adult version of the Sky Fighter Kiddie Land ride (inset). More thrilling for children than for thrill-seeking adults, passengers could change the height of their jet. Roto Jets can still be found on traditional amusement park midways that treasure older rides, most versions have a lighted, futuristic tower in the center, unlike the version here from Conklin's ride cache, circa 1960. It reappeared at Crystal Beach again in the late 1960s or early 1970s. Kaspar Klaus in Memmingen, Germany manufactured the ride first seen on North American midways starting during the early 1950s.

the hydraulic cylinders that gently sets the cars back down after flying from the ramp. Noreen Freeman, Elaine Freeman, and Christina Lagattuta happened to be sitting in the car with the stressed hydraulic that reached the breaking point after one launch too many. The cylinder snapped and the car slammed down onto the track with the full force of gravity. All three were taken to Douglas Memorial Hospital. Noreen incurred the worst injuries – a broken vertebrae, a broken ankle and a head cut. Elaine and Christina were treated for minor back injuries and released.

Left: Flying Coaster on the Looper site in front of the Giant Coaster where a hydraulic cylinder fractured sending 3 to the hospital. Below: A Flying Coaster in front of the Magic Carpet during the 1950s.

Norman Bartlett received a patent for the *Flying Coaster* in 1959 after the prototype operated in several locations, including the Canadian National Exhibition.

The ride follows a flat circular track except for a ski-jump section that launched the cars into the air. A hydraulic system allowed the cars to land softly as they continue to roll along the track for another "launch."

The Flying Coaster occupied different sites in the park whenever Conklin brought it to the park including in front of the Magic Carpet, the area occupied by the Caterpillar - where it stayed for years. The park shuffled it to the front of the Giant Coaster on the site left vacant when the Looper was dismantled. A major malfunction to the ride sent three people to the hospital on August 25, 1977. After years of operation, undetected, microscopic stress fractures developed in one of

WILD MOUSE

In 1958, Crystal Beach management was on the hunt for a new midway attraction and found one in a small, compact, wood roller coaster – the *Wild Mouse*. Patty Conklin arranged for the import of five units from their German manufacturer, Zierer.

Conklin maintained half interest in the $65,000 coaster when it debuted at Crystal Beach in 1959. Whether Conklin maintained his interest in the ride throughout its existence at the park is unknown.

Approximately a dozen cars came with the Wild Mouse, each car held a maximum of two people, one sitting behind the other without a partition between them.

Below: Front view of the Wild Mouse on a windy, and overcast morning, circa 1970. Right: The Wild Mouse as seen from the Ferris Wheel, circa 1970.

SKY RIDE

Manufactured by O.D. Hopkins, *Sky Ride* debuted in 1965. It did not operate on windy days which undoubtedly contributed to 35 seasons of flawless operation.

CALYPSO

Cathy Herbert collection.

Calypso was the first "portable" ride brought in by Conklin in 1967 to occupy the site that was the home for the Tumble Bug for more than 40 years. The earliest Calypsos from the 1960s, like this one, had a painted wood turntable. They were made by H. Speelman - Lanting from Deventer, The Netherlands. Their motion was the same as the Scrambler, but the mechanics of the rides were different. The Calypso's turntable could rotate and the car nodes remain stationary, or vice versa. The three Scrambler nodes were geared to the rotation of the entire ride. Lighting packages for the Calypso were considerably more ornate. Calypso remained on the midway through the 1968 season.

Cathy Herbert collection.

OLD MILLS AND JUNGLE LAND

After Henry Oges rebuilt his tunneled water ride Dreamland after fire destroyed it, the Dreamland moniker never appeared in Crystal Beach press again. The name Old Mill began appearing in 1917 press. For unknown reasons, the park demolished the 1917 incarnation after the 1929 season. On the same site, at a cost of $30,000 a new Old Mill opened in 1930. Additional research may reveal whether the park, Oges, or some other concessionaire owned/operated it. Changes to the Old Mill's interior scenes came in 1937 and again in 1940 for the park's 50th anniversary. The last "improvement" to the Old Mill came in 1959 with addition of a Dutch-type windmill to the roof.

People took their last rides on the Old Mill on Labor Day 1963. *"At the speed of about 10 seconds per scene, the rustic boats passed through a countryside of farms with cities [sic], a wrecked ship, water falls, and pastoral fields... The ride took nine minutes."* This brief description of some of the Old Mill scenes came from the 1964 announcement of the ride's major transformation into *Jungle Land*. The "retooling" of the ride did not affect the canals and other structural elements, however, the canal boats, exterior façades, and the interior scenes were transformed into a jungle motif.

The blades of the windmills on the Old Mill roof were removed and the roofs of the windmill towers received a fake thatched roof. Stockade fencing highlighted with jungle warrior tribal paint covered the exterior walls. The theming conveyed danger to those who dared trespass into the territory beyond the fencing. The loading/unloading platform of the Old Mill became a cannibal campground. Riders waiting to board the boats (festooned with fake leopard skin seats and a giant white swan at the bow) watched a native tribal female with a motorized head and arm dunk the head and torso of a tribal enemy into a steaming caldron. As she prepared the prisoner for cannibalizing and head shrinking, a recording of screams and moans from the victim being boiled alive played from a speaker behind the caldron. Spears, shrunken skulls, tiki gods and artificial jungle fauna added to the authenticity of the cannibal camp. Jungle sounds that included roaring lions, chirps of jungle birds and insects, and the occasional

This was the Old Mill circa 1945. By the mid 1950s the gable with the windows had been removed, and a second wind mill added in 1959.

Cathy Herbert collection.

This 1961 photo shows the Old Mill entrance with its new Jungle Land facade. Behind the elephant is the turret that was once was a wind mill now with a thatched roof.

Cathy Herbert collection.

Jungle Land natives were not afraid to stand in water in close proximity to the alligators.

"Ooh, ooh, ahh, ahh, ahh!" of a chattering chimpanzee echoed from speakers throughout the length of the canal.

Travelling trough the pitch dark tunnels, the occasional portals that once displayed city and countryside scenes became jungle scenes with Zulu warriors, alligators, snakes and snapping crocodiles framed by trees with hanging moss – all highlighted with fluorescent paint and illuminated with black-lights. Scenes open to daylight featured a hippopotamus that would rise from the water, a charging rhinoceros, and an elephant that would shoot a stream of water from its trunk at the riders in the boats.

Well done for its time, research failed to uncover the individual or company responsible for the design of the ride and the installation of the mechanical stunts.

The park deforested Jungle Land and filled in the canals after the 1977 season when Bob and Van Hall were managing the park. When questioned about the decision to remove the ride, Bob said there was so much tar on the tunnel roof from patching holes they feared it had become a firetrap and a fire would spread so fast anyone inside would burn to death or die of smoke inhalation.

Games of chance replaced the loading platform after the park evicted the cannibals. A Cinema 180 movie dome occupied a portion of the area formerly occupied by the canals. The remaining area was landscaped.

Above: A canal boat with the white swan exits the tunnel at the platform where tiki gods, skulls, and jungle flora surround a native female boiling a tribal enemy in her caldron. Left: Inside the jungle hippos are poised at the viewports of the enclosed canal.

ZUGSPITZE AND MUSIK EXPRESS

Cathy Herbert collection.

Above: Zugspitze at Crystal Beach. In the center-left side of the image is a deflated snowman. Double Octopus, Bingo Hall and Giant Coaster in the background. Below a Zugspitze at Palisades Park with a slightly different exterior and interior.

Zugspitze is the highest mountain in Germany. When German ride manufacturer Mack themed their high-speed spinning ride with a winter motif of snowy mountains, chalets, and skiers, it was appropriate to name it after highest mountain in the country.

The ride consisted of approximately twenty-four 2 to 3 passenger cars in a continuous ring that travelled an undulating circular track. Panels decorated to the theme of the ride hid the rear third of the track. In the center of the ride, a plastic snowman would inflate and deflate as the cars revolved around it. Hundreds of blue and white light bulbs outlined the interior and exterior. Zugspitze occupied a site in front of the Bingo Hall and later moved to replace the Calypso.

Musik Express was identical to Zugspitze except for aesthetics - a rectangular, colorful shell; its interior and exterior saturated with colored lights, rock star figures, and music notes. Musik Express arrived in 1980 and was a midway fixture through the 1987 season.

RoUND & SPACE WHIRL

Round-Up debuted at Crystal Beach in 1956. Manufactured by Frank Hrubetz, Round-Up uses centrifugal force to pin standing riders against the interior wall of a large disc. Unlike the Rotor where the floor drops out at nominal rotation, hydraulic pumps raise and tilt the disc to an angle of 50 degrees. The diameter of the ride varies depending upon the rider capacity. Larger units were 45 feet.

The *Space Whirl* was a uniquely themed version of the Round-up. Instead of standing, riders sat and faced a huge globe mounted in the center as if high above the earth.

ANTIQUE AUTOS

Those who remember this ride, will also remember the sign that hung on a wall that faced the loading platform that read, *"Let junior take the family for a ride."* This ride opened in 1964 – its track ran along the west side of the dance hall and between the dance hall and the *Comet*. The *Antique Autos* came from a company called Gebr-Jhle Bruchsal and they were very slow moving. The space the ride occupied could have been better used. In 1964 the park already had three car rides in operation – the Auto Speedway for younger riders, and the Turnpike and Auto Scooter for teens and adults.

Left: Images of the Space Whirl. Rock-o-Plane and Giant Coaster in the background. For a while people played "I-Got-It" in the Bingo hall. I-Got-It is a carnival variation of Bingo where players toss balls onto a Bingo-style board and hope the balls tumble into winning "Bingo" arrangements. Above: Antique Autos entrance.

CHUCKWAGON TWISTER

Sept. 13, 1932. I. J. SIEBERT 1,877,256
AMUSEMENT DEVICE
Filed June 17, 1931

Above: Chuckwagon setting up for the season. Insets - Top: Patent diagram. Left: Twister from a 1960 Allan Herschell ad. Right: Close-up of a Twister car and its high headrest.

Chuckwagon was a uniquely themed, updated version of the Hey Dey with a less complex drive system and a circular path rather than an oval. Like the Hey Dey, the cars were pivoted off-center to promote spinning. The track was tilted. It had 10 two-passenger cars made to look like buckboards with covered wagon canopies mounted on the end of sweeps that rotated about the center.

Twisters are an improved heavy duty version of the Chuckwagon capable of seating four in a car. The Twister, in comparison, had a flat track except for a slight rise and fall in one quarter of the track.

Chuckwagon and Twister ride operators used a throttle to "goose" the rotational speed to spin the cars. Operators with good timing could target a car just as it entered the upturned section of track then goose the throttle to spin the car at very high speeds. Twister cars could spin so rapidly that the back seats were equipped with headrests to prevent neck injury.

FLY - O - PLANE

Eyerly manufactured very few *Fly-o-Planes*. Perhaps they did not appear to be that thrilling of a ride so very few were ever ordered. The Fly-o-Plane is an endangered species with only one or two in left existence. Those fortunate enough to have ridden one received a ride like no other. Of all the Eyerly "o-Planes," the Fly-o-Plane reaches back to the Aeroplane putting a control in the hands of the rider(s).

Once the ride begins to turn, the planes rise and at a sufficient altitude, steering wheels inside the planes allow the riders to take control of the plane to "fly" in a normal flight or upside down, roll from side to side or barrel roll.

The Fly-o-Plane was on the Crystal Beach midway in 1970 and never returned. It occupied a site on the midway behind the Wild Mouse.

This Fly-o-Plane resides at Lake Winnepesaukah, Georgia and is one of the last of its kind.

AVALANCHE GIANT SLIDE

There was a period when Conklin would place a ride at Crystal Beach where ever there was a vacant spot on the midway. Conklin erected a giant slide from his inventory on a site that was once on the beach-side of the "Cut" before the 1924-25 expansion where the original boardwalk had been located at the base of the sand bluff.

Called *Avalanche,* the slide occupied this spot from 1970 through 1976 or 1977.

DOUBLE & SPIDER OCTOPUS

A minor variant on the Octopus, Eyerly produced the Double Octopus. It had two off-set seats at the end of each sweep doubling the ride capacity. It occupied the site next to the Comet as seen below - the loading area of the Sky Ride would eventually occupy this area. It also resided between the Zugspitze and the Giant Coaster station, visible in the background in the photo on page 198.

Spider is a re-engineered Double Octopus, but with six sweeps rather than eight. The engineering changes are evident in the sweeps and rider seats. Everything else, including the base, appears to be the same. The change provided a sturdier and anatomically correct appearance, although spiders, like octopi, have eight legs not six.

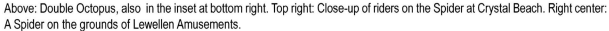
Above: Double Octopus, also in the inset at bottom right. Top right: Close-up of riders on the Spider at Crystal Beach. Right center: A Spider on the grounds of Lewellen Amusements.

Chapter 6: 1972~1982

At the age of 88, George Hall Sr. died on September 2, 1972 in Port Colborne General Hospital. With his passing, Fillmore Hall became President of the company. Fillmore's brother Edward G. Hall became the company's treasurer; George Hall Jr. became vice president.

On November 5, 1973, the Buffalo Evening News reported that Cleveland interests, armed with a commitment from a major hotel chain to build a hotel at the park, were poised to buy Crystal Beach. Closing day for the fully negotiated deal was December 1, 1973. The unidentified buyers also had plans to develop the pier into a new restaurant.

Bob Hall, son of Edward Hall, in a 1999 interview noted that by 1973 the three Hall brothers were up in age and may have been considering retirement as impetus to sell the park, but he had not heard of this particular transaction prior to this interview.

There were no details in the March 1974 announcement that the sale did not go through and all negotiations ceased. Factors that could have precipitated the collapse of the sale are too numerous to contemplate without more information. The statement noted that preliminary discussions for a sale to other groups were underway. Apparently, nothing became of those discussions either because the upcoming season announcement highlighted the passing of the guard to the third generation of the Hall family.

Robert (Bob) Hall, along with his cousin, Fillmore (Van) Hall, son of Fillmore L. Hall, would become active as managers of the company. Van terminated his employment with the Buffalo Courier Express to assume the company's business affairs through their office in the Ellicott Square Building in downtown Buffalo. Fort Lauderdale native Robert Hall was manager of Pirates' World in Dania Beach, Florida - a position he departed to manage the operations at Crystal Beach.

They faced a lethal combination of falling attendance, (not from amusement park competition, but from the ever-increasing options for people to spend their summer leisure dollars) and increasing operating expenses. If this was not enough, they also had to deal with the collision of two trains in the Comet's loading platform, and a fire in the Fantasy Land walk-through attraction in the basement of the dance hall that caused considerable damage. (Cont'd pg. 207)

Bob Hall.

Van Hall.

In 1975 from left: Fillmore Hall, Van Hall, Bob Hall, Edward Hall.

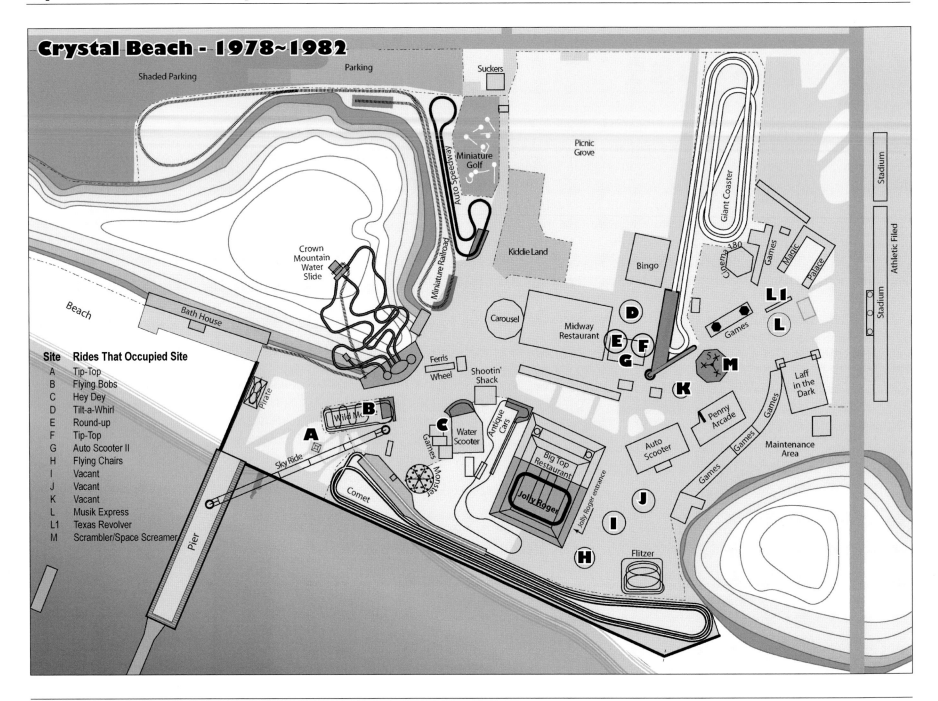

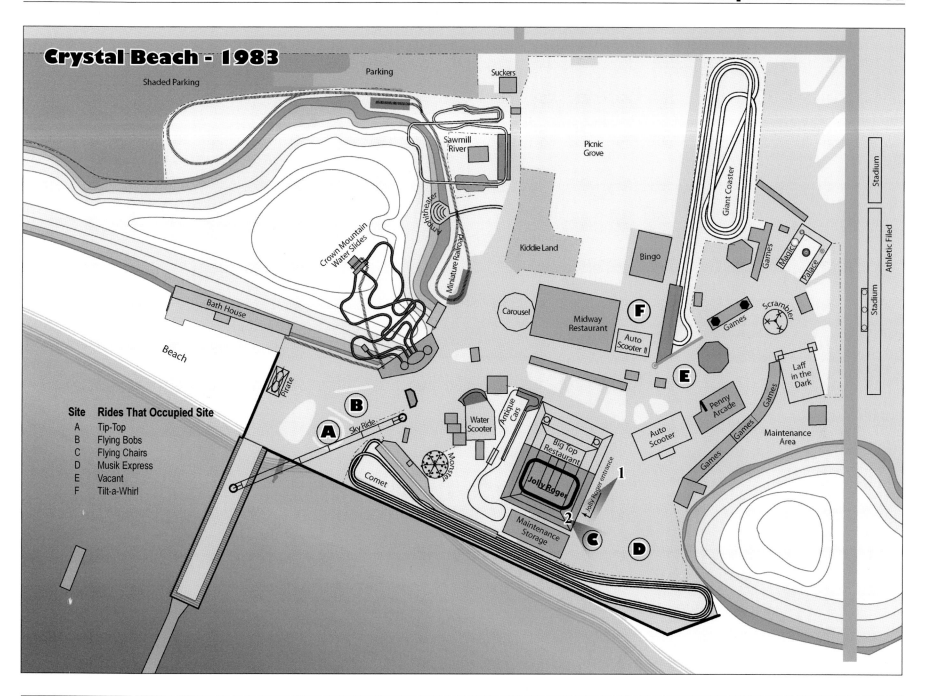

Crystal Beach - 1983

Site	Rides That Occupied Site
A	Tip-Top
B	Flying Bobs
C	Flying Chairs
D	Musik Express
E	Vacant
F	Tilt-a-Whirl

Lower Lakes Marine Historical Society collection.

Left: Smoke billows from the Fantasy Land walk through as a fireman prepares to fight the flames. Below: After the fire. Note the snow fence on the left barring access to the dance hall. The entrance to the women's restroom (left), the entrance to Fantasy Land (center) and the Wax Museum (right near the van) are blackened from smoke. Far left top and bottom: During the off-season, the dance hall perimeter that was not the dance floor was utilized for storage.

Lower Lakes Marine Historical Society collection.

Inspectors found the dance hall to be structurally sound, which assuaged fears that it had sustained serious damage that would require its demolition. Water did more damage than the fire, but it saved the building. Gone, however, were the Wax Museum and the Fantasy Land walk throughs as well as roller skating and the rest rooms. Bob Hall indicated that the fire started after someone had disposed a lit cigarette in one of the scenes.

Ready for the 1975 season the renovated dance hall had the front half converted into the "Big Top Restaurant" where for the first time in history, alcoholic beverages where permitted in the park. A New York City Troupe provided half-hour illusion shows in the back half. The $500,000 renovation included new, modern rest room facilities.

Construction of the Shootin' Shack in 1975 displaced the Flying Coaster to the former Looper site. Shootin' Shack, licensed by Walt Disney Enterprises, was a test of skill where the players aimed light-emitting guns at sensors mounted on 60 figures that lined the back wall of the shack. When hit, the sensor animated the attached figure. It was not really a game, as there were no scores or competition between players. One merely dropped quarters into the slot, grabbed a gun and fired rounds for a timed interval. With a number of people aiming at the same targets it was impossible to know which player hit the sensor when a figure became animated.

Kieran J. Glynn of Stevensville, Ontario took his last ride on the Comet when he was thrown from the train and killed. The incident garnered unwanted publicity for the park even though the coaster was cleared of any malfunctions.

At the conclusion of the 1975 season, management announced plans for the addition of a log flume, and revealed that negotiations were underway with a major motel chain to construct a hotel at the park. The hotel never materialized and the flume was still years away.

Perhaps the most controversial decision in the parks history came in 1976. Hemorrhaging money through theft and vandalism, after 86 seasons, management abandoned the open gate policy for a pay-one-price admission fee to the park. Village merchants protested that the now gated park would further reduce tourist trade that had been in a nose dive since the 1950s. Non-riding park visitors who enjoyed a stroll in the park, catching a ride on the Ferris wheel, munching on park food, or watching their grandchildren in Kiddie Land protested as well, not wanting to pay for something they did not use.

"We feel our new policy will appeal to families as well as individuals as the fixed price will enable them to determine the cost of a day's entertainment before hand," Van Hall noted. He also anticipated that the admission would be popular with children as they won't have to choose which amusements to ride with a limited number of tickets they could afford. They could ride as often as they wanted. The Comet would cost an additional 35 cents.

"Ticket sellers were giving tickets away. Bored teens and young adults would wander into the park just to damage or deface something – costing money to repair.

Teens line up at the controversial pay-one-price gate.

"The park was feeling the pinch," Hall told the press later in the season. *"We had to do something, we were facing rising costs in utilities, liability insurance, parts and maintenance. Many people came into the park and didn't spend a penny."* In order to save more money, management decided to open the season a week later than usual and cut back the park hours in June when the season is normally slack. These were perhaps the first symptoms that the park's days were numbered. Bob Hall predicted the park could wind up in a deficit if the present rate of business continued.

Riders found the admission fee of $5.50 a bargain. Non riding visitors simply stopped coming. Business in the village continued to spiral down. The open gates never returned, however, admission fees were adjusted to accommodate non-riding visitors at a considerably reduced admission rate. They also could purchase ride tickets in the park if desired.

Cinema 180 replaced Jungle Land in 1977. It consisted of a small dome where inside people stood and watched a 15-20 minute movie specially filmed for projection onto a screen that wrapped to cover the viewer's peripheral vision. It provided the sensation of being "in" the film that included scenes viewed from the eyes of someone hang gliding over the Grand Canyon, riding a roller coaster or racing through traffic as viewed from the front license plate. There was no seating in the Dome. Hand railings were in place for viewers to anchor themselves – some of the scenes where quite effective.

After a few seasons, Cinema 180 fell into disuse – perhaps the expense of licensing and maintaining the projector, Cinema 180 ceased and the dome used for storage.

Another sign of the rapidly aging park was a structural failure to the Flying Coaster that injured a woman and two children (See pg. 189).

Evidence of the decades long amusement park monopoly Crystal Beach held had ended came in the 1979 press when preseason announcements of new attractions and improvements for all the area amusement centers, Crystal Beach, Fantasy Island, and Fun and Games Park in Tonawanda were now aggregated into one synopses. Interestingly and formidably, Darien Lake east of Buffalo, was expanding to such a degree, it garnered separate press.

For 1980, in an attempt to inject live entertainment back into the park, management constructed an outdoor amphitheater. Carved it into the hillside along the miniature train, it forced the demolition of the Auto Speedway, one of the last such devices from Traver Engineering. Well intended, the amphitheater quickly fell into disuse.

An ominous sign of the future was the $7 million Darien Lake spent for the 1980 season, most on new rides. It was the first phase of a $30 million, 5-year expansion program. Annual expenditures for new rides was an expense Crystal Beach management did not concern themselves with as Conklin Rides cycled their inventory through the park. Since the gated policy, Crystal Beach had to outlay money for rides previously owned by concessionaires, and the annual flow of rides from Conklin, had dried up.

Cinema 180 dome was eventually used for storage in this image from the 1989 Crystal Beach Park auction catalog.

Park maintenance man Henry Knutson, 24 of Ridgeway, Ontario died of electrocution while on the roof of the Comet's station. Details of the incident were not clear, but he had somehow come in contact with a live wire while unplugging an electrical cord. Rushed to Port Colborne General Hospital, he was dead on arrival.

Crystal Beach treasurer Vincent McMahon noted at the end of the 1980 season that, *"It was the best year in the park's history,"* estimating attendance at 500,000. He credited the season's performance to great weather and growth of the park's Canadian market. McMahon perhaps did not realize that Crystal Beach once drew over 1 million visitors seasonally.

Already on a poor financial footing, the park trimmed its June 1981 operating hours to Thursdays through Sundays.

Competition for amusement park dollars increased considerably in 1981 with the debut of Canada's Wonderland outside of Toronto that usurped Crystal Beach's Canadian patronage. Nearby Marineland and Game Farm in Niagara Falls, Ontario was not a threat until they announced that they were going to build the world's largest steel roller coaster in 1981. On the opposite side of Point Abino, Sherkston Beach was getting into the amusement act by adding water slides and a game room to their long, sandy beach.

Clawing for business, the local amusement parks pumped up their advertising budgets. Van Hall was noncommittal on the amount Crystal Beach would spend, but revealed that it was between $500,000 and $1 million. The budget, according to Hall, was increased by 20%, half of the increase was inflationary. Canada's Wonderland had an advertising budget between $2 and $3 million; Darien Lake budgeted $2 million. Marineland's ad budget was estimated at over $1 million.

Crystal Beach added their log flume, Saw Mill River, near the Derby Road entrance to the park. This addition came at the expense of the miniature golf course – which was one of the best in the area. Its eventual replacement, erected near the site of the original in the picnic grove paled in comparison. The greens and fairways were platforms constructed of plywood that sagged when stood on to hit a ball. The original course had a variety of mechanical obstacles with hills, drops and chutes, and was landscaped. Its replacement course was flat with the cheapest of obstacles, landscaped only with crushed stone.

Anyone who had visited the park in 1981 would not have been surprised by the financial problems that befell the park in 1982. Many of the elements that Crystal Beach patrons loved about the park had vanished. The Ferris Wheel was removed after being damaged, the Hey Dey had been removed (Bob Hall said that they had a hard time getting it to operate after park superintendant Jack Roth died). Jungle Land, Auto Speedway, Turnpike, Wild Mouse, Caterpillar, and the Tumble Bug – all gone. Stunts inside the Magic Palace and Laff in the Dark that worked, worked poorly and were visually suffering from years of differed maintenance and cleaning.

The fact that Fantasy Island closed after the 1981 season did not impact attendance at Crystal Beach in 1982. Management continued to cut the early season (June) operating hours - opening only Friday through Sunday until July. And when July arrived the crowds did not, and attendance continued to slip. Rainy August weekends left the park drowning in red ink. Crystal Beach may have performed better regardless of the weather, but when Darien Lake opened for the 1982 season, it opened with a brand new roller coaster made of tubular steel with loops and corkscrews that turned riders upside down. This coaster style was relatively new expensive technology that required space and underwriting that was well beyond the limits of Crystal Beach.

Near the close of Crystal Beach's 1982 season, management was hoping the park would break even. It didn't. A spokesman for the park reported that attendance was down to 350,000. For historical comparison, attendance of 350,000 over a 90-day operating season equates to 3,890 per day. At one time in the park's history, her steamers *Americana* and the *Canadiana* were delivering 3,500 to the park every hour.

Courtesy Greg Gibbs

Courtesy Greg Gibbs

Courtesy Greg Gibbs

HUSTLER

Hustler is a variation of the Twister presented on page 172. Like the Twister, its motion resembles a taffy pulling machine, though unlike the Twister, it was not tilted. Its passenger pods were circular and free spinning. If the riders/weight were evenly distributed about the pod, it did not spin to the degree that it did when the weight in the pods was not well distributed. Hustler was a one-season-only midway ride offering during 1973 and located on the left side of the dance hall on grounds once occupied by the Turnpike.

Courtesy Greg Gibbs

Photos of the Hustler during its only season at Crystal Beach could not be located, however, presented here are images of the ride at a carnival. The front of the ride is captured in the image above. The sequence on photos on the left show the Hustler's taffy pulling machine motion. In some towns on the carnival circuit where people are sensitive to the illicit meaning of the word hustler, owners of the ride will pop-out the signage and the letters and either leave the frames open or pop in alternate "Tempest" signage (a ride with the same motion).

SKY DIVER

Rising above the trees, this is the only available image of the Sky Diver at Crystal Beach, cropped and enlarged from the photo of James Payer on the *Comet*.

Sky Divers are staples at most carnivals, county fairs and smaller amusement parks rather than large theme or major amusement parks. Built by Chance Manufacturing, Conklin's placed a *Sky Diver* at Crystal Beach for 1972.

Like Eyerly's Rock-o-Plane, Sky Diver riders control the motion of the pods they occupy. The difference being that riders on the Rock-o-Plane controlled their motion in a heels to head or head to heels tumble; on the Sky Diver, riders controlled their motion in a left-to-right or right-to-left barrel roll.

ZIPPER

Another product of Chance Manufacturing, *Zipper* first made its wicked presence known in Kansas in 1968 thanks its inventor, Joseph Brown. The Zipper is the standard to which all other "disorienting" rides are measured.

The Zipper's 12 passenger cages rotate freely on an off-center axis. All the cages are fastened to cables that drive them around the main oblong boom while the boom rotates on its own axis reaching a maximum height of 56 feet. All these rotations create intense spinning and whipping motions – especially when the cages arc around the curved ends of the boom. Without warning, the cage will stop spinning in one direction and start spinning in the opposite direction due to the oblong boom. Zipper was another 1-trick pony from Conklin rides that appeared only for the 1973 season.

TEXAS REVOLVER

TILT -A- WHIRL

A ride that has endured the test of time since their 1926 debut, Tilt-a-Whirls remain popular at parks and carnivals. Invented by Herbert Sellner, an estimated 600 Tilt-a-Whirls remain in operation world wide.

The ride consists of seven cars fixed to a pivot pin on their own platform. The platforms move on a circular undulating track that changes the centrifugal and gravitational forces on the cars, making them spin at random speeds and directions. A Tilt-a-Whirl first appeared at Crystal Beach during the 1960s, then from 1978 through 1989 and repositioned to different sites during those years.

Texas Revolver is better known to fair goes as Ring of Fire or by its generic name Super Loops.

The loop's 20 person train shuttles back and forth around the inside of a 55 foot high loop. The train is attached to an 'inertia ring' - a circular 360 degree conveyor-belt locked into a track and powered by hydraulic motors in the ride's base. It moved clockwise and counter-clockwise at the discretion of the ride's operator.

Texas Revolver was on the midway from 1977 through 1979.

FLITZER

Courtesy Robert Lindsay

Previous page left: Texas Revolver at Crystal Beach, Van Hall second from the left. Previous page upper right: Tilt-A-Whirl at Crystal Beach circa 1980. Above and right: Flitzer in the shadow of the Comet.

An all-steel, non-looping roller coaster, *Flitzer* is a mild family oriented coaster themed with race cars and mountain scenery painted on panels fastened to the coaster's frame. It's a portable, carnival style coaster with bobsled type cars that traverse a track approximately 1,200 feet long from a maximum height of 25 feet. It is a zippy coaster designed by Anton Schwartzkopf and manufactured by Zierer of Germany. The best part of the coaster is a series of hair-pin turns at ground level before returning to the loading station. Flitzer was a part of the Crystal Beach midway from 1974 to 1981.

Photos by Nick DeWolf.

HOLIDAY BOUNCE & TIP TOP

Holiday Bounce consisted of a large spinning turn table upon which sat 10 egg-shaped pods that could seat two riders each, one across from the other. Between the two riders was a wheel that the riders could grip to set the pod spinning at any speed their arms could muster.

As the turn table rotated, a compressor filled two cylinders underneath the table near the center axle to raise and pivot the turn table approximately 30 degrees. After a number of rotations in the tilted position the pressure was released with a loud hiss and the table would bounce like a trampoline as air was pumped back into the cylinders.

At night, an elaborate lighting network added another dimension to the ride. Each of four different color light bulbs were on their own circuit so a single color would bathe the ride, then switch to another color rapidly or slowly. Different color combinations could also be displayed such as blue and green without yellow and red, for example. Typically, when the table was in bounce mode, all the lights flashed rapidly in sequence.

In the 1950s, Dwayne Steck, another amusement concessionaire, moved the ride from Cuba to the U.S. on a rail barge when it was little more than the cylinders that push the turn table upward. He designed every element of the ride including the elaborate centerpiece

and lighting system. Steck brought *Holiday Bounce* to Crystal Beach during 1974 and 1975.

Tip Top, and Holiday Bounce are essentially the same ride - so similar in fact, Steck's ride could be a scrapped/discarded Tip Top. They had some differences in addition to Tip Top's comparatively spartan aesthetics. Its controls were at the front of the ride while Holiday Bounce had a separate control booth that also served as a D. J. booth. A product of Frank Hrubetz and Company, Tip Top had a 35-foot diameter turn table. It appears to be smaller than Holiday Bounce, but this could be an illusion created by the backdrop and centerpiece of Holiday Bounce. Each had the same rider capacity. Technical specs for Holiday Bounce probably do not exist since it appears to be a custom built and one of kind.

Tip Top became a Crystal Beach midway fixture in 1978, occupying various locations in the park through the 1989 season.

Photo by Nick DeWolf.

Holiday Bounce in the bounced-up mode. Previous page top: The sequence of photos show some of the constantly changing color combinations of Holiday Bounce at night. Previous page right: Postcard image of Tip Top.

ARCTIC CAT

Fort Erie Historical Museum collection.

pg. 185

Left: A great off-season view of the park from Erie Road with rides from background to foreground: Comet, Arctic Cat, Ferris wheel, Auto Speedway. Above: Close-up of the Arctic Cat.

Manufactured by Chance Rides, the production name of the coaster is Toboggan. Each Toboggan came with approximately three cars that could comfortably fit two children or one adult. Found mostly in smaller parks, carnivals and fairs, the Toboggan was unique at the time because of its vertical ascent. Once the brake released a car from the loading platform, it engaged the chain which hauled the car vertically up through a 45 foot tall iron silo. Once at the top, the track rounded the top of the silo where car would disengage the chain. The car then started down the track that spiraled around the outside of the silo like threads on a giant screw. Once it reached the bottom of the spiral, the cars lurched over a pair low profile hills, then turn back into the station. The entire length of the ride: 450 feet.

MONSTER

④ pg 227

Harvey Holzworth collection.

The ultimate of Eyerly's tentacled rides, *Monster* made its world debut in 1962 at the New York World's Fair. It operated like the other Eyerly tentacled rides, except that four, two-passenger freely spinning tubs orbited about the end of each sweep.

At night Monster glowed with green fluorescent tubes and yellow incandescent lights. Introduced to the Crystal Beach midway in 1974 (believed to be a Dwayne Steck owned-unit),

Crystal Beach wound up purchasing it. It was a midway fixture, primarily holding the site just left of the Comet's platform until moved to the open area left of the Giant Coaster's station for the 1988 season.

Even though the park owned the ride, it had been dismantled after 1988 and placed on its transport trailers. There it sat throughout the park's last season until it was set back up during October 1989 for demonstration during the park's auction.

JOLLY ROGER

The fire that ravaged the dance hall in 1974, provided the park with an opportunity to make use of the under utilized building. Installed in the lake-side half of the dance hall in 1977, the *Jolly Roger* was the last dark ride the park installed.

It consisted of a continuous sequence of cars with two benches, each facing the inside of a rectangular track route. Once beyond the loading area, riders were exposed to animated scenes of a pirate adventure, including a burning village that had been pillaged, a drunk pirate chasing a "working" woman around barrel, a ship wreck, and tropical island jungle scenes.

Deferred maintenance claimed the Jolly Roger like it claimed the other dark rides. Best viewed in total darkness, light leaks developed in the dance hall interior that lessened the experience. Like the Magic Palace and Laff in the Dark, the animated figures and lighting effects began to malfunction and fail.

The ride was removed for the return of live music and dancing.

Skull and Crossbones marked the entrance path to Jolly Roger. Comet in the background.

FLYING CHAIRS

Flying Chairs is the production name given to this ride by its manufacturer, Sartori Group of Italy. It became one of the Crystal Beach fray in 1974 and remained in operation for the next 15 years.

Unlike more sophisticated swing rides that hydraulically increase height and have mechanisms to undulate the swings, Sartori's swing rides are basic. Riders sit in the chairs, and the swings rotate around the center.

Part of the fun of this ride was holding onto the swing just ahead, or twisting the chains that suspended the chairs so they would spin as they rotated. Activities that the ride operators frowned upon.

PIRATE

Top: Pirate at its beach-front home. Center and bottom: Front and backside of the Pirate next to the Giant Coaster.

Upon its arrival at Crystal Beach in 1980 the *Pirate* occupied an appropriate spot near the beach. It was moved in 1986 to make room for the Galaxi roller coaster, moved back to its original spot in 1987 and moved next to the Giant Coaster again in 1989.

Built by Huss Rides, the 43-foot long boat could swing high enough that the right side truss could rise above the axle on the right side - same for the left side. Riders looking for the strongest sensations would scramble to the far left or right ends of the boat. The struts held the axle 57 feet above the ground.

FLYING BOBS

Photo by Karl R. Josker

Flying Bobs have a series of two-passenger cars suspended from arms that revolve around a vertical axis and follow an undulating track. Whether operating forward or backward, the suspended cars, when moving at high speed, would swing out and up like an Olympic bobsled climbing high-banked curves of the ice track they travel. The decorative panels that hid the inner mechanics were painted with winter snow scenes with "snow bunnies" on skis with exaggerated breasts and behinds.

Flying Bobs appeared at Crystal Beach for 1970, returned in 1979, then remained on the midway from 1981 through 1989.

CROWN MOUNTAIN

Courtesy Bob Hall.

Courtesy Bob Hall.

Its unlikely that any of the park visitors that sloshed down the water slides of *Crown Mountain* knew that at the stop of the stairs where water cascaded over an artificial water fall stood the east end of the Hotel Bon Air. As they waited to begin their journey down the winding chutes, people who stood in the same location seventy years earlier would not have seen the Comet as the backdrop to the midway, but another sandy ridge crowned with roller skating rink.

Crown Mountain made its debut in 1978 with four chutes: one for small children, one of "intermediate" severity, and two "adult" chutes named "River Kwai" and "Deliverance." It was the first major addition to the park since construction of the Comet. Its advertised price tag was "near" $500,000.

Added to the midway after the pay-one-price admission fee had been instituted, Crown Mountain was not included. Park patrons paid an additional dollar for a half hour "slide time." Beach-only patrons had access to Crown Mountain for $2 for a half hour.

After the first season, the natural foliage grew back to hide the construction scars to the hillside and Crown Mountain became a very attractive and popular addition to the park. Access to it, however, was a bit of challenge, made only through the bath house on the beach.

Crown Mountain became Super Duper Mountain after the park went into receivership after the 1982 season. The park sold naming rights to the water attraction to the supermarket chain just as cities sell naming rights to sports arenas to generate capital.

By the late 1980s the smooth surface of the fiberglass chutes lost their finish creating enough friction that people often had to push themselves across severely worn areas, and the intermediate slide was closed.

Flume of 1967
and Sawmill River

The precursor to *Sawmill River*, was the *Flume*. Research uncovered little information about this ride. It appeared on the midway behind the Wild Mouse in 1967 and it probably came from Conklin's inventory. Its manufacturer could have been Arrow Dynamics which was the first flume manufacturer, delivering its first flume to Six Flags Over Texas three years earlier. The portable flume at Crystal Beach had no name and had a very simple layout. It stood approximately six feet off the ground and supported by a structure that resembled scaffolding. Its footprint was square or rectangular with rounded corners that the logs could negotiate. It was not a thrilling flume. The logs moved slowly, and the two hills and drops in the layout were not more than 8 or 10 feet above the elevated troughs. The ride required constant filling as water continuously sloshed out of the trough and onto the ground below. It was a part of the midway for only one summer.

In 1981 when Sawmill River debuted, major flume rides were standard amusement park offerings. Ride manufacturer O. D. Hopkins designed Sawmill River which could have been their first flume since the company did not offer flumes before 1981. Hopkins offered to install their flumes or deliver the logs, lifts, drops, and equipment, leaving construction and set-up to the park. Whether or not Crystal Beach had Hopkins install the ride is unknown, but the park advertised the cost at $1.5 million.

The site for Sawmill River forced the sacrifice of the miniature golf course, and minor shifting of the miniature railroad's track. It incorporated the top of the sand bluff where the trough meandered through the trees and the local flora before a plunge back down.

❷ pg 227

❸ pg 227

Chapter 7: 1983~1988

By 1982 Crystal Beach started to founder. Efforts by the third generation of Halls to reverse declining attendance and revenues through major expenditures for rides were not working. To further reduce expenses, operating hours for the month of June were trimmed to Friday through Sunday from Thursday through Sunday. The park needed a resounding July and August.

Attendance continued to slip as July arrived without the crowds. Rainy August weekends killed any possibility of a successful season. Inclement weather was not the only factor behind the poor season. Darien Lake kicked off 1982 with a brand new roller coaster, *Viper*, made of tubular steel with loops and corkscrews. At the time Viper represented the state-of-the-art in roller coaster technology. Darien Lake also struck a deal with Festival East Concerts to have major entertainers perform in their new amphitheater. Crystal Beach visitors from the Golden Horseshoe perimeter of Lake Ontario had been usurped by the brand new Canada's Wonderland outside of Toronto.

Near the close of Crystal Beach's 1982 season, management hoped the park would break even - it did not. Attendance was reportedly down

to 350,000. Using the passenger capacity of the steamer *Canadiana* as measuring stick, the reported attendance amounted to a little more than a boatload per day. Few decades ago, the park was bringing in a boatload every hour and more.

The foundering U.S. economy during the late 1970s continued into the 1980s. Interest rates on loans were skyrocketing in the U.S. and Canada. Reports note that interest rates on the $7 million in loans the park had taken out had risen to 21% - implying park management signed variable rate loans, which was its ultimate undoing. Joseph Biondolillo, who would later become part owner of the park shed more light on the park's financial woes, stating that Crown Mountain cost double the $500,000 planned and Saw Mill River ran $400,000 over budget. The Canadian Imperial Bank of Commerce was unwilling to renegotiate the terms of the loans, which forced the park into bankruptcy.

The Canadian Imperial Bank appointed Peat Marwick, Ltd. of Toronto as receivers on February 21, 1983 and a month later there was press that Ramsi Tick of Buffalo was negotiating a purchase. John Charlick, vice president of Peat Marwick, said that there was no guarantee the park would open in 1983, but on March 30 came the announcement that Crystal Beach would open under the management of Ramsi Tick as negotiations for the sale continued.

During the interim, Tick promised a new spruced-up image for the park, renovation of the dance hall, and new bingo and miniature golf facilities. In consultation, Bob Hall advised Tick not to bother with Bingo facilities because the major bingo houses in Fort Erie that offered huge cash prizes had killed the park's Bingo trade years earlier. Tick turned a deaf ear to Hall's council. He also planned to re-open the pier and add an excursion boat from Buffalo on a trial basis. He had two boats under consideration: the *St. Claire* and the *Columbia* – both ran from Detroit to Bob-Lo Amusement Park.

Tick underwrote an undisclosed amount of the preparation expenses for the 1983 season out of his own pocket. The bank, through Peat Marwick bore most of the cost along with what Tick admitted was a *"very generous salary."*

Ramsey Tick welcoming visitors to Crystal Beach at the onset of the 1983 season.

Crystal Beach Park opened for 1983 on May 27. It was clean and painted, though the luster of the bright art deco paint schemes was gone. It looked waxen. The deferred maintenance issues, and the signs of neglect, however, remained. The stunts in the Magic Palace and Laugh-in-the-Dark were, for the most part, nonfunctional except for the lights that would shine on them. Cobwebs and dust in the compartments that contained the stunts were most noticeable in the Magic Palace. Paint on the carousel's menagerie was thick, cracked and chipped. The Pier was reopened, but vacant. Strollers got a lake side view of the *Comet* and the surface rust leaching through the paint on its structure.

Aided by a warm and sunny summer, everyone involved deemed the 1983 season a success with attendance up an estimated 20 percent over 1982 (still far shy of the estimated 1 million plus of the 1940s and 50s).

Belying the press that Tick and the park's receivers were in negotiations for a sale, the negotiations with Tick fell through long before the season kicked off. Tick later noted, *"So the receivers and the bank asked me to manage the park and our understanding was along about now they would advertise the park for sale and I was one of the 'interested' people."* This brings into question whether Tick used any of his money in preparation for the 1983 season as the press had indicated. According to Bob Hall years later, Tick was unwilling to negotiate a sale price with the bank so the park was put on the market.

On January 16, 1984, the Canadian Imperial Bank of Commerce announced an agreement to sell the park to the Crystal Beach Company, Ltd. Owners of the company included Edward Hall, Joseph Biondolillo and J. Allen Bernal. The undisclosed purchase price was *"well in excess of a million dollars."*

That day, Biondolillo said that the new company planned to spend $500,000 on improvements. Ed Hall told reporters at a press conference at the Buffalo Naval and Servicemen's Park that the team hoped to revive boat service to the park five-days-a-week. A plan never came to complete fruition as part of the park operations, but Ramsi Tick would eventually restore boat service independently.

As the Ontario government reviewed the transaction, Rudy J. Bonifacio became a member of the investment team. The deal was finalized in St. Catharines on April 3, 1984 and by the end of June, Bonifacio bought enough shares to have controlling interest in the park, which was critical. Bonifacio was a Canadian citizen which reduced corporate tax on the park from 50% (leveled on U.S. controlled companies) to 25% leveled on Canadian owned companies.

Renovation of the dance hall began in earnest in 1984 which was completed for the return of live music and dancing that season. The addition of a Ferris wheel to the midway filled a void since circa 1980. Management also planned to exploit the park's greatest asset, the beach, by offering sailboat rentals, parasailing and wind surfing. They also announced a plan to convert the park's Cinema 180 dome into a teenage-attraction that featured rock videos, local rock groups, and room for dancing on Wednesday nights. There is no evidence that indicates the plan for the dome materialized.

The 1984 season began on May 26th.

Noting that attendance was up 29% and profit was up 15% over 1983, the 1984 season was declared a success. Management revealed plans to spend $750,000 in 1985 and an additional $1 million in 1986 on renovations to park structures, the art deco architecture, attractions, and landscaping.

A few days later, Biondolillo announced that the park was looking for financial aid to restore the PTC #12 carousel. Mechanically, the machine was sound but the menagerie, after nearly 80 years and untold millions of riders and layer upon layer of paint, the animals were in dire need of restoration that required they be stripped of paint, disassembled, and repaired.

Biondolillo said, *"If we can't restore it I'd rather give it to a museum than continue to run it."* Biondolillo was disingenuous when he added that there were no current plans to shut down the ride and it would operate in 1985.

Charles Walker, spokesman for The National Carousel Association told a different story. According to Walker, *"Mr. Biondolillo said they*

Left: Edward Hall in 1988. Right: Joseph Biondolillo (pointing) in 1987.

wanted to sell the machine. He said they couldn't afford to have an antique taking up space."

William Baker, vice president of marketing and public relations acknowledged after weeks of rumors, that the park planned to auction the carousel piecemeal. He pointed out the park has *"not long been out of receivership,"* explaining the sale would will raise money for improvements to other parts of the park and at the same time *"keep the banks happy."*

This statement has a number of implications. One is that the 1984 season was not as successful or profitable as announced. The statement also indicates the Crystal Beach Company was still in debt with the bank. Another implication is that the auction of the carousel was just part

Front cover of the auction brochure for PTC #12.

of a long-range plan by Biondolillo to close the park permanently in the near future.

Pleas to the Crystal Beach Corporation to reconsider a piecemeal auction of PTC #12 fell on deaf ears. The carousel was unceremoniously dismantled and shipped to Fort Wayne, Indiana and auctioned on December 12, 1984.

By December of 1985, Crystal Beach management said that group bookings for 1986 were up 300% over 1985. Coming off another good season, a $5 million 3-phase improvement program was announced.

Phase 1, scheduled for completion before the 1986 season, was a "beautification" program that included ground resurfacing, ride painting, new signs and other graphics. It could be argued that these facets of the program are really general maintenance items. An international flag display was planned, but if it was built, it was innocuous to the point of invisibility. Other new projects included the opening of a "Food Fair" area carrying the international theme with ethnic foods and a staging area for ethnic entertainment. This was nothing more than reworking the building that once enclosed the Scrambler as the Space Screamer, and placing more tables in that area. Part of Phase 1 included moving Kiddieland to the area once occupied by the Cyclone and the Turnpike then build an "Arts and Crafts Bazaar" on the old Kiddieland site. It never materialized.

The more ambitious Phases 2 and 3 included conversion of a section of the bathhouse to a beach club and patio bar – this *did* materialize as Schooner's Beach Club. The upper level of the dock was to be converted into a new "full-service" restaurant; the exterior designed to resemble the *Canadiana* – a nice idea that never left the drawing board. The most ambitious project was the development of a 750-slip marina under the shadow of the *Comet*. It stayed an artist rendering.

The announcement claimed that the spending program *"marks a commitment by the management to restore the importance of Crystal Beach to the recreational and tour and travel markets of both the United States and Canada"* Whether the owners were serious about the rejuvenation of the park is difficult to ascertain. Michael Huling, executive vice president of the park was upbeat, telling the press, *"Reports of our demise have been greatly exaggerated. Crystal Beach is alive and well."*

Biondolillo reported that the owners would be negotiating with Fort Erie officials to close Derby Road between Erie Road and the Queen's Circle in the Village for the creation of a pedestrian mall with shops and other attractions. Crystal Beach would own portions of the mall including the Ontario Hotel, which the park claimed to have recently purchased to house the park offices and residences for entertainment troupes with long term contracts with the park. This was an interesting idea as it could have injected new life into the village, which had declined to a greater degree than the park. There is no confirmation if this idea was fodder for the press or a serious proposal presented to the Fort Erie government for serious consideration. Given that the park lacked any real expansion room, the idea had merit but little else.

In 1986, the Crystal Beach Corporation attempted to expand their marketing outreach by becoming members of the Niagara Frontier Tourism & Travel Cooperative Task Force, but were refused simply because the park was in Canada. Of the 49 members of the task force, 16 voted against Crystal Beach for inclusion, 10 voted in favor of Crystal Beach, 23 did not vote.

Yvonne Kay, chairman of the tourism group said it was strictly a matter of geography because the park was in Canada and the group was formed strictly for Western New York businesses. Biondolillo was understandably incensed. The park had been a part of Western New York for generations, and while the park's business did not generate as much ancillary business in Buffalo, Crystal Beach could have attracted more people *"just passing through"* Western New York to stay the night after a Crystal Beach detour. Biondolillo said the park was going to spend $64,000 to charter the Miss Buffalo, and had arranged tour packages with the Buffalo Hilton Hotel.

Michael Hulling, by the end of June, was predicting that the 1986 season would be good, having achieved 91% of his target group sales

in June alone. Hulling also sheds some light on the previous two years since the park was out of receivership by saying the new owners *"just barely made the nut, but they did."* Hulling hinted about the future of the park when he noted, *"I don't know if the marketplace will tolerate three or four parks for very long."*

The first new attraction on the midway in years was the Galaxi Coaster that stayed only one season.

Crystal Beach posted *"one of the best years we've ever had in the history of the park, noting attendance was up 54 to 60 percent and sales increased by about 1 to 1.2 million dollars,"* according to Biondolillo. He credited the continued development of Crystal Beach as a traditional amusement park, and a good advertising campaign.

The advertising was not only good, it was award winning. One spot featured Mike Ramsey and Mike Foligno of the Buffalo Sabres Hockey Team – in a parody of the Coke vs. Pepsi commercials, arguing whether riding the Comet was better facing forward or backward. The scene cuts them sitting in a Comet train being hauled up the Comet's lift hill – one facing forward, the other backward. The commercial shows Ramsey and Foligno screaming in terror through the ride. The commercial ends showing the backside of the athletes walking away from the coaster's loading platform with their pants stained as if they had wet themselves out of freight during the ride. This was the most memorable of the commercials but it was not the award winner.

The winning commercial featured David Lamb, artistic director of the Kavinoky Theater at D'Youville College bantering with Chuck Miano co-owner of the Old Man River Restaurant. Miano, dressed in a Hawaiian shirt can barely get a word in edgewise, while Lamb, dressed in a tux and speaking with a British accent, describes Crystal Beach and ends his diatribe with *"The only thing Crystal Beach doesn't have is long lines."*

The campaign set a new standard for amusement park advertisements for which Crystal Beach won an award for best commercial by a park with attendance of 250,000 to 750,000, award by the International Association of Amusement Parks and Attractions (IAAPA) during their

Artist renderings for Schooners Beach Club did come to fruition in 1987, however the transformation of the pier into a restaurant with the facade of the Canadiana never left the drawing board.

trade show that fall. The campaign won an "Effie" (effectiveness) Award – that takes into account the total campaign, the commercials themselves, and their impact on the advertiser's business. The campaign was picked over submissions from parks in California, and Florida - beating out such well-known establishments like Cypress Gardens.

Schooners Beach Club opened in 1987 built into part of the bathhouse, which had been under utilized for decades. It featured a wood sun deck facing the beach with comfortable outdoor chairs, tables with umbrellas, and live local rock bands on weekends. Schooners supplied the park with income with very little overhead, however, residents of cottages on the sand bluff that overlooked the beach complained about the loud music and noise. Schooners grossed over $750,000 annually.

Expectations for what was erroneously celebrated as the 100th anniversary of Crystal Beach were high, but the plans the park delivered were tepid. On May 15, 1988, the Buffalo News published a special 12-page advertising insert to the Sunday News Magazine about the upcoming 100th anniversary of Crystal Beach that contained a few paragraphs of the park's early years in tune with all previous accounts on the park's beginning. Also appearing in the insert were congratulatory ads purchased by the Fort Erie Chamber of Commerce, the Buffalo Bisons, and businesses in Fort Erie and Ridgeway.

The planned events included a model/talent search, a bathing suit competition, a jet ski competition, a dart throwing competition, and similar functions, but nothing that would have attracted droves of people. A disappointing line-up for the alleged auspicious year.

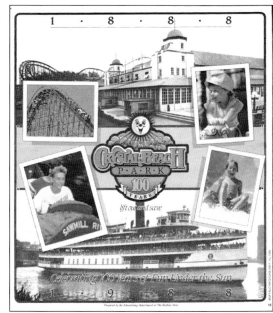

This ad erroneously celebrated the 100th anniversary of Crystal Beach 2 years prematurely - details of which are discussed in the "Origins" chapter.

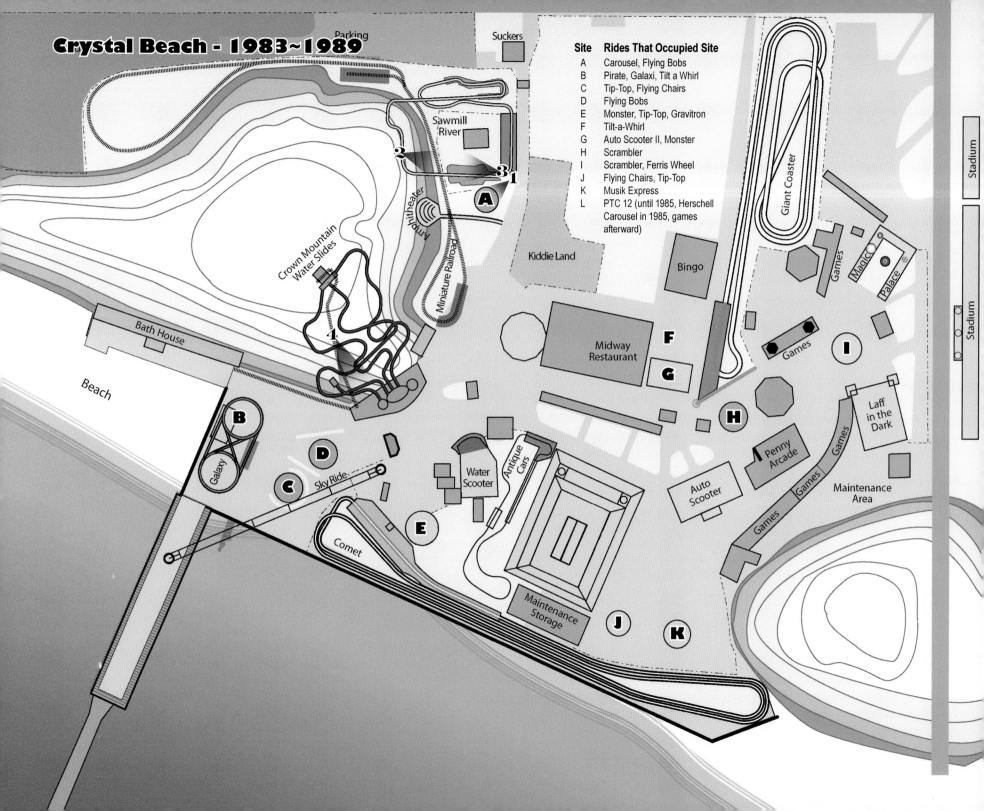

Crystal Beach - 1983~1989

Site | Rides That Occupied Site

Site	Rides That Occupied Site
A	Carousel, Flying Bobs
B	Pirate, Galaxi, Tilt a Whirl
C	Tip-Top, Flying Chairs
D	Flying Bobs
E	Monster, Tip-Top, Gravitron
F	Tilt-a-Whirl
G	Auto Scooter II, Monster
H	Scrambler
I	Scrambler, Ferris Wheel
J	Flying Chairs, Tip-Top
K	Musik Express
L	PTC 12 (until 1985, Herschell Carousel in 1985, games afterward)

Parking

Suckers

Sawmill River

Crown Mountain Water Slides

Amphitheater

Miniature Railroad

Kiddie Land

Giant Coaster

Games

Magic

Palace

Bingo

Midway Restaurant

Games

Games

F

G

H

I

Bath House

Beach

Galaxy

B

D

C

Sky Ride

Water Scooter

Antique Cars

E

Comet

Maintenance Storage

Auto Scooter

Penny Arcade

Games

Games

Games

Laff in the Dark

Maintenance Area

J

K

Stadium

Stadium

GALAXI

It appeared that Crystal Beach had turned the corner with the arrival of the *Galaxi* roller coaster in 1986. The coaster was not purchased by the park, its supplier was not revealed in the press, but could have been from the Conklin ride collection.

The Galaxies are typical portable coasters manufactured by the Italian company SDC. Because of their small footprint, they are popular at small amusement parks with limited space. They are also popular with traveling carnivals because of their modular all steel track and structure.

Galaxi coasters provide a two-minute ride that covers 1,100 feet of track with two major dips and a top speed of approximately 30 miles per hour. The trains consist of two cars, each car carried four people. Its highest point was 45 feet, largest drop - 32 feet. Crystal Beach emphasized its 720-degree and 360 degree helices. This may sound impressive, but the ride was very slow. Consider the Comet had four times as much track and covered it in the same two minutes. In spite of this, Galaxi was a good intermediate coaster for youngsters too big for Kiddieland's Lil Dipper, and not quite big or brave enough for the Giant.

Above right: This image of the Galaxi Coaster, although not sharp, illustrates how it fit perfectly on this spot overlooking the beach. It is red paint provided a needed splash of color to the midway. Right: Erecting the Galaxi Coaster in May 1986. Track of the lift hill in the background of the image curves to the right to the first drop.

GRAVITRON

Gravitron is similar to the Rotor, but it is part ride, part optical illusion. People on the outside can only see the ride, that looks like it popped out of the opening sequences to Lost in Space, rotate at a high speed. Some models have cameras inside wired to monitors on the outside so people can see what is happening.

Inside is where the illusion is created. Riders cannot see outside to notice they are spinning, and everything on the inside rotates, including the ride operator sitting at a control panel precisely in the center.

Because the riders do not see the rotation, they can only feel the g-forces pressing against them emanating from nowhere. The sense of sight is fooled.

Surrounding the inside perimeter walls are 45 vertical panels tilted to the contour of the ship each the height and width of an average human body. Riders lean back on the panels that have rollers underneath so they can roll upward as the ride approaches optimum speed. Riders are also dazzled with lights and rock music blaring from speakers.

People on the outside that can observe the inside through monitors will not see the inside spinning, they see, curiously, people pinned on the wall a few feet off the floor. They may even see brave riders turning themselves sideways or upside down as if defying gravity.

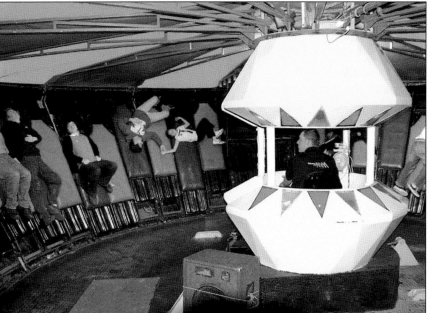

The exterior and interior of a Gravitron at a carnival.

Chapter 8:
1989...

January 1989 came with an announcement that a development team was acquiring Crystal Beach with plans to build a marina in the shadow of the Comet and pledged to keep the park open. Davis R. Tiburzi, president of DRT Development Company indicated that the first phase – 750 boat slips and a breakwater to protect them was planned for the end of 1990 or mid 1991. The original plan was set aside for lack of funding and development experience. Tiburzi deflected rumors that the park would be plowed under for residential development,

"We think the park is a profitable venture in itself with a lot of potential." He did leave open the possibility that park land would be used for residential development, but not in the near future. Tiburzi, at this time, had an agreement to buy the shares of Crystal Beach owned by Ed Hall and Rudy Bonifacio

Biondolillo had other plans and by April, Hall and Bonifacio were trying to back out of the sale of their interest in the park to Tiburzi for unknown reasons.

May had arrived and there were no season announcements in the papers of the upcoming 1989 season. And when the season was underway there were few, if any, advertisements for the park in newspapers or on television. At the park it was apparent that the end was near. On most days, including the weekends, the park was deserted. Ride operators and game attendants sat with nothing to do. The Musik Express had vanished from the midway, and the Monster sat disassembled on flatbed trailers. A concessionaire set up a go-cart track that was not included with admission to the park, was having a disappointing season.

Cathy Herbert collection.

Above: Spectators gather around the Comet as it is being auctioned. Right: Lucky bidders take home a car from the Giant Coaster.

What was not apparent was that Biondolillo had made a decision to close the park forever after the 1989 season. Tiburzi got an injunction that prevented Hall and Biondolillo from selling their shares to anyone other than Tiburzi until a court hearing and ruling, but nothing prevented Biondolillo from closing the park even though Tiburzi wanted to keep it running for at least another two seasons.

"Crystal Beach Customers Say Park's Closing Isn't Amusing" was the headline when Biondolillo went public with his plans to pull the plug on the park. Its last day of operation was Labor Day, 1989. It did open one more day the following weekend for a company that previously booked the entire park for an employee picnic.

Courtesy Richard Schwegler

Photo by Richard Schwegler

Biondolillo admitted that closing the park had been under consideration for a number of years, and a study revealed it would cost at least $20 million to make Crystal Beach competitive with Darien Lake and Canada's Wonderland.

Biondolillo had auctioned all the rides on October 17, 1989, as no apparent injunction preventing the sale of the park's assets had been issued.

The day of the auction was a stereotypical fall day on the Niagara Frontier – cold, gray, windy and rainy. The symbolism was deafening. Devotees of the park that had paid $10 just to have the opportunity to bid quickly learned that unless their pockets were deep, they would be going home cold, wet, and empty handed.

Ontario courts decided in favor of Tiburzi on December of 1989. In spite of Tiburzi's alleged desire to keep the park operating a little longer, there is nothing to guarantee that he would have continued to operate it, but with the rides sold, his intentions were inconsequential. During the next few years, the landmarks were systematically demolished, except for the Comet that was dismantled and shipped by truck to Fantasy Island to await reconstruction.

Photo by Richard Schwegler

Far left bottom: The Magic Palace looks as if it had been bombed. Top left: Look closely and find the tilted room, still enclosed by its interior walls. Left: The pedestal fountain in the Magic Palace courtyard.

A remnant of the Giant Coaster track and the remains of the coaster in the background.

The Giant Coaster a pile of timber.

Photo by Cathy Herbert

Photo by Cathy Herbert

A crane chews into the dance hall.

Photo by Cathy Herbert

Left: Dismantling the Comet. Top right: Early stages of demolition. Right center: Laff in the Dark succumbs to a backhoe. Bottom right: Aerial of the park grounds, only the dance hall remains.

By Wayne Farrar, courtesy Niagara Falls, Ontario Public Library

Chapter 9:
Postmortem

There is no single answer to the question, *"What had happened to Crystal Beach Park?"* The owners had concluded that the cards were stacked against the amusement center which was too far gone to keep on life support. The decision to close the park was based on a study that concluded it would have cost an estimated $20 million to reinvent it with a large percentage of the dollars going into repopulating the park with rides. Biondolillo did not elaborate whether rehabilitating the older rides like Laff in the Dark and Magic Palace were included. He also did not reveal who had conducted the study.

The park faced other hard realities. There was no vacant land for expansion. This was of no consequence for most of the park's existence. For decades Crystal Beach Park was the largest within a hundred mile radius or more. Competition from other local and regional outdoor amusement business became fierce with the advent of large theme parks owned by corporations. By the mid 1980s, Crystal Beach Park – inclusive of the beach, midway, picnic grove, and parking areas – could comfortably fit into the parking lot of Darien Lake or Canada's Wonderland. For most of its existence, Crystal Beach had a monopoly on the amusement park business on the Niagara Frontier and during the early years of the park, Crystal Beach had put the squeeze on the local competition just like it started to feel during the 1970s.

Weather is always a concern in the amusement park business, but by the late 1970s it had become a major component in the equation of the financial health of Crystal Beach. With increasing competition, every day of decent weather (especially on weekends) meant less pressure to make up lost business during the limited subsequent days.

Biondolillo reasoned that in order to justify the $20 million, the park would need to attract more than 10,000 visitors daily from June through August. He did not feel that was possible, and if it was, there was not enough parking.

During the late 19th Century farmers considered Crystal Beach and adjoining waterfront a wasteland, a century later the same waterfront real estate had become more valuable than the park that occupied it.

Lack of capital and expansion room, extreme competition, a three month operating season, and a business with assets not nearly as valuable as the real estate were the realities that left Biondolillo with only one course action, unpleasant as it was. But how did Crystal Beach reach the point of no return?

It could ne argued that John Rebstock, the park's founder, doomed the park once he began selling off his property that surrounded it during the 1890s, land locking it without room for growth. But in all fairness, he was not an amusement park Nostradomus and cannot be faulted for not having planned for the park a century into the future.

The sacrifice of the lake front promenade for the construction of the Comet is the event some consider the moment when Crystal Beach turned the wrong corner. While the Comet did mark a transition point in the park's history it was more of a monument to the end of the World War II era than a bad decision. (Proven by the fact when the gavel struck at the auction, the sale price was the highest ever paid for a used wood roller coaster, and since its reconstruction, it remains in the top twenty-five of wood coasters on a global survey by Amusement Today.)

One factor that contributed to the decline of Crystal Beach never considered previously, was the population decline of Buffalo and the surrounding suburbs. If Buffalo stayed at its mid 1940s and 1950s population levels, the park may have survived the onslaught of Fantasy Island, Marineland, Canada's Wonderland, Darien Lake. (Fantasy Island did go out of business for a season, but returned after one year and has remained strong since). These parks would have taken a chunk out of Crystal Beach business initially, but the park could have recovered from its wounds. No longer would it have been the predominant area park, but could have survived and remained healthy, especially after people had got tired of the crowds and exorbitant prices of the larger parks with parking fees nearly as much as a park admission.

Crystal Beach did take advantage of this pricing disparity during an award winning marketing campaign credited for bringing people back to the park during the mid 1980s. Sadly when they got there, most of what truly made Crystal Beach the amusement park that people loved years earlier was either in poor condition, had the appearance of being in poor condition, or had disappeared altogether. Gone from the midway by 1984: Caterpillar (1965), Tumble Bug (1967), Turnpike (1971c), Jungle Land (1977), Hey Dey (1978), Wild Mouse (1979), the Eli Bridge Aristocrat Ferris Wheel (1980c), PTC#12 Carousel (1984), Magic Carpet at the point became the Magic Palace (1972). The Comet looked in bad shape, even though it was not… the surface rust on the lake-facing structure looked malignant but it the structure was strong. The colorful paint and neon of its station replaced with fluorescent signage. The Giant Coaster was in decent shape as well, having received major track work in 1987. Unfortunately it had not gotten a coat of paint since 1972. Most of the fantastic neon lighting in the park had vanished. The colorful paint jobs on the building facades had been painted over with drab solid colors. Many lights on the rides were either burned out or missing entirely.

The removal of the familiar and cherished began during the Hall era of the 1960s, and while it may have made sense to remove the rides at the time (because of maintenance expenses for the fabrication of parts no longer available from defunct ride manufacturers) their absence hurt the park later. People wanted new and updated rides but not at the expense of losing old favorites, or supplanting old favorites with game booths. While it may have been expensive to maintain the old, the cost was exponentially less than the expense to maintain the sophisticated new rides and burden of debt that came with them.

The stunts inside the Magic Palace and Laff in the Dark were in poor shape. In the Magic Palace, many stunts like the "car wash rollers" were removed and the rooms left vacant. The falling wall of crates and barrels stopped falling. The slides were closed off forcing the use of the stairs, and of course, the Magic Carpet itself was gone. The stunts that remained were barely functioning if at all. None of them had been cleaned in years. Laff in the Dark stunts suffered from the same lack of diligence. The stunts in these attractions were primitive compared the technology-created illusions of today's major parks but they were effective in their intent – surprise – but they had to work.

Some feel that the pay-one-price-admission pushed the park over the edge. The long-time non-riding visitors and the village merchants were sour to the pay-one-price of the gated park. For riders it was great deal, however, it probably added cost to the park. Ungated, Conklin brought his rides to the park at no expense to Crystal Beach which received a percentage of the receipts from each of Conklin's rides. With gating, the park had to lease or buy rides. Whether or not the pay-one-price was effective at minimizing theft and maintenance costs from vandalism as Bob and Van Hall asserted will never be known.

The big ticket attractions added during the late 1970s and early 1980s certainly dug the hole the park could not get out of after a very soggy 1982 season. The refurbishment to the dance hall and modernized rest rooms were necessary after the fire. As Darien Lake expanded year after year, the outlay for the big ticket items became necessary because the park had purged most of its classic rides and had nothing left to offer. The classic rides, if they remained on the midway, would not have eliminated the need for updated rides but they would have lessened the pressure for them.

Prior to the installation of the water slides, the last major investment the park made was the installation of the Comet. During the late 1940s the park still had investors. If the park still had them during the 1970s and 1980s, they may have been more forgiving and willing to renegotiate on failed or short returns unlike a bank that had loaned the park millions at high interest rates. When Crystal Beach became entirely owned by the Hall family, the era of investors ended. By the mid 1970s all the rides were owned or leased by the park and the descendants of George Hall Sr. were expecting dividends from the park but were not required make an investment. Without capital to put back into the park, Bob and Van Hall had to turn to creditors. Clearly, the Halls had made a series of decisions that coupled with factors they could not control, painted the park into a corner. If they had made the decision not to compete with big theme parks, but improve the existing assets and redoubled their efforts as a niche, family park, it *may* have survived and strongly.

Whether or not Biondolillo made the correct decision to close Crystal Beach Park rather than invest $20 million (if a loan was even obtainable) will never be known. However, a cursory examination of another amusement park, Geauga Lake, indicates he made the right business decision.

Beginning in the 1990s, Geauga Lake was entertaining over a million visitors annually. Subsequent owners invested millions of dollars and attendance continued to soar. It was merged with neighboring Sea World, they added roller coasters and other attractions, but then attendance began to decline. Between 2002 and 2005 attendance slipped from 2.15 million to 700,000.

Geauga's final owner, Cedar Fair (also the owners of Cedar Point) announced a $26 million dollar expansion and reduction of ticket prices by $10, but that did not reverse the trend. Late in September 2007, Cedar Fair announced it was closing Geauga Lake after 119 years. There is more to the demise of Geauga Lake than that presented in this cursory account, but it does underscore that money and major rides are not a cure-all.

Crystal Beach Park aficionados vilify Biondolillo for closing the park. To his credit, he did publicize the decision to close the park while the it was still in operation. This provided a two-week window for many to return one last time to re-experience what remained and relive old memories. Partisans of Geauga Lake were not afforded the same courtesy.

Had Crystal Beach Park survived into the 21st Century, it probably would have fallen victim to the events of September 11, 2001. Before that tragic day, the border between Canada and the United States and was extremely permeable for Canadian and U.S. citizens - customs was nearly a formality. This open border was vital to Crystal Beach.

Now that passports are necessary, people who did not cross the border frequently have foregone crossing altogether – most not willing to shoulder the expense of passport. A summer day at Crystal Beach for many residents of Western New York was the only time they visited Canada. If Crystal Beach Park survived the 1980s and 1990s, the closing of the open border would have hit the park hard.

If 9/11 had not happened, Bob and Van Hall may have been forced to sell upon their old age, and possibly to someone whose only interest was development, not operating an amusement park.

At the time of this writing, Crystal Beach has been gone for 22 years. Its absence is still felt, however, for a generation of people Crystal Beach is nothing more than ancient local history.

Chapter 10: Origins

This third volume of Crystal Beach history, that taken collectively with the previous two volumes, all facets of the park from 1890 through 1989 are covered except for one - How Crystal Beach Park began. All three volumes contain references to the "romantic" or "traditional" history of Crystal Beach and its assertions of the origins of Crystal Beach Park. Those assertions are weighed against period research and circumstantial evidence which support a beginning less romantic and more realistic. Normally, a chapter about the park's inception would be found closer to the front of the book, however, since this chapter is an analysis, it works better as a conclusive piece.

The romantic history of Crystal Beach has its roots in a 1931 news article that attests John Rebstock began a religious retreat in 1888. This retreat failed after two seasons because everyone who attended it was more interested in the relief sideshow attractions rather than the religious programs and since amusement is what the people wanted, Rebstock gave them more of it and Crystal Beach rose out of the ashes. All of the iterations of Crystal Beach history since then repeat the 1931 account almost verbatim. Recent nostalgia DVD and television productions on Crystal Beach and other books perpetuate the romantic history. Some accounts have minor variances, but they all condense to these few salient details:

- John Rebstock purchased his land on the southern Ontario shores of Lake Erie to sell and barge-off off the sand for construction projects in Buffalo.
- He later reconsidered selling the sand so as not to destroy the natural beauty and decided to create a religious retreat on the grounds.
- Crystal Beach began in 1888 as a religious Camp Meeting/ Chautauqua in 1888.

- The largest hotel at the retreat was the Assembly House run by Dr. Thomas Snyder.
- The Assembly House was the headquarters for the camp meetings, residences for the speakers, lecturers, and eventually for park entertainers.
- 150,000 visited the Camp Meeting/Chautauqua assembly during each of its two seasons.

Elements of these bullet points are not necessarily false or inaccurate, but they have been woven into a story of the start of Crystal Beach that period research does not bear out.

Proponents of Crystal Beach romantic history should question romantic accounts because the terms "religious camp meeting/ assembly" and "Chautauqua" interchangeably between them. Because these are two different entities whose objectives are as far apart as Creationism and Evolutionary Theory, the romantic history comes into question as it cannot nail down whether the park started as a religious camp meeting or Chautauqua. (See Appendix for a description of these entities.)

The extended roots of Crystal Beach (park and village) extend back to the mid 19th Century and Baden-Baden, Germany, the ancestral home of John E. and Catherine (Kiepser) Rebstock – the parents of the founder of Crystal Beach. [For clarity, the father of John Rebstock the founder of Crystal Beach will be referred to as John Sr.] John Sr. and Catherine immigrated to the United States during the 1840s and settled in Black Rock, New York (later absorbed by the City of Buffalo). According to city directories their home was at the corner of Hamilton and Water Streets (Water Street has long since vanished). John Sr. earned a living as a grocer. Catherine gave birth to their first child, Mary, in 1848, followed a year later by their second daughter Catherine. John Evangelist Rebstock was born in Buffalo in 1852.

Listings for the John E. Rebstock Sr. family in the Buffalo City Directories cease after 1854. It can be concluded then that by 1855, John Sr. and Catherine had packed up their children and belongings and crossed the Niagara River to resettle near Ridgeway, Ontario. The reason for their departure from Buffalo remains largely speculative, however they may have held the belief, like many other immigrants during that period, that the inevitability of the U.S. civil war was not their war to fight. So they fled the U.S. to avoid involvement.

During their years in Canada, the Rebstock family grew. John was followed by three brothers – Albert C, Stephen, and Joseph; and three more sisters – Rachel, Emma, and Rose, not necessarily born in that order.

John Sr. supported his burgeoning family by cutting timber for a farmer named Adam Barnhardt. John accompanied his father and walked along side the cattle that dragged the logs to the Lake Erie shore at Prospect Point (the eastern cusp of Point Abino Bay adjoining the waterfront where Crystal Beach Park would be built). Then the logs were floated across the lake to lumber mills in Buffalo. It was the younger Rebstock's job to keep the cattle from straying into the lake.

Tragedy came to the Rebstock family when John Sr. died during the early 1860s. The exact date is uncertain but derived from the fact that the Rebstock name, as it relates to this family, reappears in the Buffalo directories in 1863 and lists Catherine Rebstock as a widow residing at 375 Washington Street, Buffalo. The circumstances behind John Sr.'s passing are also unknown. John was at most 11 years old when his father died. Catherine undoubtedly returned to Buffalo where there were more opportunities for her to find work and support her family. She found work as a dressmaker. The family home and business address changed a number of times during the 1860s for reasons that are not apparent.

By 1873, the 21 year old John Rebstock earned a living as a clerk in Buffalo. The directory does not indicate where he clerked, but it may have been at the firm of Hauck & Garono where he did clerk in 1876. Hauck & Garono, at 255 Pearl Street, specialized in home furnishings, primarily hardware and stoves.

When and how John met his first wife, Alice E. Mason, is another curiosity lost to time. What is known about her is that she was a schoolteacher from Highgate, Vermont (located near Lake Champlain and the Quebec border). The Reverend Babbit wed John and Alice on September 4, 1878 in Highgate – John was 26 years old and Alice was 24. The couple returned to Buffalo and resided at 106 (and/or 116) Bird Avenue and later at 92 Bird Avenue.

In addition to getting married in 1878, John became part owner in the firm of Warren, Rebstock & Company located at 540-542 Washington. His partners were Charles F. and Henry J. Warren both Buffalo. The business specialized in the sale of hardware and stoves. Two years later John started a stove and hardware business of his own that involved a number of members of his family.

It was John Rebstock's practice to register his businesses under Alice's name. A. E. Rebstock Hardware and Stoves was located at 548 Washington Street (later moved and expanded to larger facilities on Washington Street). The 1880 directory records the home of A. E. Rebstock at 116 Bird Avenue – which was also the registered home address for John. According to the 1880 directory, John managed the business and his brother Joseph was a clerk.

Joseph Rebstock departed his brother's business to become a florist, opening his own stores at 567 and 979 Main Street. Another of John's brothers, Albert, clerked at the hardware and stove store. Buffalo City Directories now listed John as president of the John E. Rebstock Stove Company, Ltd.

LARGER AND FINEST DISPLAY OF,

Stoves Ranges

IN WESTERN NEW YORK.

Best Goods and Lowest Prices.

THE REBSTOCK STOVE CO.,

(LIMITED.)

564 and 566 Washington Street.

SIX STORES ABOVE GENESEE

Pen and Ink drawing of the Rebstock Stove and Hardware Store that appeared in an advertisement.

Some of the romantic accounts of Crystal Beach origins claim that Rebstock made a considerable sum of money developing an area of Black Rock in the vicinity of Tonawanda Street and Riverside Park. There are kernels of truth to this in records of real estate transactions, however the extent to which he "developed" this area remains to be discovered. The North Park Land Company, which does not list Rebstock as a member, is credited with the actual development of the real estate in the area often credited to Rebstock. This company purchased 29 acres of land from "Mr. Rebstock, the stove dealer" in 1897. The purchase price and the precise location of the acreage were not given for publication. (Buffalo Courier 8/31/1897). Of course by this time, Crystal Beach was winding down its 8th season.

Its probable that in 1886 he sold a large tract of land to the New York Central Railroad that proposed extension of their line through lower Black Rock to Germania Park through the property Rebstock owned (Buffalo Express 9/12/1886). There are other transactions in the Riverside Park – Tonawanda Street area under A. E. Rebstock listed in the appendix. How he had come to own any of the land is unknown.

In what was then Bertie Township of Ontario, Rebstock purchased some land on Point Abino Bay from Elenor A. Dickout and his wife Melissa Eliza. Lot number twenty-five in the broken front upon Lake Erie [shoreline frontage] and contained approximately 150 acres. Rebstock paid the $8,500 for the land. Initially, he had the property recorded with Alice as the owner. The transaction occurred on June 1, 1887. Rebstock borrowed $7,500 from the Ontario Loan and Savings Company. The Mortgage required payment in full at 6.5% interest at the end of one year. It also required that Rebstock insure the structures on the property for $2,000 – presumably, this structure was the Dickout farmhouse.

Part of this acreage contained 30 acres of apple, pear and cherry tree orchards. He converted the barn on the property into an evaporating plant to dry the fruit that he sold it to food processors.

Upon the imminent opening of Crystal Beach, a report noted "... *the property was bought in the first place on account of its commercial value, by utilizing the vast quantities of sand which abound."* This serves to enforce the notion that John Rebstock had intended to barge off the sand from the lake front "wastelands" to sell for use in construction projects in Buffalo. The excavation would be conducted through The Lake Erie Sand Company (LESC) whose officers were M. J. Galvin, John Rebstock, John Johnson, Oliver Jenkins, and Erastus C. Knight. The earliest record found for the LESC is in 1890, implying that it existed as early as 1889 – a year before Crystal Beach opened. (Directories typically reflect the prior year.)

It does not appear that the Lake Erie Sand Company advanced beyond germination, possibly because the demand for sand was in decline – especially in road construction. Starting during the 1880s asphalt was becoming the predominant material for road pavement. In fact, in 1890, the stench from asphalt production brought numerous complaints to the Buffalo Mayor's office. With established sand sources at Point Abino (Fox and Holloway Sand Company) and elsewhere, there was no need for yet another supplier. Sand on Rebstock's property was abundant but limited. Given the existing market conditions, the projected gross income from a sand mining enterprise may not have justified the cost of building the infrastructure (sand hopper and horse-drawn railroad), and projected operating expenses for the LESC to turn a reasonable profit.

There is nothing to substantiate the romantic notion that Rebstock had an epiphany that gave him a sudden appreciation for the environment and prompted him to abandon the LESC for a business venture less deleterious to the waterfront. Environmental concerns during this era took a back seat to development and economic growth. There is no evidence that Rebstock's attitude toward development and the environment was any different from that of the era overall. It is unlikely that he would have changed his mind if there had been sufficient projected profit in such an enterprise. This conjecture does not impugn Rebstock for any lack of environmental sensitivity; it was just the mind set of business world at that time. Even the beauty of Niagara Falls fell victim to the objectionable encroachment of industry on the

John E. Rebstock

Erastus Cole Knight

Oliver A. Jenkins

Arthur W. Hickman

Did these men have a picnic lunch on the beach?

American side and shabby tourist attractions, pay-to-view barricades, and tourist extortion on the Canadian side years earlier. While Rebstock did not ravage his land for the mineral resources, he affected a different type of environmental damage by developing a resort on it then compounded the damage by subdividing the property and selling the parcels that would ultimately become the town of Crystal Beach.

The likely scenario behind the establishment of Crystal Beach is that Rebstock deliberated over what type of enterprise he could establish there when he reached the conclusion that the LESC was too risky financially to pursue. The resort of Crystal Beach, which would later split over time into the park and the village, was the alternative.

Some romantic accounts have Rebstock entertaining Erastus C. Knight and other prominent Buffalonians on his waterfront property with a picnic dinner. At this dinner, the men concluded that the best use for Rebstock's land was a summer resort with a bathing beach. The other Buffalonians were Oliver Jenkins, and attorneys Arthur Hickman, and William Palmer. If there is any truth to this romantic history element, then realistically,

Rebstock probably discussed potential business options with his colleagues in a more formal setting: the Buffalo Club, a restaurant, or over dinner across a dining room table at the residence of either of these gentlemen with their wives. None of these men would have been so cavalier to consider such a major undertaking as the development of a summer resort without major deliberation. The start-up costs for construction of a dock, and leasing and operating a steamer would have been considerable. The image of reserved prominent Buffalo attorneys and businessmen having a picnic on a beach is uncharacteristic to the point of being comical. These men may have walked the beach and grove to discuss the vision at best.

Crystal Beach opened for the first time on July 16, 1890.

None of the period sources from which the above history is written note John Rebstock's involvement in a religious establishment of any kind.

Romantic origin elements about a religious retreat or Chautauqua emanate from the Crystal Beach International Assembly (CBIA) that Rebstock began in 1895– five years after Crystal Beach Park opened. The CBIA disappeared after the summer of 1896. A two-year life span like the religious establishment of romantic history.

The May 1895 announcements for the development and imminent opening of the CBIA were prominent and comprehensive. The CBIA press coverage indicated that the governing body developed a constitution modeled after the original Chautauqua in Jamestown, New York. The Assembly House, still under construction, would serve as the base of operations and housing for the guest speakers.

The Assembly's officers included, as president, the Reverend William H. Main of the Emmanuel Baptist Church of Buffalo. Chancellor and Vice President of the CBIA was the Reverend Thomas Snyder, Ph. D. of Preston Ontario. The CBIA schedule ran for two months from July 1 through September 1.

According to romantic history, 150,000 visited the religious retreat each of its two seasons (1888 and 1889). Consider the logistics of transporting this many people from Buffalo to Crystal

Pen and ink drawings of William H. Main (left) and Thomas Snyder (right) chancellor and vice president respectively of the CBIA.

A very stern-looking Dr. Thomas Snyder from his obituary. Niagara Falls Gazette, February 7, 1927.

Beach in 1888 without a dock for boats or automobiles and paved roads to move large numbers of people quickly. Ridgeway could be reached easily enough via railroad, but the bottleneck would have been between there and Crystal Beach. If there had been such a retreat in 1888, and 150,000 people visited it during a 90-day season, then 1,670 people visited each day. This does not seem like it would be a big logistics problem, unless the horse and buggy was the primary mode of transport.

Two horses with a wagon capable of carrying 10 people would have required 167 trips a day. The other extreme would require 167 wagons with 334 horses to move 1,670 people in one trip (double these amounts for the return trip). So in Ridgeway there would have been a lot of people standing around waiting for a horse and buggy, or a long parade of horses and buggies on a daily basis. There is no record of such a transportation effort between Ridgeway and Crystal Beach by horse and buggy or any other contrivance, not even in folklore.

Rebstock was an intelligent man. Advertisements for his hardware and stove business appeared in Buffalo papers daily. He certainly would have advertised an 1888 religious retreat in Buffalo papers if it had

existed, but such ads were not found. Even the Buffalo Christian Advocate – a Methodist Christian newspaper did not contain ads for the mythological religious retreat, but it did for his store. (Rebstock published this paper under the name A. E. Rebstock & Co. from November 1884 through November 1885. Others assumed publication afterward.) Rebstock was a devout Methodist, so at the very least he would have advertised the 1888-1889 retreat in this paper. Romantic history notes that Rebstock wanted to "popularize" Christianity for the mental and spiritual uplift of the common people, so without advertising the retreat in newspapers the common people read, how would they have know it was there? The original Chautauqua in Jamestown, New York had regular press releases and updates printed in Buffalo papers since its 1875 inception. The Crystal Beach International Assembly regularly advertised in the common press. If the alleged religious retreat of 1888-89 that supposedly was the start of Crystal Beach had existed, it is reasonable that a search through all the Buffalo newspapers from 1887 through 1889 would have revealed at least a modicum of print about this retreat not a vacuum.

Since some of the elements from the romantic history are in fact the origins of the Crystal Beach International Assembly in 1895, and the remaining elements are not consistent with Rebstock's demonstrated business acumen, the only conclusion is that the start of Crystal Beach Park in 1888 as a religious retreat is folklore. Additionally, in June 1889, John Rebstock was appointed to a committee in Buffalo to oversee the paving of Buffalo's west side streets considered to be in his neighborhood. (If his retreat was foundering in 1889, he would have been at Point Abino Bay trying to shoring it up.)

Crystal Beach began on July 16, 1890. Subsequent seasonal announcements through the decades sequentially number each anniversary with statements like, "Crystal Beach will open for its 63rd season on May…" Then in 1984, the 1888 inaugural year of the mythological retreat became the inaugural year of the park. Even if the retreat had existed in 1888, to claim it was the start of Crystal Beach Park is as erroneous as claiming that the United States and Canada began as countries when Columbus discovered America (whether or not Columbus discovered America notwithstanding).

The park's first season was 1890, its first anniversary was 1891. Using basic arithmetic, when Crystal Beach Park closed after Labor Day 1989 it was the end of its 100th season during its 99th anniversary year. The skewed time line may have been deliberate to accelerate plans to close the park after its 100th anniversary. It trapped Rose Jankowiak Hirsch in her book, Crystal Memories, to make unsubstantiated claims to explain the incongruity. She claims that the park's actual 50th anniversary was in 1938, and the park postponed it two years because they were still reeling from the 1932 bankruptcy. Yet the park spent $10,000 one year after filing bankruptcy adding the Motorboat Speedway to the midway. An additional $25,000 created Laff in the Dark in 1936, and an estimated 2 million visited Crystal Beach that year according to park management. While the park was frugal, these expenditures are not indicative of an amusement park financially constrained in the midst of the Great Depression.

To address how the 1895 Crystal Beach International Assembly (CBIA) erroneously became the start of Crystal Beach as a religious retreat in 1888; some background about the assembly itself is necessary.

From the 1895 CBIA press releases, the assembly grounds were separate from the property owned by the Crystal Beach Steamboat and Ferry Company that owned and operated the park. Construction of the Assembly House, a three-story hotel which would serve as the Assembly headquarters, was not complete until mid July of 1895. It had eighty rooms and a price tag over $10,000. Furnished with *"new*

The Royal Hotel circa 1920. The wing on the right side was an addition not part of the original Assembly House.

furniture of the most improved style," the first floor had two parlors, one for hotel guests, the other a private parlor for the assembly officers. Staked out in *"a natural cove in the hill"* approximately 100 feet from the Assembly House was an amphitheater *"around which seats will be built."* (From this description, the amphitheater was on the Erie Road side of the sand bluff near the area of the miniature railroad's horseshoe turn that directed the train back to the station). The Board of Directors included John E. Rebstock; W. H. Montague, Secretary of State, M.P., Ottawa; Eber Cutler and C. H. Haun of Ridgeway; and Buffalo real estate developer and realtor George Chadeayne.

Regarding programs, Rev. Main reported, *"There will be two meetings every day with the best speakers and preachers that can possibly be had."* The programs were noted to have special advantages for Sunday school teachers, church workers, scholars and educators. The scheduled lecture topics included "The Building of the Bible"; "Missing a Factor in History"; "Problems of Progress"; "The Unreality of Realism"; "Conscience"; and "The Wit, Humor and Pathos of the Irish People". Planned speakers would arrive from across

An amphitheater was stated out...where there is "a natural cove in the hill around which seats will be built" abandoned circa 1900 and used for donkey rides.

John Rebstock hired two additional steamers, the *State of New York* and the *State of Ohio*, to make the Crystal Beach run in addition to of the regularly scheduled runs of the *Pearl* and *Gazelle* to accommodate a multitude of 10,000 expected for the opening exercises. Attendance on opening day, July 1, 1895 was between 400 and 500, critically short of the 10,000 – not even a boatload.

Within two weeks of its grand opening, public interest and enthusiasm for the Assembly was loosing the little momentum it may have had. Indicative that attendance remained far below expectations, the CBIA offered free tickets to anyone from Buffalo to visit the Assembly for the performance of the Buffalo Choral Society on July 10, 1895. Then officers waived all admission fees for programs during the entire week of July 12, 1895. Newspaper coverage of events and programs at the Silver Lake and Jamestown Chautauquas regularly captured substantial press. By the end of July, coverage of programs at the CBIA shrank from a half column to a small paragraph.

Eber Cutler, one the Assembly's board members, filed a Mechanic's Lien against the CBIA on August 1, 1895. This lien is a strong indication that the Assembly was foundering and that the Board was not quick to access the guarantee fund, or had already depleted it. According to the lien, CBIA owed Cutler for "Lumber and materials and furnishings… for the erection of an assembly hall for the use of said assembly and pavilion."

By the end of August, newspaper coverage of the CBIA diminished to a few lines to announce a speaker and the topic of the lecture, or a musical function. The press published the highlights of the summer season programs from the Chautauquas at Jamestown, and Silver Lake at the end of the season. The CBIA was conspicuous by the absence of

North America including Sir William Dawson, President of Queens University, Canada; Rev. W. F. Taylor, D.D. of Seattle, Washington; Dr. H. S. Lloyd of Colgate University; and Alabama Congressman Howard.

To underwrite the operating expenses, the Assembly planned to charge nominal admission fees for the programs, classes and concerts. Ultimately, the Board wanted the CBIA to be a self-supporting, non-profit organization. The Board established a guarantee fund upon which to draw in the event that the Assembly failed to generate sufficient income.

Buffalo Courier, June 29, 1923

Smoke billows from the roof of the Royal Hotel.

a similar end-of-season recap of its first season – another indicator that the first year of the CBIA was less than stellar. Innes and his Famous Band appeared at the CBIA in 1895. Innes, accustomed to first class accommodations was not pleased with the CBIA accommodations, the amphitheater, or the fact that there was not a bottle of beer to be found anywhere.

The Crystal Beach International Assembly had a number of factors working against any chance it had for success. First, was its immediacy to Crystal Beach Park. Consider this analogy: if Crystal Beach was a slice of chocolate cake and the CBIA was a plate of Brussels sprouts, most disembarking passengers at the Crystal Beach pier would choose the slice of chocolate cake. The lay back atmosphere of the grove, a frolic on the beach, the free entertainment (most live entertainment in the grove was free except theater Vaudeville), and all the other concessions and entertainment offerings could easily seduce the well-intentioned Assembly-bound passengers during the time it took to walk the length of the pier. Who would not choose a day at Crystal

Beach Park over stiff and starchy lectures?

Another factor that undermined the CBIA's chances was the other existing Chautauquas. While there was interest in the Chautauqua Movement during this era, people that pursued its spiritual, educational and cultural offerings were already involved with these long-established institutions. By 1895 the Chautauqua at Jamestown was in its 21st year, and had grown in size to a college campus with lecture and assembly halls, resident housing, and infrastructure covering over 150 acres. The Chautauqua at Silver Lake in Wyoming County, although considerably smaller than Jamestown, was also well established. In comparison, the CBIA was qualitatively and quantitatively inferior.

Poor attendance probably forced the depletion of the guarantee fund - speakers and lectures had to be paid, there was Eber Cutler's mechanic's lien, and a host of other general expenses including the salaries of the CBIA officers. If there was consensus among the board to cut their losses and not have a second season, Rebstock was not among them. Running the Assembly for a second season is a testament to Rebstock's determination, but his decision to continue with this loosing enterprise seems one more of the heart than of the head.

References to the Assembly's president, William H. Main were missing from the meager press coverage the Assembly received during its sophomore season. A holdover from 1895 was Thomas Snyder, but there were no references to his 1895 title of Vice President.

The 1896 season began on July 25 – three weeks later than the prior season with a six week agenda that was virtually nonexistent. What was probably an advertising ploy was the possibility that Republican presidential nominee William McKinley was a tentative speaker for the season – he never made an appearance. The only definite speaker was Thomas Snyder who would lecture on Rome, Italy on opening day.

Evidence that the Assembly was programmatically weak is the fact that Rebstock leased the Assembly grounds to "The Foresters, Macabees, and the Ancient Order of United Workmen" (all Fraternal Benefits Societies) for an entire weekend of private functions. As the season progressed through August, the CBIA disappeared from the press with the exception of an occasional and inconspicuous one-line announcement of a scheduled speaker. By September 1896, the Crystal Beach International Assembly disappeared from the press altogether, never to reappear. Snyder became the owner and proprietor of the Assembly House and renamed it the Royal Hotel. Exactly when he came to purchase it is unknown, perhaps as early as 1896 or just shortly afterward.

The earliest synopsis of Crystal Beach History appeared in 1924 and does not make references to a religious retreat or selling sand.

The next synopsis appeared in 1931. Rebstock was 79 years old and not in the best of health. The press quoted Rebstock, *"I was full of enthusiasm for the project and put a lot of my savings into it. But I soon found out that oil and water wouldn't mix. Even the ministers and the Sunday school teachers appeared to be more interested in my sideshows than they were in the services, concerts and lectures. So after two loosing years, I gave it up."*

Its possible that the reporter misconstrued the information Rebstock had conveyed to him, or Rebstock's memory was no longer what it once was or he was putting a positive spin on a failed enterprise (recall the discussion of the unreliability of interviews). The CBIA was not his only failed effort.

All accounts of the fabled Peg Leg railroad – the monorail built from Ridgeway

John Rebstock was an investor in the Ontario Southern Railroad, better known as the Peg-Leg Railroad. Intended to be a connector between the Canadian National Railroad station in Ridgeway, Ontario and Crystal Beach, it failed to draw critical ridership and shut down after three years. It may have lasted longer if the Crystal Beach terminus was in the grove rather than the summer colony and promoted as an amusement not a means of transportation.

to Crystal Beach in 1896 and closed after three unsuccessful seasons fail to mention that John Rebstock was a major investor, along with Thomas Snyder. Until research for this volume, Rebstock's (and Snyder's) involvement with the Peg Leg was a well kept secret for more than 110 years.

Diehard traditionalists will continue to subscribe to the romantic history of Crystal Beach in spite this analysis to the contrary. The initial research began only to find more information about the park as a religious retreat as it existed in 1888 and 1889, but nothing was found. It is curious that the "elements" of the traditional history parallel verifiable events of the Crystal Beach International Assembly of 1895/1896.

Ultimately, John Rebstock opened a resort 1890 that became the center of summer amusement and entertainment for Western New York and Southern Ontario residents for 100 seasons. At the time of this writing, the 25th anniversary of its passing is fast approaching. The three volumes that capture the history of Crystal Beach Park pale in comparison to experiencing the park. Even during its declining years, Crystal Beach Park had an ambiance that today's major theme parks will never have.

Harvey Holzworth collection.

Harvey Holzworth collection.

Appendix

Known Officials of the Lake Erie Excursion Company

LAST	FIRST	POSITION	YR START	COMMENTS
Jenkins	Oliver	Director	1899	Prior to Cleveland interest buy-in. Unknown if held through 1906
Rebstock	Joseph	Director	1899	Prior to Cleveland interest buy-in. Unknown if held through 1906
Rebstock	John E.	Manager	1899	Through 1907
Fisher	Henry S.	Unknown	1899	Stockholder - unknown if he held an office
Newman	Thomas F.	President	1907	Through 1923
Bradley	E.L.	Director	1907	Through 1923
Brown	Harry	Vice Pres	1907	
Fisher	Henry S.	General Mgr	1907	Through 1917
Green	Frank W.	Excursion Agent - Bflo	1907	
Horagan	F.J.	Transportation Mgr.	1907	
Meyers	A.J.	General Auditor	1908	
Rogers	Herbert B.	Manager	1907	Through 1912
Smith	Edward	Director	1908	
St. Mary	F.J.	Excursion Agent - Bflo	1909	
Stagg	George H.	Excursion Agent - Bflo	1910	At least through 1914.
Fagan	Walter E.	General Passenger	1911	
McAlpine	M.J.	Assistant Park Mgr	1912	
Worthington	George W.	Director	1912	
McAlpine	M.J.	Park Mgr	1913	Through 1917
Brian	H.J.	Auditor	1914	At least through 1918
Klehn	William H.	Excursion Agent - Bflo	1914	At least through 1918
McAlpine	M.J.	General Mgr	1918	Through 1923
Nagel	Jacob	Park Superintendent	1918	Through 1923

Principals of the Crsystal Beach Steamboat and Ferry Company, 1892

LAST	FIRST
Boland	James
Fell	George E,
Galvin	Michael A.
Green	Walter D.
Harris	Jabesh
Hickman	Arthur W.
Jenkins	Oliver
Johnson	John
Knight	Erastus
Leslie	William H.
Little	Henry H.
Minard	Dayton A.
Rebstock	John E.

A New Ferry Company.
RDC, January 26, 1892

Crystal Beach Officials Prior to Buy-in by the Lake Erie Excursion Company

Last	First	Title	Start	Coments
Knight	Erastus C.	Secretary	1891	
Blackman	D.C.	General Passenger Agent	1892	At least through 1893
Cribb	F. R.	Superintendent	1892	
Hickman	Arthur	President	1892	At least through 1895
Rebstock	John E.	General Mgr	1892	Through 1907.
Willats	A.C.	Amusement Director	1892	
Clark	Charles A.	General Passenger & Ticket Agent	1893	
Clark	Charles A.	Secretary	1894	
Fitzpatrick	John C.	General Manager	1895	
Jenkins	Oliver	Park Manager	1897	
Palmer	William	Secretary	1897	
Jenkins	Oliver	Treasurer	1898	
Cummings, T.F. and Dendy, Mr.		Midway Managers - carousel, bowling alley, boating, fishing, the pony ring, and a new ride – the aerial swings.	1900	Of Nashville, TN, and Omaha, NE.
Garfield	B.M.	Assistant Park Manger	1901	Through 1907.
Doyle	J. P.	Press and advertising agent	1902	
Lee, Mr.		Manager	1905	
Rebstock	Stephen	Bathouse Manager	1905	At least through 1906
Willats	Arthur C.	Park Superintendant	1907	

**Local resorts in competition with
Crystal Beach during its early years.**

RESORT	LOCATION	OFFICIALS	YEAR	AMENITIES/COMMENTS
Bedell House	Grand Island, NY - Just north of Elmwood Beach on the East Channel of Niagara River	Ossian Bedell, John W. Bedell	1876-1988	Hotel, restaurant, concerts, boating, fishing bathing, cycling, dancing
Seabreeze	Rochester, NY	Norris Family	1879 - Present	Initially a picnic grove. Rides start appearing circa 1900.
Fort Erie Grove Later known as Fort Erie Beach and Erie Beach	Fort Erie, Ontario	Benjamin & Edwin Baxter and W.B. Pierce, Fred Weber, Frank Bardol	1885-1930	Hotel, dancing, baseball, boating, bathing, fishing, amusement rides.
Eagle Park	Grand Island, NY, south of Windsor Beach	M. Miller	1891-1912	
Lotus Point	Farnham, NY	International Ferry Company	1891	Camping, cottages
Queen's Hotel	Navy Island, Ontario	Harbrecht & Bailey	1891, 1892, 1893	Hotel
Sheenwater	Grand Island, NY - midway on west side of Grand Island shore.	Oliver C. Howard	1891, 1892	Hotel, Picnic Grove, roller coaster, toboggan slides, steam riding gallery
Sour Spring Grove	Grand Island, NY - Across from Tonawanda	Leonard Hauenstein	1891, 1892, 1893	Large Pavillion, Picnic grove, 4 bowling alleys, baseball grounds, concerts
Woodlawn Beach	So. Shore of Lake Erie (Lackawanna)		1892 - 1899	Beach, concerts, dancing pavillion, dining hall, picnic grove, camp grounds, merry-go-round, hotel
Eldoraro Beach	Grand Island		1892-1893	Athletic grounds, bathing beach, bowling alleys, concerts, dancing, water toboggan, restaurant
Edgewater	Grand Island - North Grand Island Shore across from North Tonawanda.	William Voetsch, Jr.	1893 -1904	Hotel, picnic grove, boating, fishing, restaurant, bowling alleys, billiard & pool rooms, toboggan slide,
Elmwood Beach (Elmwood on Niagara, 1901)	Grand Island		1894 - 1901	Vaudeville, Dancing, beach, boating, fishing, bowling. Later Beaver Island State Park
Windsor Park	Grand Island - On west Channel of Niagara River, south of Navy Island.		1894	Beach
Iroquois Beach	Port Colborne, Ontario		1894	Managed by J.H. rebstock, offices at Room 6, Main & Niagara & 584 Main Street.
Niagara View Grove	Grand Island, across from Tonawanda Island		1894	
Coney Island	Probably Grand Island		1901	Vaudeville, dancing, bowling, fishing, athletic field, picnic grounds.
Olcott Beach	Lake Ontario north of Lockport		1902 -1913	Concerts, beach, row boats, hotels, fishing, dancing, restaurants, lunch rooms, picnic grove.
Athletic Park (Changed to Luna Park - 1907) (Changed to Carnival Court)	Buffalo, NY. Main & Jefferson)		1904, 1905 1906 1907 1918-1926	Figure 8, old Mill, Carousel, Vaudeville, dancing, Circle Swing, Katzenjammer Castle, House of Trouble, Dante's Inferno, Trip to Mars, Cave of the Winds, Myth City, Temple of Myrth.
Idlewild	Grand Island	B.M. Garfield, Manager, President Lee, Secretary Maxwell.	1904	Dancing, bowling alleys, hotel, restaurant, ice cream and theater buildings, baseball grounds, swings and tables.
Bay View Beach	So. Shore of Lake Erie, south of Woodlawn beach		1908-1911	Beach, roller skating, Roller coaster "Drop the Dip", restaurant, hotel, dance hall

1946 CRYSTAL BEACH ROSTER

Crystal Beach Transit Company

George C. Hall	President and G.M.
Charles Laube	Vice President
Charles Diebold Jr.	Secretary
F.L. Hall	Acting G.M.
Edwin Stumpf	General Passenger Agent
Francis Coghlan	Assistant Passenger Agent
Jacob Nagel	Park Superintendent
James T. Mitchell	Assistant G.M.

Concessionaires

Concession Amusement Company		Crystal Beach Co. Ltd.	Aeroplane Swings
George C. Hall	Owner		Auto Racer
Francis Coghlan	Manager with		Caterpillar
	Edward Hall and		Giant Coaster
	George C. Hall Jr.		Ferris Wheel
Owns and operates:	Miniature Golf		Old Mill
	Octopus		Laff in the Dark
	Kandy Land		Bathing Beach
	Candy Stand		Crystal Ballroom (Managed by Harold Austin)
Mrs. Leo Smith	Archery, Check Stand 1		
Nik-o-Lock Co.	Automatic toilets		
Carrie & John Seubert	Bathhouse	**Hey Dey Co. Ltd.**	Hey Dey
Herbert White	Bowling Alleys		
Mike Provino	Billiard Tables	**LeJeune Brothers**	Miniature Railway
Ella May Sherrif	Check stand	**Stewart H Gibson**	New Water Scooter
Harriet Devine	Devine Darts	**Thomas F. Dillon**	Pony Track
D.B.H. Co. Ltd.	Dodgem	**Patty Conklin**	Kiddie Land
Crystal Scooter Co.	Carousel	**John O. Dexter**	Roller Rink
Cyclone Coaster Co.	Cyclone Coaster	**William O. Bruce**	Shooting Gallery
		Bug Company Ltd.	Tumble Bug
Slim Nugent	Fascination Game		
	Pin Game	**Canadian Amusement Company**	
	8 smaller games	**4 Knapp Bros.**	Owner
			Penny Arcade
Midway Restaurant Ltd.			Fun House
Charles Laube	Owner		New Magic Carpet
	Lunch Pavilion		
	Hot Dog Stand	Source:	
	Ice Cream Stand	Crystal Beach Hits New record Business	
	10 stands total	Billboard. August 3, 1946	

Some of these concessionaires were probably owned by George Hall Sr., including the Cyclone Coaster Co. which was under the operation of Concessions Amusement Company at the time of the Amos Weidrich tragedy in 1938.

Rebstock Canadian Land Transactions

Rebstock U.S. Land Transactions

Description	$	Source
The proposed extension of the NYCRR through lower Black Rock to Germania Park through the propoerty owned by Mr. Rebstock will be convenient for shipping.		BX. 9/12/1886
AER to Louisa D Schults East side of Tonawanda St near Bush	$200	BX 8/3/1888
AER to Jennie Tilson Roesch Ave north side, east of Tonawanda St	$162	BX 7/3/1889
AER to Mary C Moffatt Roesch Ave north side east of Tonawanda St	$150	BX 7/3/1889
AER to Abram Watty Tonawanda St east side south of O'Niell	$500	BX 7/3/1889
AER to Frank T Burns West Ave west side North of Bird ave	$8,500	BX 1/17/1890
AER to Alicia Hughes West Ave west side north of Bird Ave	$3,500	BX 1/3/1890
Mrs. Alice E. Rebstock is building three frame cottages on Bradley Street near Hawley Street.		BX 2/21/1891
The North Park Land Association purchased 29 acres of land in North Buffalo from Mr. Rebstock, the stove dealer. The purchase price and the precise location of the acreage was not given for publication.		BC 8/31/1897.

AER = Alice E. Rebstock

1956 Crystal Beach Park and Village Riot Arrests
(Excludes Canadiana Incidents)

Name	Abjudication
Michael Guzzio	Failed to appear at trial. Bail ($250) forfieted and a warrant issued for his arrest though could only be served if Guzzio returned to Canada.
Tony Pinto	Convicted of creating a disturbance, fined $350, and deported.
Peter Giglia	Convicted of creating a disturbance, fined $250, and deported.
Leo DiGiulio	Convicted of creating a disturbance, fined $300, and deported.
Reginald James	Convicted of carrying concealed weapons. Charges of creating a distrubance were dismissed. Fined $300 and deported.
James Carswell	Convicted of carrying concealed weapons. Charges of creating a distrubance were dismissed. Fined $200 and deported.
Maxwell McCullough	Charges of creating a distrubance were dismissed.
James Pickens	Charges of creating a distrubance were dismissed.

Source: "5 Youths Fined for Roles in Crystal Beach Clash" BCE 6/14/1956

Instr. Number	Date						1st Party		2nd Party		$	Type	Comments
	Transaction			Recorded									
	M	D	Y	M	D	Y	Last	First	Last	First			
5,488	6	1	1887	6	11	1887	Dickout	Elenor and Melissa	Rebstock	Alice	$8,500	Deed	
5,489	6	1	1887	6	11	1887	Rebstock	Alice and John	Ontario Loan & Savings Co.		$7,500	Mortgage	
6,642	12	20	1890	1	3	1891	Rebstock	Alice and John	Lake Erie Sand Company Ltd.		$1	Deed	35 Acres composed of parts of lots 25 and 26
6,643	12	20	1890	1	3	1891	Rebstock	Alice and John	Lake Erie Sand Company Ltd.		$1	Deed	Same as above for NYS record
7,231	3	18	1892	5	2	1892	Lake Erie Sand Company		Palmer	William	$1	Deed	35 Acres composed of parts of lots 25 and 26, plus 39 acres under water.
7,232	3	28	1892	5	2	1892	Palmer	William	Crystal Beach Steamboat & Ferry Co.		$70,000	Deed	35 Acres composed of parts of lots 25 and 26, plus 39 acres under water.
7,233	3	28	1892	5	2	1892	Crystal Beach Steamboat & Ferry Co.		Palmer	William	$287,000	Mortgage	35 Acres composed of parts of lots 25 and 26, plus 39 acres under water.
7,233	3	28	1892	5	2	1892	Crystal Beach Steamboat & Ferry Co.		Palmer	William	$100,000	Mortgage	cb-land, building, docks, improvements, furniture and fixtures in buildings, all small boats, tools, implements
7,233	3	28	1892	5	2	1892	Crystal Beach Steamboat & Ferry Co.		Palmer	William	$13,000	Mortgage	steamer pearl
7,233	3	28	1892	5	2	1892	Crystal Beach Steamboat & Ferry Co.		Palmer	William	$74,000	Mortgage	ferry rights cash
7,233	3	28	1892	5	2	1892	Crystal Beach Steamboat & Ferry Co.		Palmer	William	$100,000	Mortgage	ferry rights bonds
8,408	8	1	1895	8	2	1895	Cutler	Eber	Crystal Beach International Assembly		$243.66	Mechanics Lien	
12,400	11	17	1906	12	31	1906	Rebstock	Alice & John	Lake Erie Excursion Co.		$1.00	Deed	
274	9	18	1922	9	22	1922	Rebstock	John & Mamie	Lake Erie Excursion Co.		$2.00	Deed	1/4 interest to LEEC
276	8	29	1922	9	22	1922	Rebstock	John & Mamie	Lake Erie Excursion Co.		$2.00	Deed	All interest in land to LEEC
275	9	11	1922	9	22	1922	Mason	Louise	Lake Erie Excursion Co.		$2.00	Deed	1/4 interest to LEEC. Per last will & testament

Mamie Rebstock is John Rebstock's second wife.

Fort Erie Historical Museum Files.

A Day at Crystal Beach in 1935

A special interest reporter, Roseberry traveled to various attractions throughout the Niagara Frontier and wrote about the attraction and the associated expense of what he considered a typical day trip. On August 10, 1935, he spent a day at Crystal Beach. He rode the Cyclone, Lindy Loop, Dodg 'em, Old Mill, and the Fun House. He considered the injuries he endured from tumbles he had taken while roller skating to be far worse than any discomfort he felt on from the rides which vanquished all his inhibitions about riding them. He itemized the following expenses:

Trolley Fare .... 20 cents
Boat Fare .... 35 cents
Bathhouse use .... 25 cents
Two hot dogs .... 20 cents
Orangeade .... 10 cents
Ball throwing games 35 cents
Dart throwing game .. 10 cents
Penny Arcade .... 20 cents
Roller skating .... 40 cents
Amusement Rides.... 60 cents
Dancing .... 25 cents
TOTAL $3.00

Crystal Beach Ride Inventory

Big Eli Wheel 5, serial no 784-47 was a pale comparison to the Aristocrat.

Aerial Swings (Next to Razzle Dazzle partially seen in photo on page 20) 1900c – 1910c
Aerolite Swing 1895?
Aeroplane Swing 1925c – 1937c
Aeropractor 1934
Airborne (Paratrooper) 1964-1966; 1971-1972
Antique Cars (alongside dance hall) 1964-1989
Arctic Cat 1974
Auto Racer 1929-1941
Auto Scooter 1948-1989
Auto Scooter II 1977-1987
Auto Speedway 1942-1980c
Avalanche 1970-1977c
Backety-Back 1908-1926
Bug House 1920c-1929c
Bump the Bumps 1906-1924
Cake Walk 1910-1911c
Carousel (Unknown Mfg.) 1904-1911c
Carousel (Herschell) 1985-1989
Carousel (PTC#12) 1912-1984
Carousel (Steam) 1892c-1903c
Caterpillar 1924-1964 (absent 1931-1938c for Lindy Loop)
Chuck Wagon 1969
Cinema 180 1978-1981c
Circle Swing 1905-1924c
Circus 1930-1939
Comet 1948-1989
Crystal Mirror Maze 1955-?
Custer Cars 1925-1934c
Cyclone 1927-1946
Dodgem 1922-1924c
Ferris Wheel 1985-1989 **(see auction Brochure for Mfg.)**
Ferris Wheel (On Beach) 1896c-?
Ferris Wheel (at Backety-Back) 1914c-1924c
Ferris Wheel (Eli Bridge) 1925-1980c
Ferris Wheel (Replaced Eli Bridge) 1984c
Figure 8 1907-1916
Flitzer 1974-1981
Flume 1967
Flying Bobs 1970; 1979-1989 (possibly absent for 1980)
Flying Chairs 1974-1989

Flying Coaster 1962-1977 (possibly absent 1964)
Flying Scooters 1942-1961c
Fly-o-Plane 1967
Fun House 1927-1948
Galaxy 1986
Giant Coaster 1917-1989
Gravitron 1988
Hey Dey 1926-1979c
Holiday Bounce 1974-1975
Hot Rod Racer 1957-1959
House that Jack Built 1910-1924
Hurricane/Saturn 6 1952; 1972-1974 (possibly absent 1973)
Hustler 1973
Jolly Roger 1977-1983c
Joyland 1920c-1929c
Laff in the Dark 1936-1989
Lindy Loop 1931-1938c
Looper 1952-1974c
Magic Carpet 1946-1971
Magic Palace 1972-1989
Merry Mix-up 1924 (possibly 1923-1925)
Miniature Railway (Steam Locos) 1908c-1947
Miniature Railway (Streamliner) 1948-1961
Miniature Railway (Frontier) 1962-1989
Missouri Mule 1929-1933c
Monster 1974-1988
Moon Rocket 1950; 1958-1959; 1972-1973
Motorboat Speedway 1931-1947
Musik Express 1980-1988c
Mystery 1917 (possibly 1916-1919)
Octopus 1938-1953c
Octopus (Double) 1960-1967c
Old Mill 1914c-1964
Old Mill as Dreamland 1910c-1913
Old Mill as Jungle Land 1965-1977
Old Mill as Scenic Rivers 1908c-1910c
Olympic Bob 1964-1965
Pirate 1980-1989
Razzle Dazzle 1895-1907c
Rocket Ships 1947-1959c
Rock-o-Plane 1950-1952; 1955; 1968-1969; 1972-1973
Roll-o-Plane 1943-1948c; 1963-1965; 1970-

1973c
Roto Jet 1961-1962; 1972c
Rotor 1956-1959c; 1972-1974
Round-Up 1955c; 1971-1973; 1977-1978c
Saw Mill River 1981-1989
Scrambler 1957-1989
Sea Swing 1922-1938c
Sky Ride 1965-1989
Sky Diver 1972-1973
Space Whirl 1968-1969
Spider 1968-1973
Spook Alley 1940-1944c
Steeple Chase 1917-1929c
Texas Revolver 1977-1979
Tilt-a-Whirl 1978-1989c
Tip-Top 1977c-1989
Tractor Ride 1928 possibly 1927-1929
Tumble Bug 1926-1966
Turnpike 1961-1971c
Twister 1954-1959c
Twister (Hey Dey style) 1975
Water Scooter 1947-1989
Crown (Super Duper) **Mountain** Water Slide 1978-1989
Whip 1918c-1929c
Wild Mouse 1959-1980c
Zipper 1973
Zugspitze 1966-1969

Gadabout
Over the Falls
Switchback Railway 1893?
Trip to the North Pole 1910
Water Bike 1934-1937

The Tractor Ride took riders around the midway in viewing wagons that must have been difficult to negotiate through the crowds on busy days. An obvious home-made concession, its life span was unlikely more than a season.

This inventory was compiled from ride names appearing as part of the park's line-up in newspaper advertisements, park press releases, photographs. Years designated with a "c" are approximate for the year it appeared, or its final year on the midway. It is not intended to be a definitive inventory, only comprehensive.

Carousel Auction Prices	
Piece	Final Bid
Chariot 1	$4,000
Chariot 2	$4,000
St. Bernard	$29,000
Wolf	$8,500
Lion	$28,000
Giraffe	$22,000
Horse in Armor Plate	$19,500
Tiger	$18,500

1989 Auction - Major Items	
Ride	Final Bid
Comet	$210,000
Pirate	$200,000
Monster	$30,000
Ferris Wheel	$11,000
Scrambler	$11,000
Laff in the Dark	$8,000
Bumper Cars	$8,000
Magic Carpet	$5,500
Giant Coaster	$2,500
Lil Dipper (Kiddieland Coaster)	$2,250

Mystery Rides

Gadabout

This was a bumper car ride invented by John Stock. Its predecessor was the "Glideabout" that consisted of three circular 10-passenger cars driven by an operator in each car. Three large battery powered motors put the car in motion.

Only one Glideabout was made in 1918 and was a failure because the cars were heavy, and lumbering. Stock made a number of changes: downsize the cars to four passengers, replace the batteries with power supplied by a pole making contact with the electrically charged ceiling. The name was changed to Gadabout.

All that can be learned about the Gadabout at Crystal Beach is what can be gleaned from an out of focus image (below). Whether its one of Stock's original rides or a transplant from another park remains unknown. It may be a bumper car of a different manufacturer with "Gadabout" painted on the façade. Even the year(s) it was on the Crystal Beach midway is a mystery – if it was in fact at Crystal Beach at all. There is no press relating this ride to the park - its not even certain that the image was photographed at Crystal Beach. Apart from the white-painted tree trunks, there is nothing in the image that definitively identifies this location as Crystal Beach.

Over the Falls

There are references to this ride in other sources, but no images or period documentation that conclusively puts this ride at Crystal Beach.

Mill Chutes are similar to the various Old Mills at Crystal Beach except at the end of the ride on the Mill Chute, the canal boat is hauled up a hill similar to a roller coaster, then it slides down a trough into a pool of water like today's log flume rides. Over the Falls is most likely a Mill Chute, but no evidence exists of a Mill Chute at Crystal Beach. Euclid Beach near Cleveland, Ohio had a mill chute called "Over the Falls." Erie Beach had a mill chute as well, but its name is unknown.

Trip to the North Pole

New for 1910 at Crystal Beach was an attraction called "Trip to the North Pole." Rides with such names typically created the illusion that the riders (sitting in a stationary car) were actually being transported somewhere. There were a number of such "rides" at the Pan Am and other amusement parks with names such as "Trip to the Moon." An advertisement for Crystal Beach called Trip to the North Pole *"very entertaining and instructive."*

Water Bike

This advertised attraction from 1934 through 1937 could have been the Sea Swing that sat in the water on the beach, but descriptions and details remain elusive.

Chautauqua vs. Religious Campground Assembly/Retreat

Religious camp meetings were a Methodist phenomenon, with a platform that was entirely religious. At these meetings, fire and brimstone preachers emphasized the universality of human depravity, compelled sinners to repent and experience salvation by God's grace. During such preaching, the penitent would walk to the front of the auditorium where they would be surrounded by exhorters who would sing and pray over the sinner until he experienced the "conversion" of God's grace, relieving despair.

Night preaching was tribal. The mournful cries of sinners overpowered the roar from the flames of the fire altars. Reaching fever pitch at the moment of conversion, the repentant would fall to the ground and tremble like an epileptic having a seizure. There was none of this at the Crystal Beach International Assembly.

The platform of the Chautauqua was improvement of Sunday school teaching techniques and administration through Bible study, teacher training classes, and lectures. Instruction and lecture topics included "Language and Illustration in Teaching" and "Helps of Science in Religious Teaching." Cultural enrichment activities consisted of concerts, recreational activities and devotional exercises. The target participants were primarily Sunday school teachers and church ministers.

After three years the Chautauqua founders recognized that if it was to survive, the instructional programs had to expand and attract a wider and less secular audience. The Chautauqua, for a period, evolved into an accredited university which did not last beyond a few years, but the original Chautauqua survives today as the Chautauqua Institution – a nine week summer center for the arts, education, religion, and recreation.

Known/Confirmed Injuries and Fatalities at Crystal Beach (Park and Beach)

Date	Name	Age	Residence	Incident
08/24/1907	Elmer Metzler	18	Buffalo, NY	Drowned.
06/29/1910	Louise Koch	17	Orchard Park, NY	Died from injuries sustained when thrown from Backety-Back train.
07/05/1910	Harry Croker			Drowned. Broke back while diving.
08/17/1913	Charles Greene	15		Drowned. Broke back while diving.
08/13/1916	Carl Warner	19		Injured while diving.
08/26/1922	Stanley Paine	38	Nia. Falls, Ont.	Drowned. Caught in undertow.
1922	Florence Beam	19	Ridgeway, Ont.	Drowned. Tossed in water when canoe tipped that she stood up in.
09/03/1921	Anna Konowalski		Buffalo, NY	Drowned while swimming near pier.
09/03/1921	Edward Green	30	Buffalo, NY	Drowned while trying to save Anna Konowalski.
07/08/1928	Albert Jarzeniecki	14	Buffalo, NY	Drowned.
06/24/1929	Morris Donahue	22	St. Mary's, Pa.	Drowned following a heart attack.
07/25/1930	Margaret Brady	8	Buffalo, NY	Injured when thrown from Giant Coaster.
08/01/1930	Marian Kormilo	19	Winnipeg, Manitoba	Drowned while learning to swim.
08/10/1936	Marjorie Weber	16	Kenmore, NY	Injured while exiting Ferris Wheel.
05/30/1938	Amos Wiedrich	23	Buffalo, NY	Thrown from Cyclone, crushed by train.
07/12/1940	John Barnes	11	Buffalo, NY	Drowned.
07/17/1964	Anthony Serra	14	Buffalo, NY	Drowned. Broke back while diving.
06/26/1966	Joan Seply		Welland, Ont.	Fell from Airborne ride. Severe head injuries and compound leg fractures.
07/01/1969	Bobbie Hurst	7		Drowned diving off pier.
07/01/1969	Danny Hurst	9		Drowned diving off pier.
06/16/1974	Vicky Langley		Welland, Ont.	Injured from Comet train collision.
06/16/1974	Christine Langley		Welland, Ont.	Injured from Comet train collision.
06/02/1975	Kieran Glynn	26	Stevensville, Ont.	Died from injuries sustained when thrown from Comet.
08/25/1977	Noreen Freeman	28	Hamburg, NY	Injured; Flying Coaster structure failure.
08/25/1977	Elaine Freeman	8	Hamburg, NY	Injured; Flying Coaster structure failure.
08/25/1977	Christina Lagattut	8	Angola, NY	Injured; Flying Coaster structure failure.
07/14/1980	Henry Knutson	24	Ridgeway, Ont.	Park maintenance man electrocuted.
06/03/1990	John Shave	28	Wainfleet, Ont.	Crushed by safe in Penny Arcade during park demolition.

Excludes all incidents involving park steamers.

25 Incidents involing 28 people. 8 incidents involving rides; 15 water incidents; 2 freak accidents.

19 fatalities: 14 involving water; 3 involving roller coasters; 2 freak accidents.

Assets and Liabilities of the Buffalo and Crystal Beach Corporation at Bankruptcy Filing

Assets

Real Estate in Buffalo & Canada	$951,592
Steamer (Canadiana)	$205,330
Auto Race Cars	$7,101
Aeroplane Swing	$4,964
Giant Coaster	$11,610
Ferris Wheel	$4,400
Lindy Loop	$7,809
Penny Arcade	$1,146
Bath House Equipment	$450
Broadcasting Equipment	$2,532
Check stands and ticket booths	$1,766
Ballroom*	$3,325
Playground Equipment	$965
Tables & Benches	$4,042
Fountain & Stand	$2,093
Consessions Amusement Co.**	$100,000
Bflo & Crystal Beach Corp. Capital Stock	$10,000

Liabilities

Taxes	$13,203
Secured Claims	$628,749
Unsecured Claims	$99,925
147 1st Mortgage Bond Holders	$331,700
Walter P. Mattich $18,300	
Second Mortgage Bond Holders	$147,000
Geroge Hall $18,500	
Other Claims	
M&T Trust	$128,000
Erie Beach Co.	$47,500
Steven J. Rebstock	$5,000
Charles Diebold, Jr.	$5,000
George C. Hall	$5,000
Walter P. Mattich	$5,000

*Was most likely the old ballroom used for roller skating starting in 1925.

** Concessions owned and operated rides in Crystal Beach including the Cyclone.

Crystal Beach Lists Assets at $1,756,376. Liabilities of $774,177 Scheduled in Bankruptcy Proceedings by Amusement Concern. BEN May 13, 1932.

Side Friction Track

Under Friction Track

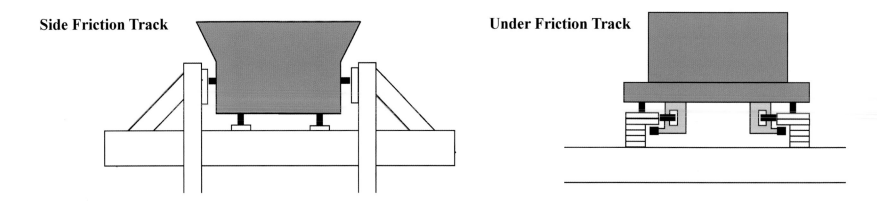

Backety-Back Functionality
These drawings illustrate how the Backety-Back trains "switched" track levels and reversed direction.

The small, round, black dots (A) are special side wheels on the train cars that are captured by a special side rail (B) illustrated by the thin, black parallel lines. The combination of A & B carries the train over the gap in the track until the special side rail ends and the main wheels drop back to the base track (C). The train continues to roll until it stalls at the incline (D). The special side wheels are clearly visible in Figures 8 and 9 on the previous page.

After the stall, the train reverses direction (E). Because the train "dropped" off the special rail at (C), the special wheel is below the side rail at (F) and can not re-engage it. This allows the train to continue in the reverse direction through the gap in the track to the level below (G).

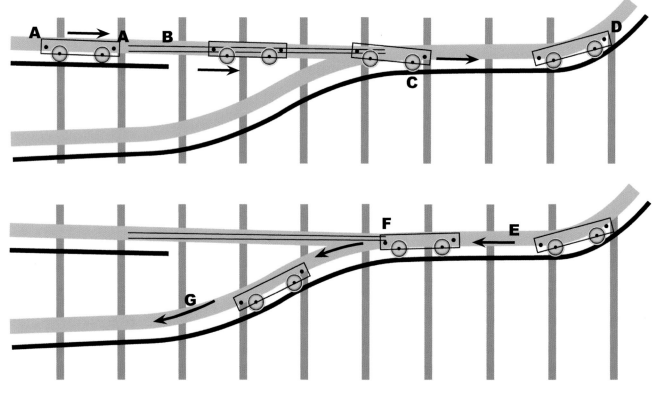

Bibliography

NEWSPAPERS Key:

AEJ – Albany Evening Journal
BC – Buffalo Courier
BCE – Buffalo Courier Express
BCM – Buffalo Commercial Advertiser
BEN – Buffalo Evening News
BET – Buffalo Evening Times
BT – Buffalo Times.
BX – Buffalo Express
FET – Fort Erie Times Review
NFG – Niagara Falls Gazette (NY)
NFR – Niagara Falls Review (Ont)
NYT – New York Times
OSN – Oregon Statesman Newspaper
RDC – Rochester Democrat and Chronicle
SCS – St. Catharines Standard
SJ – Syracuse Journal
SMJ – Statesman Journal, Salem, Oregon
SPS – Syracuse Post Standard.
TDS – Toronto Daily Star
TT – Toronto Telegram
WDT – Watertown Daily Times
WT – Welland Evening Tribune

1890
New Pleasure Resort to be established at Point Abino. BDC, April 12, 1890
Crystal Beach Advertisement. BC, July 16, 1890

Complaining of Asphalt Stench. BX, July 16, 1890

A New Summer Resort. Crystal Beach Near Point Abino to be Made Popular. BC, July 13, 1890.

At Crescent Beach – A New Buffalo Company formed to Make a Coney Island of It. BC, August 17, 1890

1891
An Excursion Steamer Bought to Run to Crystal Beach. BC, March 19, 1891

Crystal Beach Advertisement. BC, June 23, 1891

Crystal Beach Hotel Now Open For the Season. Advertisement. BC, August 14, 1891

Dancing at Crystal Beach. BC, August 28, 1891

1892
Crystal Beach Steamboat and Ferry Company. BX, January 25, 1892

A New Ferry Company. RDC, January 26, 1892

The Shore Resorts. BX, May 2, 1892

Chautauqua is Open. BX, July 3, 1892.

Crystal Beach Advertisement. Select Dancing in the Pavilion. BX, September 13, 1892

1893
Crystal Beach Hotel. It Was Completely Destroyed by Fire Yesterday. BX, May 4, 1893

Lake and River Resorts – The Crystal Beach Line. BX, May 8, 1893

Buffalo Yacht Club's Annual Regatta at Crystal Beach. BX, August 13, 1893.

1894
On the Other Side. BC, August 8, 1894

1895
At Crystal Beach. International Assembly on the Chautauqua Plan. BC, May 13, 1895.
A Gigantic Project. The Crystal Beach International Assembly. BC, June 8, 1895.

Well Known Men. The President and Chancellor of the New Assembly. BC, June 10, 1895.

Crystal Beach Assembly. Preaching at the Auditorium by the Colored Demosthenes. BC, June 29, 1895

Summer Programme. Exercises to be Held at Crystal Beach Assembly. BC, June 30, 1895.

The Opening Day. The Inauguration of the International Assembly. Buffalo Courier. July 2, 1895.

Sermons and Songs. Doings at Crystal Beach's International Assembly. BC, July 10, 1895.

Over the Water. Large Audiences at the Daily Sessions of the Assembly. BC, July 12, 1895.

At Crystal Beach. BC, July 19, 1895

Interesting Days. Proceedings of the International Assembly Across the Lake. BC, July 24, 1895.

At Crystal Beach. Programme of Concerts to be Given at the Assembly. BC, August 2, 1895.

Crystal Beach Assembly. BC, August 16, 1895.

At Crystal Beach. Congressman Howard of Alabama and Evangelist. BC, August 21, 1895.

Sam Jones at Crystal Beach. BC, August 22, 1895

At Crystal Beach. BC, September 6, 1895.

1896
Point Abino. Its Beauties and People to be Found There. BX, July 13, 1896.

Camp Life. BX, July 18, 1896

1897
Crystal Beach Hotel. Now Open For the Season. BC, August 27, 1897.

1898
None

1899
Stock Companies – The Lake Erie Excursion Company. RDC, May 25, 1899

At Crystal Beach. Season Will Open on Saturday. BX, May 26, 1899.

Boats Were Crowded. BX, May, 31, 1899.

Not Enough Boats. BX, June 5, 1899.
For the Union Station, BX, June 4, 1899.

1900
Crystal Beach. Buffalo's Coney Island Open for the Season. BX, May 29, 1900

Storm's Havoc in Buffalo. NYT, Sept. 13, 1900

Won't Delay The Fair. Buildings Damaged by the Storm. BX, September 13, 1900

Crystal Beach All Right. BX, September 14, 1900

High Winds Troubled Boats. BX, November 12, 1900

1901
Crystal Beach's Opening. BX, May 24, 1901

1902
Crystal Beach for $48,000. Buffalo's "Coney Island" Sold to the Lake Erie Excursion Company." TDS, February 28, 1902

Boat Was Crowded. BX, May 31, 1902

Crystal Beach. BX, July 17, 1902.

Fifty Boats Beached. Many Wrecked in Buffalo by Severe Storm. SJ, August 8, 1902.

1903
Crystal Beach Boats. Three Good Ones Promised. Dock Rebuilt. BX, April 26, 1903

1904
Crystal Beach. BC, June 11, 1904.
Vast Improvements at Crystal Beach. BC, July 30, 1904.

1905
None

1906
Crystal Beach Line. Big Improvements. BCM, April 6, 1906.
Crystal Beach Ready For Opening. BC, June 22, 1906.

Crystal Beach Rights to be Sold to the Detroit & Buffalo Line." BET, November 1, 1906.

Buy Crystal Beach – Buffalo Company to Purchase Canadian Resort. TDS, November 2, 1906.

1907
For Crystal Beach. Lake Erie Excursion Company Seeking Boats at Detroit. BX, February 20, 1907.

Crystal Beach. Many Improvements Will be Observed There When the Season Opens. BCM, March 28, 1907.

Crystal Beach Opening Is On Decoration Day. BC, May 26, 1907

Crystal Beach Opens Tomorrow. BCM, May 29, 1907.

Crystal Beach Advertisement. 4th of July at Crystal Beach. BC, June 30, 1907.

To Manage Crystal Beach Line. BX, December 8, 1907

1908
Crystal Beach. Steamer Americana scheduled to make her first trip tomorrow. BX, May 28, 1908

Crystal Beach in New Dress is Drawing Thousands. BX, June 7, 1908.

At Crystal Beach. BX, July 4, 1908.

1909
Crystal Beach Welcomes Crowds Tomorrow. BC, May 28, 1909.

Crystal Beach Open. BX, May 30, 1909.

New Attractions – Crystal Beach. BC, June 6, 1909.

1910
Crystal's Opening. BX,. May 22, 1910.
Opening Night – Saturday May 28th, 1910. Crystal Beach Advertisement. FET, 1910

Crystal Beach Endless Fun Along the Midway. Advertisement. BX, June 19, 1910.

Schoolgirl Crushed Dead. BX, June 23, 1910

Girl Crushed Dead. BX, June 23, 1910

Buffalo Girl Victim of Scenic Railway. SPS, June 23, 1910.

Miss Louise Koch will be buried on Sunday. BX, June, 25, 1910.

A Terrible Accident. FET, June 30, 1910.

Buffalo Times Special Children's Day at Crystal Beach. Advertisement. BT, July 3, 1910.

Advertisement. BT, July 3, 1910.

1911

Crystal Beach In Spring Blizzard Widening the Cut. BC, Week ending April 9,1911.

Crystal Beach to Open. BX, May 7, 1911.

At Beaches and Resorts. BX, May 28, 1911,

Beaches and Resorts. BX, August 27, 1911.

1912

May 29th is Opening Day. BX, May 5, 1912

First Trip to Crystal Beach to be Made on Wednesday. BX, May 26, 1912.

Crystal Opens Today. BX, May 29, 1912.

Thousands Visit Beach. BX, May 31, 1912.

$14,000 Blaze at Crystal. Dreamland Damaged by Fire. BX, July 12, 1912

1913

To Manage Lakeside Park. RDC, February 17, 1913.

Crystal Beach to Open May 29. BC, May 11, 1913

1914

Beach Soon to be Open. BX, May 10, 1914
Crystal Beach to Open May 28. BC, May 10, 1914.

Opening of Lake Beaches. BX, May 24, 1914

Maple Beach Park to be Again on the Map. AEJ, June 20, 1914.

Thousands at Beach. BX, July 5, 1914.

1915

$60,000 Fire at Crystal, Business Block at Beach is Wiped Out. BX, May 21, 1915.

At Beaches and Resorts. BX, May 23, 1915.

1916

Crystal Beach Opens Saturday. BX, May 21, 1916.
At Beaches and Resorts. BX, August 6, 1916.

1917

Crystal Beach Open May 29th. BX, May 6, 1917.

Crystal Beach Opening. BX, May 20, 1917

Crystal Beach. Buffalo's Popular Lakeside Resort to Offer Many New Attractions. BT, May 27, 1917.

Crystal Beach Season Opens Next Tuesday. BC, May 27, 1917.

Crystal Beach Opens Tuesday. BX, May 27, 1917.

Great Throng Passes Day at Crystal Beach. BC, May 31, 1917.

Crystal Beach in Full Swing. BX, June 3, 1917.

At Beaches and Resorts. BX, June 16, 1917.

1918

Crystal Beach to open for season next Wednesday. BX, May 19, 1918

At Beaches and Resorts. BX, May 26, 1918.

1919

Crystal Beach Sewers. BX, April 14, 1922.

New Dance Hall to be Built at Crystal Beach. BX, April 27, 1919

Crystal Beach Opens Wednesday For New Season. BC, May 25, 1919

Thousands Watch Thrilling Rescue at Crystal Beach. BX, July 14, 1919

Record Crowd at Beach, 50 Faint in Jam at Dock. BX, July 24, 1919

1920

Crystal Beach to open for season coming Thursday. BX, May 23, 1920.

Crystal Beach Opening. BX, May 25, 1920.

1921

Recreation Pier at Crystal Beach Ready for Season. BX, May 15, 1921.

Giant New Pier is Dedicated at Crystal Beach BX, May 27, 1921.

1922

Crystal Beach Will Open on the Queen's Day. BX, May 7, 1922

Subway to the Docks. BX, March 12, 1922.

1923

Dynamite Used to Prevent Spread of Flames at Resort. AEJ, June 28, 1923

Fire Destroys Crystal Beach Hotel (Royal) BC, June 29, 1923.

Used Dynamite to Stop $90,000 Fire at Crystal Beach. BC, June 29, 1923

Crystal Beach Fire Stopped by Dynamite. BX, June 29, 1923

Crystal Beach Resort is sold for $2,000,000. TDS, November 23, 1923

1924

New Incorporations. NYT, January 27, 1924.
Plan Big Improvement at Crystal Beach Park. BC, March 30, 1924

New Crystal Beach Promise of Management. BX, March 30, 1924.

Crystal Beach Changes Hands for $1,000,000. BX, March 27, 1924

Crystal Beach Prepares for Automobilists. BX, April 6, 1924

Crystal Beach Docks Reached by New Subway. BX, May 4, 1924.

Crystal Beach Opens Season on Victoria Day. BX, May 18, 1924.

1924 Season Now Open at Crystal Beach. BX, May, 25, 1924

Many Forms of Enjoyment at Crystal Beach. BX, July 27, 1924

Bathing Beach Popular With Picnic Throngs. BX, August 3, 1924

At Crystal Beach. BX, August 7, 1924

Roller Rink is Wrecked First. BT, October 12,1924.

1925

New $250,000 Dance Hall at Crystal Beach. BX, May 10, 1925

Crystal Beach Will Present New Features. BX, May 17, 1925

Crystal Beach Season Opens on Thursday. BX, May 24, 1925

Crystal Beach Dedicates its New Ballroom. BX, June 22, 1925

$250,000 Ballroom at Crystal Beach is Formally Dedicated. BX, June 24, 1925.

Cooling Ride Sunday Night on Americana. BX, July 12, 1925.

1926

Crystal Beach Season Opens This Thursday. BX, May 23, 1926

1927

Crystal Beach to Open May 28th. BCE, May 8, 1927.

Crystal Beach Ready For Opening Saturday. BCE, May 24, 1927

Preparing for Opening. BT, May 15, 1927

Crystal Beach Ready to Open. BT, May 22, 1927

Crystal Beach Season Opened. BT, May 29, 1927

Large Crowd at Opening of Crystal Beach. BCE, May 29, 1927.

Two Lake Trips Today on Crystal Beach Line. BCE, May 29, 1927

Thousands at Beach Opening. BET, May 29, 1927.

Take Ride on Crystal Beach Boat. BT, June 5, 1927 (CYC rapidly approaching completion)

Crystal Beach's Latest Thriller. BT, July 3, 1927. (Final Tests July 1, 1927).

Largest All-Steel Coaster Ready at Crystal Beach. BCE, July 3, 1927.

Cyclone Coaster. New Feature at Crystal Beach Ready Monday. BET, July 2, 1927.

Crystal Beach Ready for 4th. BT, July 3, 1927.

Crystal Beach – A Delightful Place for Healthful Summer Pleasure. BET, August 7, 1927.

1928
None

1929

Crystal Beach to Open 1929 Season May 29. BCE, May 26, 1929

Hundreds Take Advantage of Crystal Beach 'News' Day. BEN, June 21,1929.

Crystal Beach Whoopee Rides Cut Fares for New Coupons. BEN, July 9, 1929.

1930

Crystal Beach Midway Daily Becomes Bigger. BCE, May 11, 1930.

First Boat Leaves for Crystal Beach. BEN, May 28, 1930.

Thousands Gather at Crystal Beach. BEN, July 3, 1930.

1931

Only One Criminal Case on Calendar at Spring Assizes. NFG February 25, 1931.

$8,000 Damages Allowed by Jury For Girl Injuring Girl. NFG, March 6, 1931

Crystal Beach Plans Outlined For 1931 Season. BCE, April 26, 1931.

1932

Resort Operators File Bankruptcy. BEN, April 8, 1932.

Joseph Becker Names Crystal Beach Trustee. BEN, April 23, 1932.

Prepare to Name Receivers for Beach. BT, April 23, 1932.

Crystal Beach Lists Assets at $1,756,376. BEN, May 18, 1932.

Ready for Opening. BCE, May 21, 1932.

1933

Canadian Resort Will Open May 29. BEN, May 17, 1933.

Crystal Beach Adds Power Boat Course. BEN May 24, 1933.

First Crystal Beach Coupon To Appear in News Saturday. BEN, June 23, 1933.

1934
Remember Beach Coupons Before Summer Slips By. BEN, July 24, 1934.
1935
Crystal Beach Firm Opposes Taxing Method. BCE, May 17, 1935.

Many Amusements Open to Crystal Beach Coupons. BEN, June 27, 1935.

Vacation Thrift at New High as Reporter Goes to Crystal. BEN, August 10, 1935.

1936
Coupons for Crystal Beach Again Offered by News. BEN, June 22, 1936.

Uncanny Thrills Furnished by Ride at Crystal Beach. BEN, July 15, 1936.

Crystal Closes Its Best Season in 9-Year Span. BCE, September 8, 1936.

1937
Crystal Beach to Offer New 1937 Feature. BCE, May 23, 1937.

Crystal Beach Ready for Opening Monday. Buffalo's Coney Island Will Celebrate 47th Gala Season." BCE, May 28, 1937.

47th Season at Crystal Beach is Begun Gaily. BCE, June 1, 1937.

$3,000 Damage Action Brought Against Beach. BCE, June 18, 1937.

Girl who sued Crystal Beach awarded $1,500. BCE, June 19, 1937.

News Coupons Cut Costs of Crystal Beach Rides. BEN, July 19, 1937.

1938
Crystal Beach Adds Octopus to Fun Devices. BCE, April 17, 1938.

Crystal Beach to Open With Gala Program. BCE, May 15, 1938.

Tragedy Seen by Scores at Crystal Beach." BCE, May 31, 1938.

Man Dies in Plunge from Roller Coaster." Buffalo Evening News, May 31, 1938.

Inquest to be Held Monday in Coaster Death. BCE, June 1, 1938.

$100,000 to be asked for Coaster Car Death." Courier Express, June 18, 1938.

Estate of Dead Buffalo Man Now Suing for $25,000 in Fatality at Crystal Beach." Fort Erie Times Review, November 30, 1938.

Safety Bar Failed, Witness in Coaster Death Suit Says." Buffalo Courier Express, November 30, 1938

1939
Liquidation of C&B Company Wins Approval. BCE, May 27, 1939.

Buffalo's $2,000,000 Playground Celebrates is 49th Successful Season. Crystal Beach Advertisement. BCE, May 29, 1939.

15,000 Persons Go to Beach as Season Begins. BCE, May 31, 1939.

Buffalo Nickel Day. Crystal Beach Advertisement. BCE, August 23, 1939.

Safety Bar Failed, Witness in Coaster Death Suit Says. BCE, Nov. 30, 1939.

1940
Crystal Beach to Celebrate Jubilee Event. BCE, April 28, 1940.

Laffing Man's Debut Awaits Beach Opening. BCE, May 26, 1940.

Harry S. Hall, Beach Figure, Dies Suddenly. BCE, June 15, 1940

Jubilee Dance is Planned at Crystal Beach. BCE, July 14, 1940.

Beach to Mark Anniversary With Costume Ball Tonight. BCE, July 16, 1940

1941
Saturday, June 14th is Nickel Day at Crystal Beach. Crystal Beach Advertisement. BCE, June 13, 1941.

1942
Crystal Beach All Set For Memorial Day. BCE, May 28, 1942

Thursday August 27 is Nickel Day. BEN, August 24, 1942.

1943
Opening of beach Set for Tomorrow. BCE, May 28, 1943.

Clip News Coupons Saturday for 1st Bargain Day at Crystal. BEN, June 16, 1943.

Where to go for Fun. BEN, August 28, 1943.

1944
Crystal Beach to Reopen for Season Saturday. BEN, May 23, 1944

1945
Crystal Beach Will Open 55th Season on May 26. BEN, May 12, 1945.

Monday Will Be First News Coupon Day at Crystal Beach. BEN, June 15, 1945.

$50,000 Bathhouse at Crystal Beach Opens Saturday. BEN, June 28, 1945

1946
Crystal Beach will open early with 4 new attractions. BEN, May 11, 1946.
Crystal Beach Will Open On Victoria Day. BCE, May 12, 1946.

Girl Badly Hurt in Park Ride Fall. BCE, June 27, 1946.

Whistles Blow for Last Time on Miniature Trains at Crystal Beach. BEN, September 3, 1946.

Thrill King 20 Seasons Comes Down. TT, September 16, 1946. Fort Erie Museum Files, Ridgeway, Ontario.

Dismantling Famous Cyclone Coaster at Crystal Beach. FET, 1946. Fort Erie Historical Museum Clipping Files.

1947
Beach will Open May 24 with 2 New Attractions. BEN, May 3, 1947.

Advertisement. BEN, May 23, 1947.

Summer's Coming – and so are News Crystal Beach Coupons. BEN June 19, 1947.

1948
Giant Crystal Beach Coaster to Give Most Thrilling Ride. BEN, January 9, 1948.

Cheering Workmen First Riders on New Crystal Beach Comet. BEN, May 12, 1948.

Its Opening Day Once More at Crystal Beach. BEN, May 22, 1948.

Look of Newness Belies 58 Years of Crystal Beach. BEN, June 5, 1948

Coupons for Beach in News tomorrow. BEN, June 23, 1948

1949
Crystal Beach Set for Grand Opening. BCE May 20, 1949

Bright and Shining, Crystal Beach Open for Season. BEN, May, 28, 1949.

70,000 Enter Ft. Erie Bridges too Small for Gigantic Influx. TDS, July 4, 1949.

1950
Crystal Beach Will Present Paved Midway. BCE, May 14, 1950

Crystal Beach Dolls Up, Adds 3 New Thrill Rides. BEN, May 25, 1950.

Crystal Beach Votes to Allow Sunday Sports. BCE June 27, 1950

Amusement Rides at Crystal Beach Now Run Sundays. BEN July 1, 1950

1951
Canadiana Sailing May 26 to Mark Opening of Beach. BEN, May 19, 1951.

Crystal Beach to be Opened Next Saturday. BCE, May 20, 1951

61st Season Opens at Crystal Beach on Full 7-Day Basis.. BEN May 25, 1951

Once-Lively Passenger Trade All But Gone From Lakes. BEN, September 1, 1951.

1952
Crystal Beach Opens May 24. BCE, May 18, 1952.

Crystal Beach Set for Opening Today. BCE, May 24, 1952

Save With Coupons at Crystal Beach; News Day Friday. BEN, June 18, 1952.

2 Miniature Crystal Beach Trains for Sale. BCE, July 6, 1952.

1953
21 Bargain Days Scheduled at Beach for News Readers. BEN, June 17, 1953

Jacob H. Nagel, 78. Crystal Beach Figure. BEN, December 15, 1953.

1954
Sounds of Spring Heard at Crystal. BCE, April 29, 1954.

Roth Heads Crystal Beach Park. BEN, May 5, 1954.

1955
Crystal Beach Opens Season Saturday. BCE, May 25, 1955

1956
Crystal Beach Will Open $55,000 Bingo Building. BCE, May 11, 1956.

Crystal Beach Plans Opening. BCE, May 20, 1956

Terror Marks Boatride. BCE, May 31, 1956.

.Dozen Arrested, Six Injured in Wild Disorders. BEN, May 31, 1956.

50 to 100 Fights Says Injured Man. BCE, May 31, 1956.

Governor Voices Grave Concern, Mayor Calls Parley. BCE, June 1, 1956.

Psychologists Blame Riots on Economic, Social Ills. BCE, June 3, 1956

Attempt to Free Trio set Off Beach Battle. BCE, June 4, 1956.

Fireworks Sale Banned at Beach. BCE, June 5, 1956.

Trial of Beach Rioters is Postponed. BCE, June 7, 1956

5 Youths Fined for Roles in Crystal Beach Clash. BCE, June 14, 1956.

18,400,000 Passengers Later, Canadiana Calls I Quits. BEN, November 11, 1956.

Steamer Canadiana Will Run to Crystal Beach No More. BEN, November 27, 1956.

1957
None

1958
Crystal Beach to Reopen With New Rides Featured. BCE, May 20, 1958

M. McAlpine Dies; Resort Developer. BCE, September 1, 1958

1959
Crystal Beach Adds Lights, Wild Mouse. Billboard, April 27, 1959.

1960
None

1961
New Crystal Beach Offering – the Hot Rod Turnpike Ride. BEN, May 12, 1961

1962
Beehive of Activity Prepares Crystal Beach for Opening. BEN, May 17, 1962.

1963
Lee Eyerly, Businessman, Pioneer in Aviation, Dies. OSN, March 25, 1963

Business Leader Succumb" Oregon Statesman newspaper, March 28, 1963

2 New rides at Beach; Park Opens on Saturday. BEN, May 22, 1963.

1964
Addition at Crystal Beach. Photo Caption. BEN, May 22, 1964.

Crystal Beach to Unveil its $250,000 Remodeling. BEN, May 22, 1964.

Crystal Beach Has New Rides. BCE, May 24, 1964.

Fun for the Whole Family. Advertisement. BCE, June 11, 1964

Louis Lejeune Has a One Track Mind: Crystal Beach Line. BCE, July 1, 1964

Crystal Beach For Family Fun. Advertisement. BCE August 9, 1964

1965
Giddyap Old Paint Photo Caption. BCE, May 20, 1965.

1966
None

1967
Earmuffs for Now – But Crystal Beach has Summer Fun in Sight. BEN, May 17, 1967

1968
Crystal Beach Sparkling for Season Opening Saturday. Amusements readied for 79th Year. BEN May 22, 1968.

Crystal Beach Sets New Hours. BEN June 20, 1968

Crystal Beach. Advertisement. BCE June 23, 1968

Photo. BCE, July 20, 1968.

1969
It's Crystal Clear: Summer's Here! BEN, May 22, 1969

Merger Set for crystal Beach Park. BCE, May 24, 1969.

Crystal Beach to Merge with Florida Company. BEN, May 24, 1969

Crystal Beach Now Open. Advertisement BCE, June 3, 1969.

Crystal Beach 1 Ticket Bargain Day. Advertisement. BCE, August 27, 1969

Amusement Park Planned. BEN, September 23, 1969.

1970
Its Clear as Crystal (Beach) The Fun Will Resume Saturday. Buffalo Evening News, May 21, 1970.

Crystal Beach ready for Visitors. BCE May 22, 1970

Crystal Beach, Just Arrived the fantastic Fly-o-Plane. Advertisement. BCE, June 9, 1970.

One Ticket Day. Advertisement. BCE August 28, 1970.

1971
Elephant Will Soon Lose Home Ballroom Will Buzz to Skaters. FET, May 7, 1971.

New Coat of Paint Spruces Up Crystal Beach. BEN, May 20, 1971

1 Ticket Bargain Days. Advertisement BCE, August 29, 1971.

1972
A Bigger Crystal Beach Opens Season Tomorrow. BEN, May 19, 1972.

Two Hurt in Roller Coaster Crash. BCE, June 17, 1974.

George C. Hall is Dead; Operated Crystal Beach Park. BEN, September 5 1972.

1973
Old and New Combine to Offer Fun at Crystal Beach Opening. BEN May 17, 1973

Cleveland Interests Buying Crystal Beach Park. BEN November 5, 1973

1974
Hall Family Revamps Setup at Crystal Beach. BEN March 12, 1974.

Halls Retain Crystal Beach, Set Expansion. BCE March 12, 1974

85th Season at Crystal Beach Opens Saturday with New Rides. BEN, May 15, 1974.

Getting Ready. Photo Caption. BCE, May 16, 1974.

Crystal Beach 5 More in '74. Advertisement. BCE, June 1, 1974.

Crystal Beach Fire. FET August 16, 1974.

Fire Damages Ballroom at Crystal Beach. BEN August 16, 1974

4 Rescued From Fire at Crystal Beach BCE August 16, 1974

½ Price Days. Advertisement BCE, August 25, 1974

1975
Crystal Beach to Open Season; Adds 2 Restaurants, Live Show BEN, May 15, 1975

Niagara Frontier Industries. New Amusements Planned at Crystal Beach. BCE, June 1, 1975.

Thrown from Roller Coaster, Stevensville Man is Killed. FET, June 22, 1975.

Comet Coaster Cleared of Blame In Man's Death. BEN, June 23, 1975

Ride Found In Order After Death. BCE, June 23, 1975
Inquest to Be Weighed In 'Comet' Ride Death. BCE, June 24, 1975

1976
New Ticket Policy at Crystal Beach. BEN, January 20, 1976

Amusement Park Set Flat Fees. BCE, February 22, 1976.

1977
$250,000 Facelift at Crystal Beach" BCE, April 30, 1977.

Crystal Beach Roller Coaster Rates High with Builder, Buffs. BCE, June 12, 1977

Expansion Means More Grins at Fun and Games Park. BCE, June 15, 1977

Woman, Two Children Hurt on Ride at Crystal Beach. BCE, August 26, 1977.

1978
Crystal Midway Adds Riding Gear. BCE, May 23, 1978

Marineland Pushes Ahead With $75 Million Expansion, BCE, July 8, 1978

Reporter Tests Suicidal Thrills in New Fun Rides. BCE, July 29, 1978

1979
Paul Snyder's Recreation Goldmine. BEN, May 27, 1979.

Area Parks Spend Heavily to Groom for New Season. BCE, June 12, 1979

Area's 3 Amusement Parks Offer Thrills, Chills, Eats. BCE, August 18, 1979.

1980
Area Amusement Parks Alter Attractions. BCE, May 21,1980

Darien Lake is Envisioned Disney World of the East. BEN, June 22,1980

Worker Dies After Touching Wire at Ride. BEN, July 25, 1980

1981
Toronto's New Theme Park is a $115 Million Dream Come True. BEN May 17, 1981.

Fun, Fun , Fun. Amusement Parks Pour On Attractions for All Ages , Tastes and Budgets. BEN May 22, 1981.

It's Time for Whoopee!!! At Darien Lake and Crystal Beach. BCE, May 23, 1981

Ontario Place has Attractions to Entertain Kids of All Ages. BEN, May 24, 1981

For All the Highs. Crystal Beach Advertisement. BEN, May 24, 1981

Fast Growin' Fun in the Country. Advertising Insert. BEN, July 5, 1981.

Ad Budgets Expand Along with Area's Amusement Parks. BEN, July 21, 1981

1982
Troubled Fantasy Island Reaches End of the Line. BEN, May 14, 1982.

Coaster Fanatics Foam at Mouth. BCE, July 20, 1982.

Disappointing Season for Crystal Beach – Not For Darien Lake. BEN, September 6, 1982

1983
Sale is Near for Crystal Beach. BEN, March 11, 1983

End of the Line for Crystal Beach? BEN, March 11, 1983

Crystal Beach Will Open With Excursion Boat, Pier. BEN, March 30, 1983.

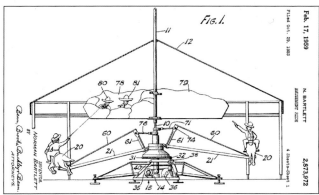

Images of the Kiddieland ride "Rodeo." Riders pointed guns at the Indian Targets. If a target was hit, a lamp in the background was turned on. The patent illustration shows these figures mounted overhead, instead of in a ground-level shed as seen on the left side of the top photo.

Cathy Herbert collection.